Joomla! 1.5
Beginner's Guide

Build and maintain impressive user-friendly websites the fast and easy way with Joomla! 1.5

Eric Tiggeler

PUBLISHING

BIRMINGHAM - MUMBAI

Joomla! 1.5

Beginner's Guide

First published: February 2010

Production Reference: 2230210

Published by Packt Publishing Ltd.
32 Lincoln Road
Olton
Birmingham, B27 6PA, UK.

ISBN 978-1-847199-90-4

www.packtpub.com

Cover Image by Vinayak Chittar (vinayak.chittar@gmail.com)

Credits

Author
Eric Tiggeler

Reviewers
Jose Argudo
Jennifer Marriott

Acquisition Editor
David Barnes

Development Editor
Rakesh Shejwal

Technical Editor
Hithesh Uchil

Indexer
Monica Ajmera Mehta

Editorial Team Leader
Akshara Aware

Project Team Leader
Lata Basantani

Project Coordinator
Poorvi Nair

Proofreader
Jeff Orloff

Graphics
Geetanjali Sawant

Production Coordinator
Melwyn D'sa

Cover Work
Melwyn D'sa

About the Author

Eric Tiggeler is an experienced writer of tutorials on Joomla! He writes how-tos for computer magazines and for the Dutch Joomla! community website. He has published a Dutch Joomla! manual, which got excellent reviews. Over the last ten years, Eric has developed numerous websites, big and small—many of them using Joomla!.

Eric is fascinated by the Web as a powerful and creative means of communication, and by revolutionary software such as Joomla!, enabling anybody to create beautiful and user-friendly websites without requiring any technical knowledge.

On a daily basis, Eric works as a consultant and copywriter at a communication consultancy company affiliated with the Free University of Amsterdam. Over the last few years, he has written more than ten Dutch books on writing and communication. His passion is making complex things easy to understand.

Eric Tiggeler is married and has two daughters. He lives and works in Hilversum, the Netherlands. On the Web, you'll find him on www.schrijfgids.nl (in Dutch) and www.joomm.net (in English).

Turning an idea into a book is by no means something you do all by yourself. I would like to thank the Packt team—David, Rakesh, Poorvi, and Hithesh—for their encouraging commitment to this project. Thanks also to both reviewers Jose Argudo and Jennifer Marriott for their helpful comments and detailed feedback.

I especially want to thank the three beautiful women in my life who managed to put up with my hours of invisibility during the writing of this book. Big truckloads of thanks go to my personal proofreader whose harsh, but honest "You've lost me heres" helped me to keep this book clear, down to earth, and focused on what real people want to know.

About the Reviewers

Jose Argudo is a web developer from Valencia, Spain. After finishing his studies he started working for a web design company. Then, six years later, he decided to freelance.

Now that some years have passed as a freelancer, he thinks it's the best decision he has ever taken because that let him work with the tools he likes, such as Joomla!, CodeIgniter, CakePHP, jQuery, and other known open source technologies.

His desire to learn and share his knowledge has led him to be a regular reviewer of books from Packt, like Joomla! With Flash, Joomla! 1.5 SEO, Magento Theme Design, and Symfony 1.3 web application development.

Recently, he has even published his own book, CodeIgniter 1.7, which you can also find at Packt's site. If you work with PHP, take a look at it!

If you want to know more about him, you can check his site www.joseargudo.com.

To my girlfriend and to my brother, I wish them the best.

Jennifer Marriott is a Canadian musician and a web designer/developer now located in Oklahoma, USA. She has studied Broadcasting and Communications, has been involved in Information Technology since the mid-1990s, and has been a long-time contributor and community member of the Joomla! Project.

Jennifer, along with her business partner Wendy Robinson, runs Marpo Multimedia—a boutique multimedia/web development company.

Jennifer is currently busy with her own book and two new music projects to be released in 2010.

I would really like to thank the Joomla! Project and the entire Joomla! Community for such a great software!

Table of Contents

Preface

Joomla! is one of the most popular open-source Content Management Systems, actively developed and supported by a world-wide user community. It's a free, fun, and feature-rich tool for anyone who wants to create dynamic, interactive websites. Even beginners can deploy Joomla! to build professional websites, although it can be challenging to get beyond the basics and build the site that completely meets your needs. This book will help you to start building websites with Joomla! quickly and get the most out of its advanced features.

What this book covers

In Chapter 1: *Introduction: A New and Easy Way to Build Websites*, you'll learn why you want to use Joomla! to create an advanced, cool-looking site that's easy to expand, customize, and maintain.

In Chapter 2: *Installation: Getting Joomla! Up and Running*, you'll learn how to install Joomla! on your own computer or on a web server, and how to create a sample site.

In Chapter 3: *First Steps: Getting to Know Joomla!*, you'll get familiar with the basic concepts of Joomla!, the Joomla! interface, and the principles of a website constructed out of 'building blocks'.

In Chapter 4: *Web Building Basics: Creating a Site in an Hour*, you'll face a real-life challenge of using Joomla! to build a basic but expandable website fast. You'll customize Joomla!'s default sample site to fit your needs, adding content, menu links, and change the site's look and feel.

In Chapter 5: *Small Sites, Big Sites: Organizing your Content Effectively*, you'll make it easy to add and find information on your site by designing a clear, expandable, and manageable structure for your content.

In Chapter 6: *Creating Killer Content: Adding and Editing Articles*, you'll learn to create content pages that are attractive and easy to read, and you'll learn about different ways to tweak the page layout.

In Chapter 7: *Welcoming Your Visitors: Creating Attractive Home Pages and Overview Pages*, you'll create a home page and overview pages to entice visitors to actually read all your valuable content.

In Chapter 8: *Helping Your Visitors Find What They Want: Managing Menus*, you'll learn how you can help the visitor to find what they want easily by designing clear and easy navigation through menus.

In Chapter 9: *Opening Up the Site: Enabling Users to Contribute and Interact*, you'll learn how to enable users to log in and allow them to create content and manage the website.

In Chapter 10: *Getting the Most out of Your Site: Extending Joomla!*, you'll learn how to extend Joomla!'s capabilities using all sorts of extensions—using an image gallery to attractively display pictures, automatically showing article teasers on the home page, or enhancing your workspace by installing an easier content editor.

In Chapter 11: *Creating an Attractive Design: Working with Templates*, you'll see how templates will give your site a fresh look and feel, and make it easy to create an individual look, different from a "typical" Joomla! site. You'll also learn to install and customize templates.

In Chapter 12: *Attracting Search Engine Traffic: Tips and Techniques*, you'll see how to increase your site's visibility for search engines by applying Search Engine Optimization (SEO) techniques, such as creating friendly URLs.

In Appendix A: *Keeping the Site Secure*, learn some simple, common sense steps you can take to keep your site safe from hackers or data loss.

What you need for this book

To follow the tutorials and exercises in this book, you'll need a computer with Internet access. It's recommended to have a web hosting account so that you can install Joomla! online.

Who this book is for

The Joomla! Beginner's Guide is aimed at anyone who wants to build and maintain a great website and get the most out of Joomla!. It helps you build on the skills and knowledge you may already have of creating websites—but if you're new to this subject, you won't have any difficulty understanding the instructions. Of course, we'll touch upon basic terms and concepts (such as HTML and CSS), but if you're not familiar with these, you'll also find references to some Web resources.

Conventions

In this book, you will find several headings appearing frequently.

To give clear instructions of how to complete a procedure or task, we use:

Time for action – heading

1. Action 1

2. Action 2

3. Action 3

Instructions often need some extra explanation so that they make sense, so they are followed with:

What just happened?

This heading explains the working of tasks or instructions that you have just completed.

You will also find some other learning aids in the book, including:

Pop quiz – heading

These are short multiple choice questions intended to help you test your own understanding.

Have a go hero – heading

These set practical challenges and give you ideas for experimenting with what you have learned.

You will also find a number of styles of text that distinguish between different kinds of information. Here are some examples of these styles and an explanation of their meaning.

Code words in text are shown as follows: "Change the `width` and `height` values to reflect the size of the new image. To shift the image a little to the left-hand side, decrease the `margin-left` value."

New terms and **important words** are shown in bold. Words that you see on the screen, in menus or dialog boxes, for example, appear in the text like this: "Click on **Save** and click on **Preview**".

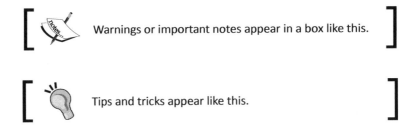

Warnings or important notes appear in a box like this.

Tips and tricks appear like this.

Reader feedback

Feedback from our readers is always welcome. Let us know what you think about this book—what you liked or may have disliked. Reader feedback is important for us to develop titles that you really get the most out of.

To send us general feedback, simply send an e-mail to feedback@packtpub.com, and mention the book title via the subject of your message.

If there is a book that you need and would like to see us publish, please send us a note in the **SUGGEST A TITLE** form on www.packtpub.com or e-mail suggest@packtpub.com.

If there is a topic that you have expertise in and you are interested in either writing or contributing to a book, see our author guide on www.packtpub.com/authors.

Customer support

Now that you are the proud owner of a Packt book, we have a number of things to help you to get the most from your purchase.

Errata

Although we have taken every care to ensure the accuracy of our content, mistakes do happen. If you find a mistake in one of our books—maybe a mistake in the text or the code—we would be grateful if you would report this to us. By doing so, you can save other readers from frustration and help us improve subsequent versions of this book. If you find any errata, please report them by visiting http://www.packtpub.com/support, selecting your book, clicking on the **let us know** link, and entering the details of your errata. Once your errata are verified, your submission will be accepted and the errata will be uploaded on our website, or added to any list of existing errata, under the Errata section of that title. Any existing errata can be viewed by selecting your title from http://www.packtpub.com/support.

Piracy

Piracy of copyright material on the Internet is an ongoing problem across all media. At Packt, we take the protection of our copyright and licenses very seriously. If you come across any illegal copies of our works, in any form, on the Internet, please provide us with the location address or website name immediately so that we can pursue a remedy.

Please contact us at copyright@packtpub.com with a link to the suspected pirated material.

We appreciate your help in protecting our authors, and our ability to bring you valuable content.

Questions

You can contact us at questions@packtpub.com if you are having a problem with any aspect of the book, and we will do our best to address it.

1

Introduction: A New and Easy Way to Build Websites

You want to build a website. It should look great, and it should be easy to use and maintain. Keeping it up-to-date should be effortless, not a lot of work. Changing the appearance of your site should take minutes, not hours. You don't want to manage it all by yourself, but you want to enable other people to log in and write new content without having to understand HTML or other coding languages. And when your site grows, it should be easy to extend it with new functionality—maybe adding a forum, or a newsletter.

If that's what you're looking for, welcome to Joomla!. When it comes to creating a great, professional looking website that's easy to use, you really can't beat the power of a **Content Management System (CMS)** such as Joomla!. Using Joomla!, you don't have to be a web professional to create a state-of-the-art website. Without writing a single line of code, you can create any kind of site, featuring a variety of cool and advanced features.

Join the CMS revolution

Maybe you have some experience building websites the traditional way. That basically meant creating HTML documents—web pages—one by one. As the site grew, you'd end up with a bunch of HTML documents, trying to keep all of them organized and making sure all menu links stayed up-to-date. You'd probably maintain the site by yourself because anyone else who added content would have to know their way around in the structure of your particular site, and be proficient in the web editing software you use.

Enter the Holy Grail of web building: the Content Management System! A CMS is an application that runs on a web server that allows you to develop and maintain a website online. It comes packed with tools and features, from basic features to add and modify content to advanced functionality such as user registration or site search capability. In short, a CMS makes it possible to build sites that would normally involve a full team of web professionals with a massive amount of time, money, and expertise at their disposal.

All that magic is made possible because a CMS is really an advanced set of scripts (written in a scripting language, such as PHP) that uses a database to store the content of your website. From that database, it retrieves bits and pieces of content and presents them as web pages. This dynamic way of storing and presenting content makes a CMS very flexible. Do you want to show only a selection of articles from a specific category on a page? Do you want to display only the intro texts and images of the most recent articles on the home page? Do you want to add a list of links to the most popular contents? Do you want to limit access to registered users? It's all possible—just pick the right settings. Additionally, a CMS allows you to integrate all sorts of extra features, such as contact forms, picture galleries, and much more.

The best part is that CMSes like these are yours to download and deploy today. You can pick your CMS of choice from a range of freely available open-source products. Your new CMS-powered site can be online tomorrow. Now how's that for a great deal?

Why would you choose Joomla!?

There are many open-source CMSes around. They're all great tools, each with its own typical uses and benefits. Why would you want to choose Joomla!?

- People tend to choose Joomla! because they find it easy to use. It has a clear and friendly user interface. It makes it easy to manage content and easy to create and publish articles to keep your site current—anytime, anywhere—using a web browser.

- Adding new features takes just a few clicks. There are thousands of extensions available, from menu systems to commenting systems and forums.

- It's very easy to change the site's appearance—templates are abundant and can be installed within minutes, giving your site a fresh look and feel.

- Joomla! is actively developed and it's well supported by a huge worldwide community of users and developers. It is updated frequently, adding new features, security enhancements, and other improvements.

Apart from these typical Joomla! benefits, it comes with all of the advantages of a state-of-the-art CMS. Just a few examples are:

- It's really easy to add or edit content and to keep it organized (even if there's lots of it).

- Keeping hyperlinks up-to-date is greatly automated. For example, if you add a new web page to a category a new link will automatically appear in pages pointing to that category.

- You don't have to maintain the website all by yourself. Other users can add content, add new menu items, and much more.

The numbers seem to indicate that Joomla! is the open-source CMS of choice for web builders worldwide. It's the engine behind some 20 million websites worldwide and this number is still growing rapidly day by day. Joomla! is one of the biggest open-source software projects around, supported by a huge user community and constantly being developed further by an international team of volunteers.

What kind of sites can you build with Joomla!?

Let's have a look at some great real-world examples of sites built using Joomla!—if you're anything like me, that's what makes you want to get started right away, creating something equally cool (or preferably, something even better!). These are just a few examples from the Web and from the Joomla! site showcase (`http://community.joomla.org/showcase`). They are very diverse sites from very different organizations, each with their own goals and target groups. What they have in common is that they deploy Joomla! in a way that you could too. They all create a great Web appearance by adapting the CMS to their specific needs, making it perfectly suited for the content they present and the impression they want to make.

Here's an example from a non-profit organization: Green Energy Solutions (`http://masteringgreen.com`). It shows a clean corporate design, displaying a few highlights from the site's contents combined with simple and clear navigation.

The following example is a relatively small website of a specialized company (www.abbeyfloor.co.uk). The site offers a clear and attractive overview of the services and products. The design is a customization of a freely available Joomla! template.

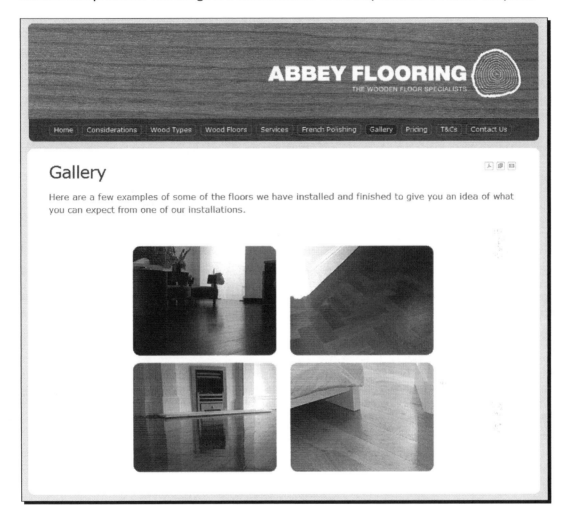

Of course, Joomla! can handle much more content; complex sites with thousands of pages are no exception. Here's an illustration of a content-rich site with a made-to-measure design, offering its various target groups different ways to reach the site's contents: the University of Nebraska website (`http://nebraska.edu`):

One final example demonstrates that Joomla! sites don't have to look anything like a typical Joomla! site. If you want to take customization to the max, you can use an entirely different design—and still take advantage of Joomla!'s default functionality to power the site. The following is a site of a Dutch freelance cook (www.tijskookt.nl):

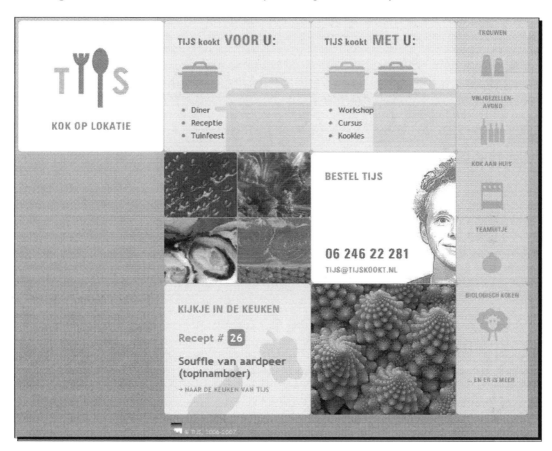

 If you're looking for some more inspiration, browse the official Joomla! showcase: http://community.joomla.org/showcase or go to www.bestofjoomla.com and look around the *Best of Sites* section.

Learning to use Joomla!

It may sound too good to be true. Does Joomla! really make creating state-of-the-art websites side splittingly easy? Let's be honest—it will make it *reasonably* easy, but of course it does require you to invest some time and effort. After all, working with Joomla! (or any CMS) is very different from building websites the traditional way. You'll notice this as soon as you start installing the system. Compared to setting up a simple static website consisting of a few HTML pages, building a Joomla!-powered site takes a bit more preparation. You'll need hosting space that meets specific requirements and you'll need to set up a database. It's very doable, and this book will run you through the process step by step. But it does take some commitment and isn't really the most exciting part of working with Joomla!

Once you've got Joomla! set up, you'll soon get the hang of creating a fine, basic site. However, it can be challenging to get things just right for your particular goals. After all, you don't want "just any Joomla!-powered site"—you want to build a specific site, aimed at your specific target audience. The Joomla! Beginner's Guide will help you to go beyond a basic site with default settings, and it will help you make the choices that fit your goals.

One last challenge you should be aware of; in some ways, Joomla! will make it almost too easy to add any functionality you like. There's nothing to stop you from adding dozens of extra functions to your site or stuffing your pages with eye candy. Of course, that's not really what makes a good site, nor is it what makes your visitors tick. Customizing a site to your needs while keeping an eye on user experience is something a CMS can't do for you. But if you're serious about creating an excellent website that your visitors will want to read and use, then this book will help you find your way.

In short, even with Joomla!, it will take a lot of time and effort to create and maintain great websites. The site won't run itself, but Joomla! will make it much easier and much more fun for you (and your web team members) to keep it evolving.

What you'll learn using this book

The Joomla! Beginner's Guide is designed to make it as easy as possible for you to get the most out of Joomla!. It's focused on learning by doing—the structure of the book reflects the process of building a website. First, you'll install Joomla!, take a tour of the system, and get a feel for what it's like. After that, you'll start building your own site step by step:

◆ You master the fundamentals by creating a basic website with lightning speed.

◆ You'll adapt and expand this basic site to meet your (and your visitors') growing needs. You'll set up a structure for the different sorts of content you want on your site, and you learn how to add different types of pages.

- You'll learn how make that content easy to find through well-designed menus and design an attractive home page that directs people to the content they might be interested in.

- You'll learn how to engage your web visitors and turn them into active users who can register and add content.

- You'll extend Joomla!'s capabilities and add features (such as a picture gallery) to the site.

- You'll change the site layout and make it more attractive.

- You'll find out how to tweak the site to attract search engine traffic and to keep the site safe.

About the example site

The Joomla! Beginner's Guide focuses on building a realistic example site step-by-step. Instead of just learning about Joomla!'s capabilities in general terms, you'll meet real-world web building challenges. Throughout the book, you'll achieve all of your fictitious client's goals (that is 'I want a website that my web team members can update themselves' or 'I want a website that makes it easy to navigate through a large amount of content').

Now who's that client of yours? It's the Society for the Reappreciation of Ugly Paintings, also known as SRUP. They just love amateur paintings that mostly end up dumped in the trash heap or turn up in charity shops. You'll have to agree that it's a terrible waste. The SRUP think that bad painting is good. They argue it's creative, it's the ordinary peoples' artistic view on reality, and it can be valuable art—in its own, ugly way. The SRUP people need a website to inform the public about their goals, showing fine examples of ugly paintings, and encouraging people to join and participate.

You'll take the SRUP site through different stages of development. First you'll base the site on Joomla!'s default design and layout.

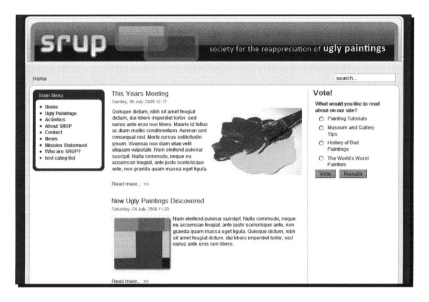

Later on, you'll add advanced features and shape the site's contents and design to meet the changing needs of your client.

The SRUP site is a good example of what you can do with Joomla! You start out with a basic website and add sophisticated features as you go. Of course, you can follow along in this book without having to actually perform all of the actions described—but you'll find it's a good and fun way to learn building a site and honing your skills as you go.

Summary

In this chapter, you've been introduced to the wonderful world of the Joomla! CMS. You've learned about:

- ◆ The difference between building a website the traditional way and using a CMS. You don't have to create HTML documents (web pages) one by one, instead you use a web application to develop and maintain your site. Using the tools and features of the CMS, you can create more powerful sites that are easier to maintain.
- ◆ The benefits of using Joomla!, such as its ease of use, the ability to add extra features, and the ability to change the look and feel of the site fast.
- ◆ The structure of this book; step-by-step, you'll learn how to build a realistic example site with Joomla!.

That's enough theory for now—let's get started! In the next chapter, you'll install Joomla! and get it up and running. After that, you'll get familiar with the way Joomla! works and start building.

Installation: Getting Joomla! Up and Running

2

Joomla! isn't just an ordinary software package that you can install on your own computer: it needs a web server to run. If you're new to Joomla!, installing a web application may seem daunting. And well, let's be honest, running the installation procedure is probably the least exciting part of working with Joomla!. However, if you just follow the required steps, it's pretty straightforward. It does take a little preparation, but if you've got everything ready, you can walk through Joomla!'s user-friendly setup wizard that takes most of the hassle out of the installation.

In this chapter you'll learn about:

- ◆ What you need to install Joomla!
- ◆ How to install Joomla! on a web server
- ◆ What's in the box: what do you get when you install Joomla!?
- ◆ Where to find help if you get stuck

You'll install Joomla! on a web server, allowing you or anyone else with Internet access to immediately see, and visit your Joomla!-powered site. Your site will be accessible via your own web address (URL), such as http://www.example.com. When you build and customize the site you'll access the site through your browser.

So let's get started!

Don't fear the technical mumbo jumbo

Joomla! will make it really easy for you to build a state of the art website—but installing the program will inevitably introduce you to some technical names and acronyms. Don't let this intimidate you. If you've never heard of PHP, MySQL, and the like, you may be tempted to call in your computer geek nephew to carry out the installation for you, allowing you to jump ahead to the fun and creative part—creating a beautiful site. But rest assured, you can pull this off yourself. It's like following directions to a destination in a city you're new to. If you keep to the instructions, you're certain to get there. Moreover, as you'll do this more often, you'll get to know the city map better and better. It will take you less and less time to get a new Joomla! site up and running.

What do you need to start?

To be able to install and run Joomla!, you'll need hosting space and a few tools. Here's your shopping list.

1. Hosting space

First of all, you'll need hosting space; a place on a web server where you can set up your site to make it accessible to anyone with Internet access. Your hosting account should support the PHP scripting language (as Joomla! is written in PHP); it should support the type of database that Joomla! uses, called MySQL; and it has to run the Apache server software. Specifically, these are the system requirements for Joomla! 1.5:

- PHP 4.3.10 or above
- MySQL 3.23 x or above
- Apache 1.3.x or above

You shouldn't have any difficulty finding hosting accounts that meet these system requirements. If you're not sure, any hosting provider should be able to tell you if they support Joomla!.

You can find detailed system requirements at the Joomla! official help site: `http://help.joomla.org/content/view/1938/302.`

And what if you don't have hosting space?

If you don't have a hosting account yet, you can install Joomla! on your computer. This does involve installing the web server software first. This means you'll make Joomla! run on your computer as if it were a real, "live" web server.

- ◆ The quickest way to do this is to use an all-in-one installation package. Go to `http://bitnami.org` to download the free, open-source "BitNami Joomla! Stack" that will automatically install both web server software and Joomla! in one go.

- ◆ Another option is to first install the web server software, and then install the Joomla! software on your computer. There are several free web server software packages available, such as WampServer for Windows, and XAMPP for Windows, Linux, and Apple computers. See `www.wampserver.com` or `www.apachefriends.org`.

Although this approach is OK for testing purposes, there are some drawbacks. You'll only have access to Joomla! from just one computer, and when your site is ready for the world, you'll have to install it on a real web server anyway. In this book, we'll focus on installing and running Joomla! on a web server.

2. FTP software

To transfer files from your computer to a web server, you need special **File Transfer Protocol (FTP)** software. An FTP program is comparable to the Windows file Explorer or the Mac Finder. You use it to manage files and move them from one place to another—the only difference being that the FTP program allows you to move files from your computer to your hosting space on a web server (and vice versa).

If you're new to FTP, perform a Web search for 'FTP Tutorial' to get familiar with the basic procedures. See for example `http://www.freewebmasterhelp.com/tutorials/ftp`.

Looking for FTP software? Check out the free (open-source) FileZilla software, available for computers running Windows, Apple, and Linux. You can download it from `http://filezilla-project.org`. If you're using the Firefox you might be interested in FireFTP, an FTP plugin for your browser—as explained next.

3. A great browser (think Firefox)

If you're perfectly happy with whatever your current browser may be, you won't have any trouble managing your Joomla! site with it. However, people creating websites often install more than one browser on their computer. Apart from the ever-popular Microsoft Internet Explorer (www.microsoft.com), you might want to install the up-and-coming Google Chrome (www.google.com). But you'll definitely want to use Mozilla Firefox (www.mozilla.org). Having more than one browser allows you to check if your site looks OK in all of the major browsers.

A special benefit of having Firefox at your disposal is that there are many extensions for this browser that will make your web developing life much easier. One of these is Firebug that helps you to style your web pages (more about Firebug in Chapter 11 on templates). Another great Firefox plugin is FireFTP that turns your browser into a full-blown FTP client. Go to http://fireftp.mozdev.org to see how it works and to download a copy.

Installing Joomla! in four steps

If you have set up a web hosting account and got the tools you need, you're set to go. Installing Joomla! takes these steps:

1. Download the Joomla! files from www.joomla.org
2. Place the files on the web server
3. Create a database
4. Install Joomla! itself, using the installation wizard

It doesn't get more simpler than this. The rest of this chapter will give you a detailed walkthrough of this procedure.

Time for action – step 1: Download the Joomla! files

Let's download the current and stable version of Joomla!.

1. Point your browser to www.joomla.org. On the home page, click on the **Download Joomla!** button:

2. You'll be taken to the download page. Select the latest release (at the time of writing this is 1.5.15).

Make sure to download the Full Package (the other versions are upgrades for existing Joomla! installations).

3. The default download file is a ZIP file. If you're using Windows, download this file to your hard drive. If you're using another operating system, click on the **Download other Joomla! 1.5.x packages** link to select the appropriate package file.

4. Unpack the compressed file to a folder on your hard drive. If you don't have a software program for unpacking files, check out `http://www.7-zip.org` for an open-source file extraction program.

What just happened?

You've now got all of the files required to install Joomla! in a folder on your computer.

Time for action – step 2: Place the files on the web server

Start up your FTP program (see *What do you need to start?* earlier in this chapter) and upload all of the unzipped files in the folder to the web server. This is how you do it:

1. In your FTP program, browse to the folder containing the unzipped Joomla! files. Select all of the files (do not select the folder, only its contents).

2. Select the target directory, the root directory of the web server. The root directory is often called `httpdocs`, `htdocs`, `httpd`, `public_html`, or www. If you can't find that folder, your web hosting company should be able to help you out.

Don't worry about the name of the root folder (httpdocs or any of the other names listed above). This name won't show up in the Web address of your site. Visitors don't have to type www.example.com/httpdocs, just www.example.com will take them to your site.

If you create a folder within httpdocs, this folder name *will* show up in your web address. So, if you create a folder httpdocs/Joomla! and install Joomla! in this folder, your site will be accessible only through www.example.com/Joomla!. This means you should only create such a subfolder if this is what you want (for example, when you're just testing Joomla! and you want to keep using the root directory for your existing site).

3. In your FTP program, select all of the files in the Joomla! folder. The list of files should resemble the one in the left half of the screen shown in the following illustration. The illustration below shows the FireFTP screen, but if you're using another FTP program this shouldn't look much different.

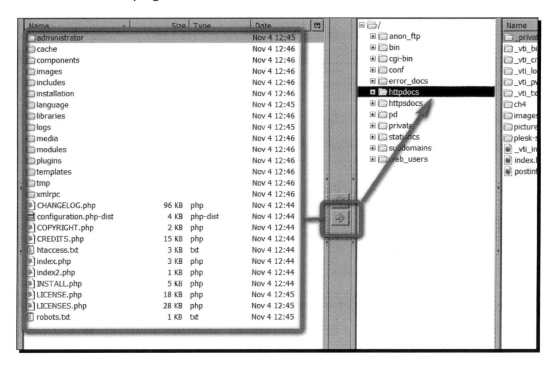

4. On the web server, select the destination folder (httpdocs). Click on the right pointing arrow to upload the Joomla! files to the web server root directory.

What just happened?

You've just got your FTP program to copy all Joomla! files from your computer to the web server. Don't worry if this takes some time, as uploading thousands of Joomla! files can take 10 minutes or more depending on the speed of your Internet connection.

Time for action – step 3: Create a database

The next step is creating an empty database for Joomla!. If you're new to Joomla!, the concept of a web application using a database may take getting used to. The database isn't a regular file that you can create (or copy, move, or delete) on the web server. To create and manage a database, you use special software. Most web hosting companies offer you database access through a web interface (usually called a control panel). Popular control panels are Plesk and CPanel. You'll find details on the control panel that's available to you in your hosting account information.

In the following example, we'll use Plesk to create a new database. If your hosting company provides another control panel, the basic procedure won't be very different. However, if you're not sure how to access your web server control panel your host should be able to provide you with the details.

> Sometimes web hosting providers don't allow their users to create their own database. Instead, they provide a pre-installed database. If this is the case, you can go on to Step 4, running the Joomla! installation wizard. You will need some database details for this: the database name, the database user name, and a password for this user. Check the account information you received from your host.

1. Log in to the Plesk control panel with the account information you have received from your hosting provider. To add a new database, click on **Databases** and then click on **Add New Database**.

2. Enter a name for the new database for example, **joomladatabase**. Click on **OK**.

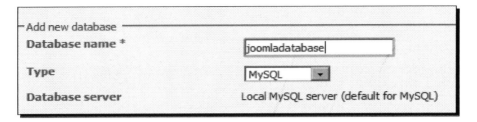

3. Create a new user for the database. Click on **Add New Database User** and enter a login name and password for the new user:

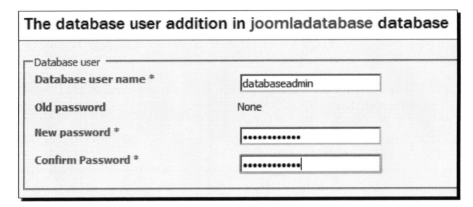

4. Make a note of the information you used to install Joomla! later on: the database name, the database user name, and password.

What just happened?

Using a web control panel, you've set up an empty database and created a database user. You're almost there; this is the last step in preparing the Joomla! installation.

Time for action – step 4: Run the Joomla! installation wizard

You've got all Joomla! files copied to the web server, and you've got a database ready to be filled. Let's finally install Joomla!!

1. Enter the URL for your site (for example, `http://www.example.com`) in your browser. The installation screen will come up:

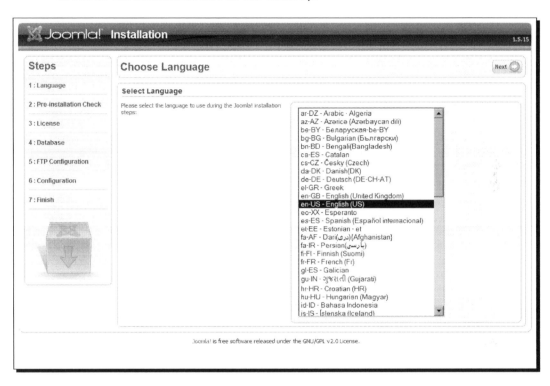

2. Select the language you want to use during the installation.

3. Click on the **Next** button. Joomla! will now verify if all of the web hosting settings are correct:

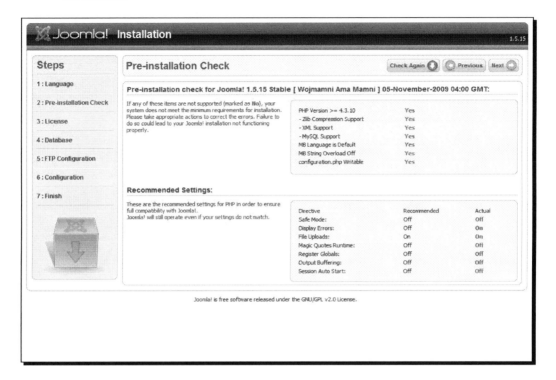

If any of the settings in the top row doesn't meet the requirements, you can correct this and click on **Check Again**. If configuration.php is not writable, this means Joomla! can't access your install directory. If this is the case Joomla! won't be able create the required configuration.php file during installation. To make the installation directory writable, use your FTP program to change directory access permissions. After the installation you can change permissions back to their old (safer) value. To read more about file permissions, check Appendix A (*Tip 4: Protect files and directories*).

Sometimes the settings your hosting provider uses don't match Joomla!'s recommended settings (the bottom row in the previous screenshot). For example, many providers set **Display Errors** to **On**. You can safely ignore Joomla!'s warning.

4. Click on **Next**. The installer will display the Joomla! license:

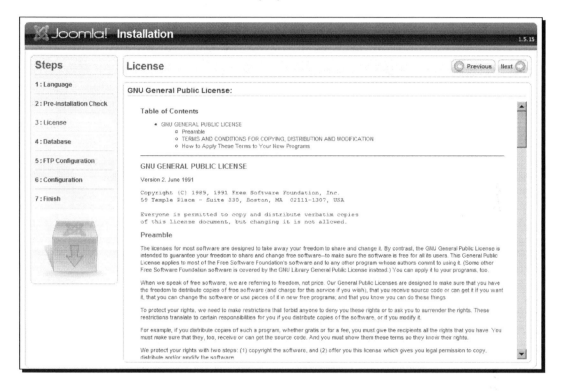

5. You'll probably want to agree to these license restrictions (you may scroll down to read the full 3000 words, if you feel like it) and click on **Next**.

6. Now you're getting somewhere! In the next screen, you'll fill out the critical database information.

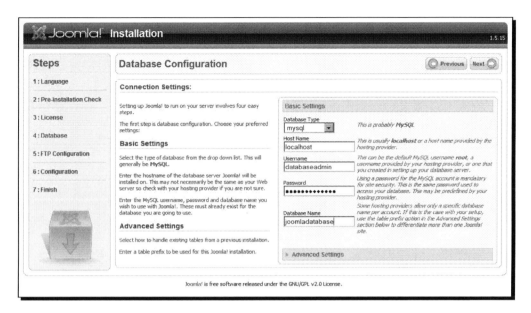

In the **Database Configuration** screen enter the following details:

- ❑ **Database Type**: Leave this set to the default value, **mysql**.

- ❑ **Host Name**: Usually this is **localhost** (unless your web hosting company has provided you with another name).

- ❑ **Username**: Enter the user name for the database you've created before. If you haven't created the database yourself, your hosting provider should be able to provide you with the database and user details. In our example, the user name is **databaseadmin**.

- ❑ Enter the database user **password** you've created when setting up the database.

Clicking on **Advanced Settings** reveals some extra options:

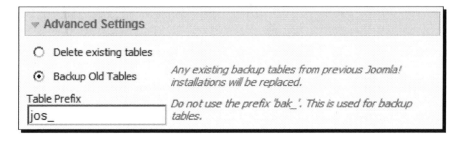

You can usually leave these unchanged:

- ❑ The option to **Delete existing tables** is only relevant when you've installed Joomla! before and want to empty the tables (the contents) of a previous database.

- ❑ Select **Backup Old Tables** to backup existing tables from a previous Joomla! installation.

- ❑ Enter a **Table Prefix** only when one database is shared by several Joomla! installations. This way, each of them can look up the appropriate data by checking for the correct prefix.

7. Once the **Database Configuration** screen is complete, click on **Next**. Joomla! will now check if it can connect to the database.

- ❑ If you see an error message you've probably made a typo when entering the database details. Make sure you have typed the password correctly. You can go back to the database details screen, enter the correct data, and click on **Next** again.

- ❑ If all goes well you are taken to the **FTP Configuration** screen:

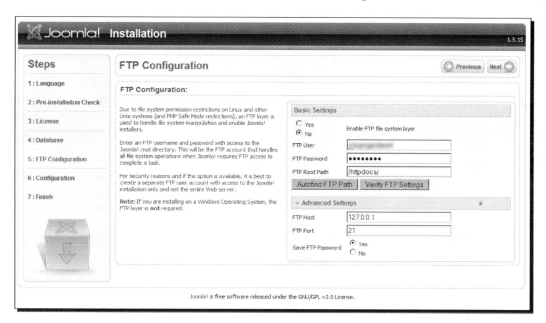

If you want, you can skip the FTP Configuration screen. It's also possible to enter the FTP details after you've installed Joomla! (in the site configuration screen). These settings allow Joomla! to have direct FTP access to your web server, for example when you want to install an extension. To enter this information right now:

8. In the **Basic Settings** section enter the FTP details you have received from your web hosting provider. Click on **Autofind FTP Path** to have Joomla! automatically detect the root directory of your site. Click on **Verify FTP Settings** to check if FTP works OK.

9. In the **Advanced Settings** section, you can skip to the third option. It's a good idea to select **Save FTP password: Yes**. If you don't you'll have to enter the password manually every time you want to upload files using Joomla!'s FTP facility.

10. Click on **Next**. You're almost done! The next step is **Site Configuration**:

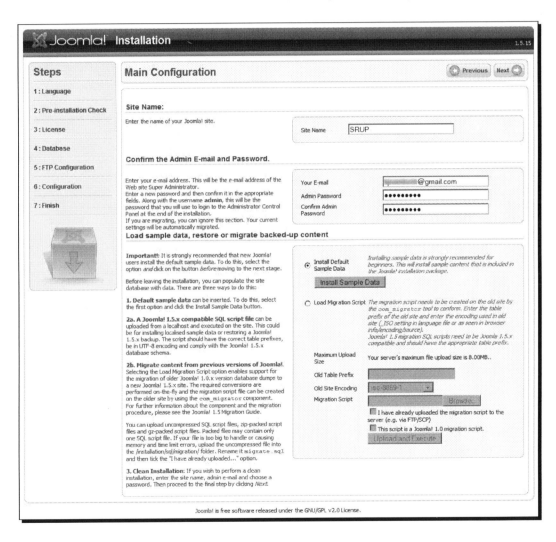

- **Site Name**: Enter the name for the website; this will be displayed in the browser title bar (and in some cases in the site header). You can change this later. In this example, we've entered **SRUP**. You'll learn more about this esteemed client for your example site in the later chapters.

- **E-mail address**: Enter a valid e-mail address. Joomla! will use this to send system messages.

- **Admin Password**: Enter the site administrator password. This is a different password from the one you've entered previously for the database user. This new password is created here and now; you'll use this to log in to Joomla! after the installation. Make a note of this!

- **Install Default Sample Data**: When you first create a Joomla! site, it's a good idea to click on **Install Sample Data**. This way, you'll get a ready-made sample site to build upon, already filled with example pages, menus, and extras. If you want to follow the exercises in this book, click on **Install Sample Data**.

- If you don't install sample data, you have to create all of the content from scratch. You'll prefer this option when you're Joomla!-savvy and know where to start.

11. Click on **Next**. You're done! Joomla! congratulates you on your success:

You're good to go now—only one thing left to do. Before you start using Joomla!, you should delete the folder named `installation`. This contains information that's needed for the installation, but it's now no longer required (and you do not want to reveal its contents to malicious hackers). You can find this in the root directory on the web server where you installed Joomla!.

12. Using your FTP program, go to the root directory of the Joomla! installation. Select the `installation` directory and delete it.

What just happened?

Congratulations! You've installed Joomla!. On the **Finish** screen, click on the **Site** button to see what your Joomla! site looks like. It will be displayed in a new browser window:

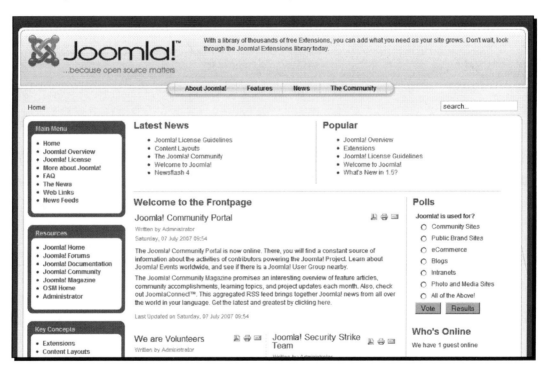

But there's more to Joomla! than meets the eye of the web visitor. On the **Finish** screen, click on **Admin** to go to the "secret" login page of your site. You can also enter your site URL in your browser address bar, adding the word `administrator`:
`www.example.com/administrator`.

You'll see this page:

Here you can log in to the backend of the site using the **Username** (that should be **admin**) and the **Password** that you've created during installation (make sure you enter the site administrator password, not the database user password). Click on **Login** to reveal the Joomla! web interface:

Protecting your site

You've just installed Joomla! so you probably want to get to the fun stuff right away and start creating cool sites. You're right of course, but still it's is a good idea to keep an eye on security issues from the very start. As soon as you've got your site set up, it's really important to make sure you don't leave any doors open to people who like to break into other peoples' websites. One important file to protect is `configuration.php` that has just been created in the root directory of your Joomla! installation. It contains critical information, such as usernames and passwords. Check Appendix A (section *Tip 4: Protect files and directories*) to learn how you can protect this file by changing access permissions.

Got stuck? Get help!

Looking for more help and tips on installing Joomla!?

- Visit the Joomla! help site `http://help.joomla.org` and check the **Joomla! 1.5. Documentation** menu.

- Check the Joomla! beginner's documentation on `http://docs.joomla.org/Beginners`. This contains links to installation tutorials.

- Don't forget there are many free video tutorials on YouTube; search for "install Joomla! 1.5" and you'll be presented with a truckload of installation guides:

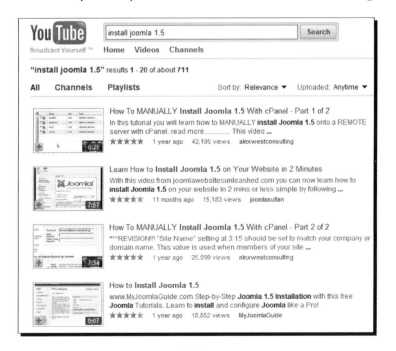

◆ If you're having trouble installing Joomla!, chances are your problem has already been solved on the official Joomla! forum dedicated to installation issues. On `http://forum.joomla.org`, look for the **Installation** section:

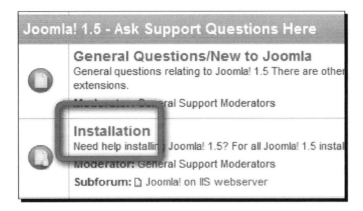

You can also point your browser directly to `http://forum.joomla.org/viewforum.php?f=429`.

 Point your browser to `www.joomm.net`, the website accompanying this book, to find answers to frequently asked Joomla! questions.

Pop quiz – test your knowledge of installing Joomla!

1. Why do you need FTP software before you can install Joomla!?

   a) To unzip the installation package.

   b) To upload files from your computer to the web server.

   c) To backup your site.

2. What are the main steps in installing Joomla!?

   a) First upload the Joomla! files, then run the web installer.

   b) Download Joomla!, upload the files, create a database, then run the web installer.

   c) Download Joomla!, upload the files, run the web installer, create a database.

3   What username and passwords do you have to enter in the Joomla! web installation wizard?

a)   The username and password needed to log in to the Joomla! backend.

b)   The username and password needed to access the MySQL database.

c)   The username and password needed to access the MySQL database, and the password needed to log in to the Joomla! backend.

Summary

In this chapter, you've learned how to install Joomla!. Specifically, we covered:

◆   The most common way to install Joomla!—using a web server. This way, the site you build is accessible through the Internet immediately. For testing purposes, you can also install Joomla! on your own computer.

◆   To be able to install and run Joomla!, you'll need hosting space and FTP software to put the required files on a web server. You might want to install a few different browsers.

◆   Installing Joomla! takes four steps:

❑   First, you get the current Joomla! file package from www.joomla.org.

❑   Then, using FTP, you place the downloaded files on your hosting space.

❑   The last step before actually installing Joomla! is creating a database; for this you can use the control panel provided by your web hosting provider.

❑   The final step is running the Joomla! web installer in your browser. This guides you through the installation process.

◆   The output of the Joomla! installation has two faces. The Joomla! frontend displays an example website that is publicly accessible, whereas the backend is Joomla!'s web management interface where just one VIP is allowed to login—you!

Now that you've got Joomla! up and running, it's about time to find out what this great new web development tool can do. In Chapter 3, you'll explore the Joomla! frontend and backend, and you'll get a first taste of building websites the Joomla! way.

3
First Steps: Getting to Know Joomla!

Congratulations! You have just installed Joomla!. This means you can now step into Joomla!, and start using one of the most exciting and powerful web building tools. Before you begin building your own site in the next chapter, let's take some time to get acquainted with the way Joomla! works. The system has a clean, user-friendly interface that's easy to learn and fun to work with; you'll be amazed at how fast you can perform content management magic in just a few clicks. This chapter introduces you to Joomla!'s basic functions.

In this chapter you will:

- Get acquainted with the Joomla! way of building and maintaining websites.
- Explore the user interface; try out the main screens and toolbars.
- Examine the Joomla! example website that you've installed. What are the main features and special functions that Joomla! offers out of the box?
- Get your feet wet and try out some of the most common administration tasks. Publish your first content, change a few things, and tweak a few settings.

This way you'll get a taste of what it's like to use Joomla! as your web tool box and get ready to build your own site in the next chapter. So let's get started!

Making the switch: Building websites the Joomla! way

If you're new to Joomla! and to Content Management Systems (CMSes), you'll find creating sites using a CMS takes a bit of getting used to. Even if you have some experience building websites, you'll have to adapt to a different way of working. But it's worth your while, and Joomla! will make it easy on you—really! Before we explore the example site you've installed in the last chapter, we'll have a brief look at just what's so different about building websites with Joomla!.

As you may know, ages ago—at least before 2005 when Joomla! came to be—most websites were handcrafted. Creating a website meant creating pages. For every web page you needed, you had to create an HTML document. You would design a basic page layout and reuse that over and over again, adding new pages and adapting the layout to fit the type of content. Whatever tool you used—Adobe (then Macromedia) Dreamweaver, Microsoft FrontPage, or maybe a plain text editor—you would be designing, coding, editing, or building the same web page your visitors would see on your website.

Getting anything published on the Web meant uploading pages (HTML documents) to a web server. Adding and updating content or managing hyperlinks was basically handicraft. You'd open a page in an editor, make changes, and upload it to the web server again. Those were the bad old days of static websites.

However, those days are long, long gone. Today, most websites are dynamic. They use a CMS to make it easier to create and manage content. These CMS-based sites are either built from scratch (by web programmers creating a custom CMS to meet specific client requirements) or based upon a generic CMS such as Joomla! that can be customized and expanded. And it's that dynamic bit that makes working with a CMS so all-new and different.

Sorry, web pages have ceased to exist

Okay, now brace yourself for the main difference between the static old school approach and building websites using a CMS such as Joomla!: there are no web pages.

Of course, a visitor browsing your site still experiences that website as—basically—a collection of pages. In Joomla!, however, the page your visitor sees isn't really a page. Rather, it's a collection of little blocks of interactive data that the CMS pulls from a database. These blocks can be arranged and combined into web pages in many different ways.

As soon as your visitor clicks on a link, he actually sends a request to Joomla! to assemble bits and pieces of data to present a full web page. If your site visitor clicks on **Home**, he'll see a page consisting of headings, images, and teaser texts. If he clicks on a **Read more** link, a new mix of data is displayed. This can consist of the same article heading from the home page, possibly the same intro text and image (now combined with the full body text) links to related articles, banners, and different menu options.

When creating static websites, the HTML page you designed would be the exact same HTML page the site visitor would see. This one-to-one relationship has gone out the window. Behind the scenes, in Joomla!, you won't be editing pages—after all, there are no pages in Joomla!. To change the output (the web page) you edit the different building blocks. These blocks can be any part of the final page: the main article, a menu entry, a banner, or a list of hyperlinks to related items.

A CMS is like a coffee machine system

In a way, a CMS works like a big multi-option coffee machine. The user presses a button to select any of the available options; the machine invisibly fetches all of the required ingredients and mixes these to serve a cup of fresh coffee, latte, frappuccino, or decaf.

This is similar to the way a CMS serves content. The user clicks on a link, the mighty machine gathers whatever combination of content parts is needed from the database to complete this particular order and it pours the output into a coffee cup—I mean, a web page.

Why is this a good thing?

The dynamic approach of CMSes, such as Joomla!, makes creating websites much more flexible. You don't have to manually create dozens of rigid content pages, copying menus and other common elements from page to page as you extend your site. Instead, you'll choose a basic page layout and add any combination of building blocks you need:

- ◆ Do you want a home page with four headings, teaser texts, Read more links, a main menu, a random image, a login form, or a list of links to popular articles? You can do this easily, as the Joomla! CMS allows you to combine different blocks of content into your home page. No programming skills needed!

◆ If your site has a section about digital photography, do you want all content pages about DSLR cameras to display a special banner to attract attention to your special newsletter on the subject? In Joomla!, it's a breeze.

◆ Would you like to have different items on your home page on every day of the week? Do you want to set a particular starting date and an ending date for publishing your articles? It's all possible. While you're on a holiday, you can have your home page automatically updated with the articles you prepared beforehand!

To summarize: you've got the power! You determine what "content blocks" Joomla! packs together onto any specific page and you also set the order and the layout of these blocks on the browser screen.

All of this magic is made possible by Joomla!'s built-in PHP wizardry. It uses the powerful PHP scripting language to communicate with a database, gathering just the blocks of data you need and presenting them the way you want.

A website built of blocks

Now what does this building blocks thing look like in real life? The following is an illustration of Joomla!'s page building system dissected:

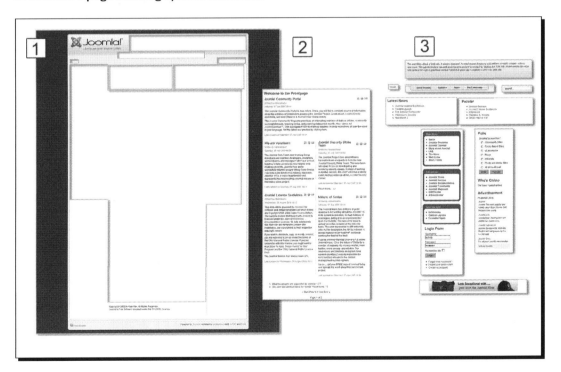

A web page in Joomla! basically consists of these three parts: a base layout (**1**), the main content block (**2**), and as many function blocks as you like (**3**).

- ◆ **(1) The base layout**: This defines the presentation of all content (the amount of columns, background colors, header graphics, and so on). This base layout also contains "positions" (spaces Joomla! can fill with its content blocks). In Joomla!, this base layout is defined in a template. Generally, you set the template once and forget about it. It controls the graphic design; it's not part of your daily routine of content management. You'll learn more about using templates in Chapter 11.

- ◆ **(2) The main content area**: This is the essential part; it contains the cold hard content. Whether you'll publish an article, show a contact form, or a photo gallery it will appear here. In Joomla!, this area is called the **mainbody**. In most cases, the mainbody appears in the middle of the page.

- ◆ **(3) The blocks around the main content area**: Examples are the Main Menu in the left-hand sidebar, Latest News, and so on. These blocks are called **modules**. Modules can contain advanced functionality: menus, polls, login forms, dynamic lists, random images, slideshows, and so on. Anything in the top, left, right, or bottom of a Joomla! page is displayed using modules. The default Joomla! installation comes with dozens of modules; the system is very extensible.

To summarize: the template functions as a frame; the mainbody is the central and essential building block that fits right in the middle; and modules are blocks that you can add and arrange around that, just the way you like, to add essential functions (or just fun and pizzazz) to your site.

Introducing frontend and backend: The Joomla! interface

Okay, so how does all this joomling around with building blocks work? How do you get the mainbody to show content the way you want to? How do you work with modules? To answer these questions, we'll first have a look at the toolkit Joomla! offers you to manage your site. The Joomla! interface features a workspace that contains all tools and controls you'll need for any web building magic.

The following screenshot shows the two faces of the Joomla! example site: the frontend and the backend.

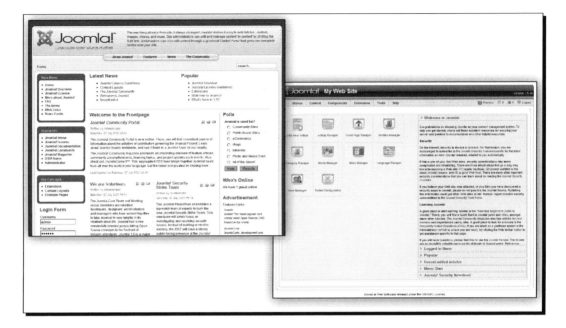

Your workspace: The backend

As you know, Joomla! is a web application. It's a software tool that's installed on a web server and that's accessed through a browser. Creating and managing a site with Joomla! is an online activity. Wherever you are, if you have Internet access you can log in to the Joomla! administration interface to manage your site.

This means every Joomla! site has a "staff entrance" your site visitors will never get to see. It's the administration interface or **backend** of your site. By default, only the site administrator has permission to log in to the backend; later on, the administrator can give other contributors access. Although there's also such a thing as frontend editing, generally you will administer your site using the backend. The backend is the interface for all site management tasks, such as adding content, changing menus, or customizing the layout.

And what's that frontend thing, then?

The public face of your Joomla! site is called—you might have guessed it—the **frontend**. That's just another word for "your website as the visitor sees it".

In the rest of this chapter, you'll learn more about these two basic notions in Joomla!. First, we'll take a closer look at the frontend (the final output of whatever you do in Joomla!).

Exploring the Joomla! example website, we'll check out the many features the CMS offers you right out of the box. After that, we'll examine how the backend works and get our hands dirty with some real life content management activities.

The frontend: The website as the user sees it

Let's first explore the elements of the default Joomla! example site home page. This will give you a good overview of the different modules that Joomla! features out of the box.

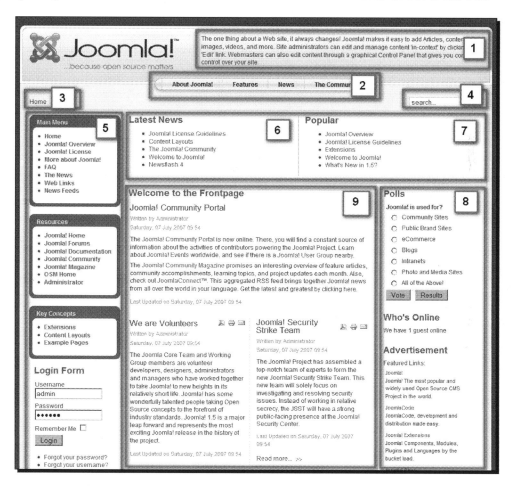

The example site that's part of the default installation is just one of the many types of sites you can build with Joomla!. As you can see, the example is focused on presenting quite a lot of (some might say, too much) information, the home page pulling the reader towards the content through intro texts, banners, link lists, a poll, several menus, and so on. It's very much focused on text; the only image you'll see is a banner ad at the bottom.

The previous picture of the home page shows the following elements:

- ◆ **News Flash**: Shows a random news flash each time the page is loaded
- ◆ **Top Menu**: A menu at the top of the page
- ◆ **Breadcrumbs**: The pathway to the current page
- ◆ **Search**: The search box—the search results are shown in the main content area
- ◆ **In the left-hand side column**: Three different menus, and a login form
- ◆ **Latest News**: Links to the most recent news items
- ◆ **Popular**: Links to the most read articles
- ◆ **In the right-hand side column**: Three separate blocks—Poll, Who's Online, and Advertisements
- ◆ **Mainbody of the Front Page**: Introductory text of selected articles

This site perfectly demonstrates what Joomla! is capable of. The fact that it's already packed with articles, menus, and extras gives you a great opportunity to try out Joomla!'s capabilities and decide for yourself which features fit your site's needs.

You're certainly not limited to building the kind of information-rich sites the example site demonstrates. In Chapter 1, you've seen a few other examples of Joomla! sites ranging from small personal blogs to huge corporate and e-commerce sites. Later on, you'll learn how to customize the sample site to create a much cleaner look that might better fit your needs.

Time for action – tour the example site

Let's take a closer look at the demo site and see some real life examples of page layouts. You'll see how the content in the mainbody and the modules in the surrounding content area change depending on the menu hyperlink you click:

1. Enter the URL of your site (for example, `http://www.mysite.com`) in your web browser. If in Chapter 2 you have installed Joomla! into another folder, the URL would be `http://www.mysite.com/otherfoldername`. You'll recognize the home page, as displayed in the following screenshot. The mainbody (the visible part of it outlined in the screenshot) consists of several article intro texts; above it, to its left-hand side and right-hand side, are modules.

2. Let's explore how the layout changes on a different page. In the **Main Menu**, click on **Joomla! Overview**. You'll notice that the mainbody displays what Joomla! calls an article, the most common type of page content (the mainbody is again outlined in the following screenshot):

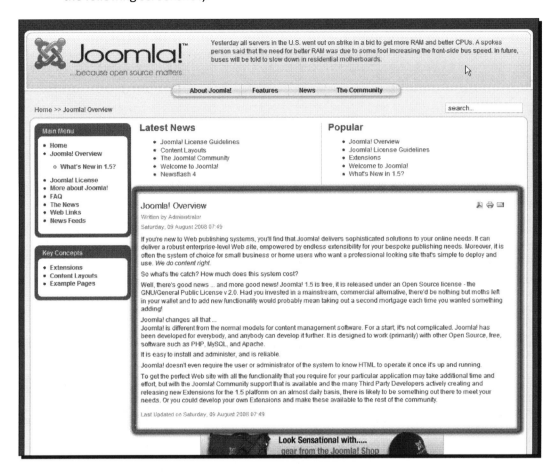

The mainbody takes up more screen space this time. On the right-hand side column, the home page modules have disappeared. This is part of the site design; the right-hand side column doesn't display when it contains no content.

3. In the **Main Menu**, click on **More about Joomla!**. You'll see another type of page layout. The mainbody now contains a short list of links to content sections: **The Project**, **The CMS**, and **The Community**.

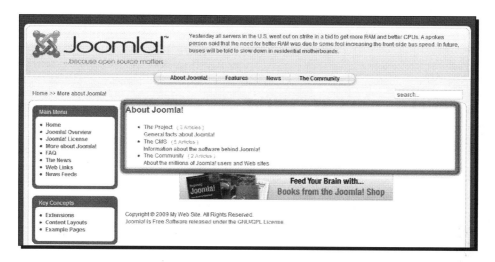

4. Now check out one last type of page layout. On the **Main Menu**, click on **The News**. As you can see, the mainbody displays a series of short introductions (or teasers). Below each intro is a **Read more** link that shows the full article.

What just happened?

At first sight, the Joomla! example site may seem overwhelming. There are many bits of content, many hyperlink lists, menus, and many different types of web page layouts. But in fact, many pages on Joomla! sites are built around the four page layouts you've just discovered: the home page, content pages (with one main article in the mainbody), and two types of "pages in between". These "pages in between" function as hyperlink lists combined with either short descriptions of the content section or introductory texts to the articles themselves. These "in-betweens" help users discover the site contents by offering them an overview of articles on related topics.

You've also discovered how the mainbody can be combined with different modules. In the example site, the home page is jam-packed with modules. All of the other pages just show a few module items in the top bar and left-hand side column. On those pages, the right-hand side column has no content and its place has been taken by the mainbody content.

Have a go hero – get familiar with the example site contents

Take some time to browse your example site. By now, you'll be able to see the framework behind the different pages and understand how different combinations of mainbody and modules are put together to create unique web pages.

You'll also notice that there is more to explore than just pages with "classic content" (articles, text, and images) that we've seen so far. Although classic content pages may be at the core of many websites, in a dynamic site all kinds of dynamic content can be displayed in the mainbody. Have a go at the Poll on the home page, or try out the Search box. You'll see the mainbody will show the (dynamic) poll and search results.

For now, we won't go any deeper into these different types of dynamic content—though it's important to realize that they exist and that they take Joomla!'s capabilities much further than just plain old "presentation of text and images". We'll cover this subject in more detail in the next few chapters.

Taking control: Administering your site in the backend

The backend is the cockpit of your Joomla! jet. It's the administration interface that lets you take your website to new heights. From the backend, you manage your site. It's organized quite neatly, so you'll learn to find your way around it pretty fast. Let's have a closer look at the backend interface right now.

Time for action – log in to the backend

1. To access the backend of your site, you'll add /administrator to the address of your website. If your site is http://www.mysite.com, type http://www.mysite.com/administrator in the address bar of your browser.

2. There it is, the secret entrance to your site! You'll see a login prompt:

3. Enter your username (by default, that's **admin**) and the password you've entered when installing Joomla! (see also Chapter 2). Click on the **Login** button.

4. After you've successfully entered your credentials, you'll enter the actual administration interface: the backend home page (the Control Panel). This interface provides access to all of the functions that you need as a site administrator, (such as adding content, changing menus, customizing the layout, and so on):

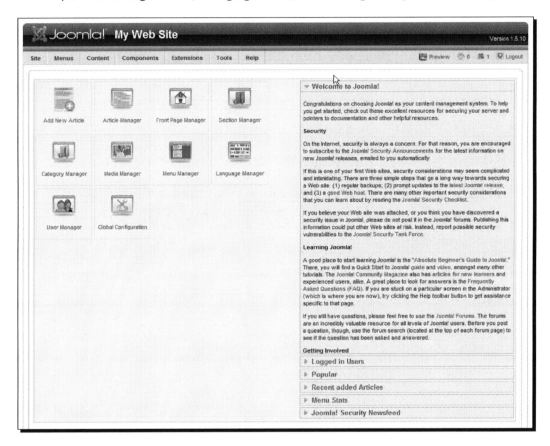

What just happened?

You've logged in to the backend of your site, and—lo and behold!—you've entered the **Control Panel**, only accessible to users with special access rights. You'll be coming back there for every site management activity. As the site administrator, you'll probably want to make a shortcut in your browser to the /administrator URL.

Taking a closer look at the Control Panel

Let's look at the Control Panel in more detail. In the following screenshot, the four main screen areas of the Control Panel are outlined:

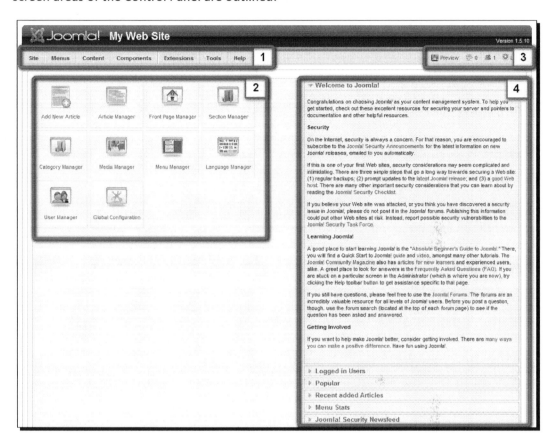

1. Menu bar

The top menu bar is an essential feature of the Control Panel. This is really where all of the action is. The seven items in this drop-down menu (listed as follows) give you access to all of Joomla!'s content management tools and functions:

- ◆ **Site**: User access management, file management, global configuration

- ◆ **Menus**: Menu management

- ◆ **Content**: Add or change articles, change site structure

- ◆ **Components**: Manage special features, such as banners and polls

- ◆ **Extensions**: Manage extensions and templates which extend the functionality and capabilities of your website

- ◆ **Tools**: Send simple e-mail messages to site users (private messages), clear site cache, and so on
- ◆ **Help**: Joomla!'s online help function

This top menu is the one you'll use over and over again when working on your site. For now, we'll first have a look at the other panels and controls; after that we will start exploring the wide range of capabilities hidden behind all of the top menu items.

2. Shortcut buttons

A series of buttons that offer quick access to frequently used functions (which you can also access through the top menu), such as adding a new article or changing site settings.

3. Preview and Info Bar

In this part of the Control Panel you'll find the following functions:

- ◆ **Preview**: Open the website's home page in a new browser tab or window
- ◆ Information on the number of private messages (messages sent to you by other users of the site) to be read by you, and the number of users logged in
- ◆ **Logout**: Logout from the backend

4. Information panels

Click on the title of these six information panels to show their content. The **Welcome to Joomla!** panel contains helpful links for new users. The other panels are self-explanatory. Click on the title (such as **Logged In Users** or **Popular**) to browse up-to-date information on your site's users and content. The **Joomla! Security Newsfeed** panel keeps you informed on security issues.

Understanding backend tools and controls

The Control Panel is the home page of the backend. Whatever action you want to perform, the dozens of links on the Control Panel page lead you to the appropriate tools or *Managers,* as Joomla! calls them. Examples are the **Article Manager**, the **Menu Manager**, and the **User Manager**. That's where the real action takes place.

Although there are many different Managers and other types of administration tools, it's quite easy to grasp the way they work. All of the interface pages share the same base layout and show a toolbar in the top right position of the screen. In the following screenshot you can see the control buttons of Joomla!'s **Article Manager** toolbar:

Many Managers share commonly used features, such as **New**, **Edit**, **Copy**, and **Trash**. Let's look at the functions of the toolbar buttons in more detail:

It's pretty straightforward to grasp what the buttons are about:

- **Unarchive**, **Archive**: Archive articles and make these accessible only through a special archive menu
- **Publish**: Make an article visible to your visitors
- **Unpublish**: Make an article invisible to your visitors (without throwing it away)
- **Move**: Move an article to another content category
- **Copy**: Create a duplicate of an article
- **Trash**: Send an article to the Trash (to delete it)
- **Edit**: Edit an article
- **New**: Create a new article
- **Parameters**: Change general article settings
- **Help**: Browse to Joomla!'s online help

The toolbar is context sensitive. It will display the buttons relevant to the current activity. When you click on the **Edit** button in the **Article Manager** you'll be taken to the article editor screen. In this screen you'll see the following set of toolbar buttons:

- ◆ **Preview**: Open a pop-up screen giving you a rough impression of what the formatted article will look like

- ◆ **Save**: Save changes and close the current window (this takes you back to the **Article Manager**)

- ◆ **Apply**: Save changes, without closing the current window

- ◆ **Close**: Cancel without saving any changes

- ◆ **Help**: Browse to Joomla!'s online help

As you can see, most toolbar buttons are self-explanatory. Note, however, the difference between the **Apply** and **Save** buttons. Click on **Apply** to save changes without leaving the current page. You'll find that when editing the text of an article, it's easiest to click on **Apply** and **Preview** to check the results in a new browser window. To correct a typo or change the article layout you don't have to re-select the article and open it again for editing. When you're satisfied with the results, click on **Save** to leave the editing screen. The same applies to any occurrence of **Save** and **Apply** on other Joomla! interface screens.

Clicking on the **Apply** button every now and then, when writing a long article, will ensure your article contents are saved. You can lose all of the unsaved changes when you leave the article editor open (without action) for more than 15 minutes. Later in this chapter you'll learn how to change this 15 minute setting to allow you to take some more time for your well-deserved coffee breaks.

Getting your feet wet: Start administering your site

We have had a first look at the Control Panel screen layout and the main backend toolbars. You're probably dying to try out how the thing actually works! I'll test your patience just a little more. First, we'll make some more sense of the Control Panel and find out what you really need to know to get started on this impressive tool box. After all, its main menu bar consists of seven menu options with more than 40 submenu items. That's a wealth of CMS power—but it's also quite daunting.

We won't go into all of the menu items and their capabilities here; rather, you'll learn how to use the important menu options as you go along building your site in the next chapters. For now, let's go ahead and see what the primary functions are.

Three types of backend actions

Roughly, the seven options in the Control Panel menu bar consist of three clusters. Some you'll use on a daily basis, some you'll only have to deploy every now and then. In the following diagram you can see what these three groups are. In the rest of this chapter, we'll have a closer look at them not in the order they appear on the menu bar, but in order of their relevance in your day-to-day content management activities.

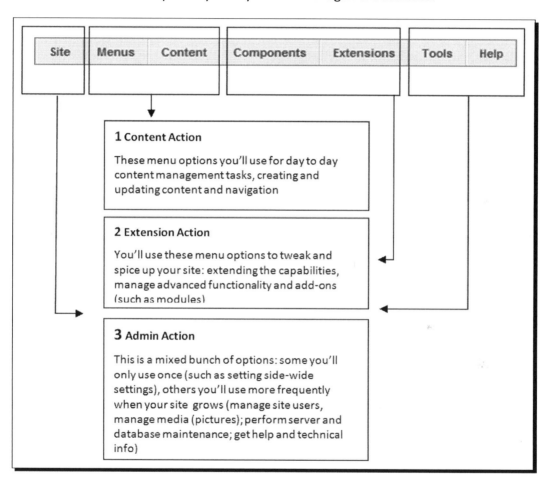

Let's try out an example of each of these three types of content and site management actions:

- **Content actions example**: Publishing actual content
- **Extension actions example**: Working with extensions or, rearranging modules
- **Admin actions example**: Changing site settings

Content actions example: Let's create some content!

It's fine to have an example site filled with some dummy content about Joomla!, but you probably want to make your mark by adding your own content. Publish something, anything, to your own Joomla! website. Go ahead!

Time for action – publish your first article

1. Navigate to **Content | Article Manager** (you can also use the **Article Manager** shortcut in the Control Panel).

2. In the toolbar, click on the **New** button (the green one with the big plus sign).

3. In the **Article: [New]** screen, fill out the **Title** and **Alias** field as shown in the following screenshot (the **Alias** will help Joomla! create user-friendly URLs; you'll learn more about that in Chapter 12 on Search Engine Optimization):

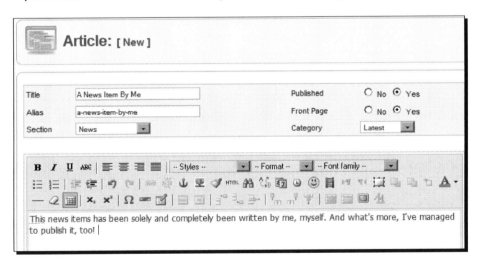

4. In the **Section** drop-down box, choose **News**. In the **Category** drop-down box, choose **Latest**. This will make your article turn up among the other articles in the News section of the site.

5. Joomla! uses a structure of sections and categories to organize content. In this example, the News section holds the Latest category, which holds articles. You'll learn more about this principle of organizing content in the next two chapters.

6. Make sure **Published** is set to **Yes**. This is the default option.

7. Click on **Front Page: Yes** to make sure your news will be shown on the home page.

8. Add some text in the text editor box. Any text will do; for now we're just playing around in the example site.

9. Click on the **Apply** button (with the green tick) in the toolbar in the top right-hand side of the page. Joomla! will inform you that it has successfully saved changes to your article.

10. Click on **Preview** in the Preview and Info Bar section of the page. This will take you to the home page of your site.

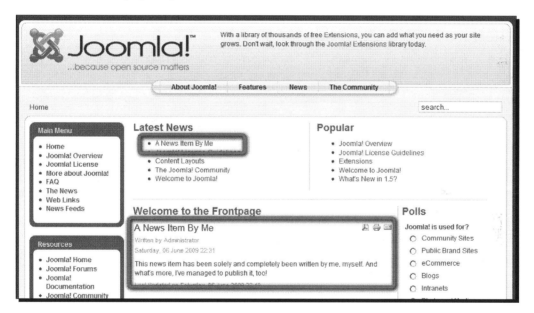

You're done! As you can see, you news item is published on the front page. What's more, Joomla! has automatically added your feature to the **Latest News** links too.

There's even one other way the visitor can navigate to your news item. Because you've added the article to the **News** section, clicking on the menu link **The News** in the **Main Menu** will also reveal your new article:

What just happened?

In a few steps you have created and published brand new content. By categorizing your new article in the right way, and clicking on the **Show on Front Page** option, the article text is added to the home page. Moreover, the article title is added as a hyperlink to the dynamic **Latest News** list, and finally the article also turns up on the page that shows items from the **News** category.

Extension actions example: Managing modules

A good web page shows a clear structure. The Joomla! example site presents lots of content in quite a crowded layout; every single space is filled with text. The site displays more than ten little blocks of content around the main content area (the mainbody). There are four menus, three of which are shown in the left-hand side column. Putting that many blocks on the page will almost certainly distract the reader from the main content. We're going to give the content some breathing room and help the reader scan the page.

Let's clean things up a little. We'll rearrange our screen and remove some unnecessary items. In Joomla!, you use the **Module Manager** to change the position and other settings of the site's modules (building blocks).

Time for action – rearranging page layout

In our left-hand side column, we'll discard the **Resources** menu and the **Page Layouts** menu, leaving only the **Main Menu**. To get an uncluttered left-hand side column displaying only the main menu we will also move the **Login Form** to the right-hand side column.

1. Navigate to **Extensions | Module Manager**.

2. As you can see, there's an impressive list of installed modules. To find just the instances of the menu module we'll apply a filter. Above the table column headings there are four drop-down list boxes. In the **Select Type** drop-down list, select **mod_mainmenu**:

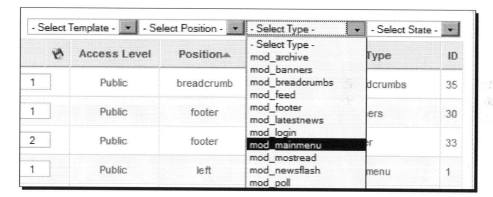

 No matter how many menus are displayed on the site, every menu module is of the **mod_mainmenu** Module Type. In other words, not only the "Main Menu" uses this module.

3. As a result, only the six instances of **mod_mainmenu** are shown:

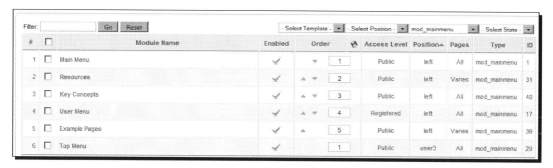

4. Click on the **Enabled** icon (a green check mark) in the column to the right-hand side of **Resources**. Clicking on the icon will toggle it to a red cross indicating this module item is now disabled.

5. Now click on the **Enabled** icon in the column to the right-hand side of **Key Concepts** and **Example Pages** too. These menu modules are also now disabled.

6. Click on **Preview**. You've cleaned up the left-hand side column. There is just one menu left, the **Main Menu** (this should never be removed or hidden; it's essential for Joomla!—and for your visitors).

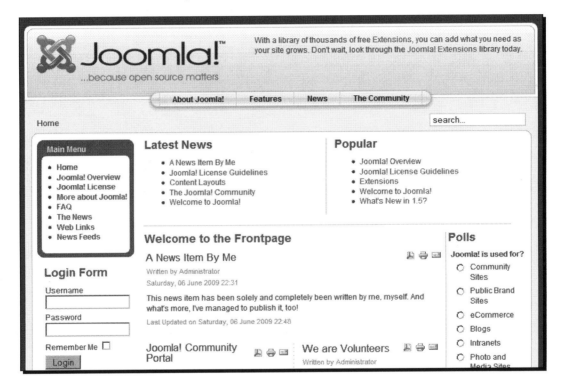

7. To finish our job, we'll switch back to the **Module Manager** in the backend to move the **Login Form** to the right-hand side column. In the **Select Type** drop-down list, choose **mod_login**.

8. In the **Module Name** column, click on **Login Form** to edit the login form settings:

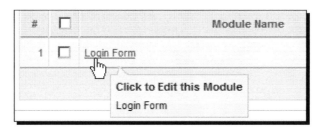

9. In the **Module: Edit** screen, select **Position: right** to make the module appear in the right-hand side column:

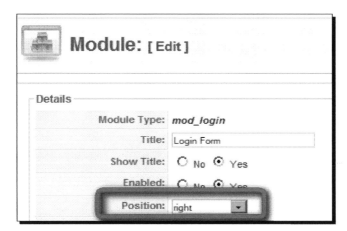

10. Click on **Save** to apply the changes and click on **Preview** to view the results. You've successfully cleaned up the left-hand side column. There's one menu left; the login form has been moved to the right-hand side of the screen:

What just happened?

You've just experienced the power of the **Module Manager**. Enabling a module displays it on your website, disabling hides it. That means you can easily switch screen items "on" or "off" and still leave them around in the backend, just in case. Also, you've seen now how quickly and easily you can move things around on the screen by choosing another **Position** in the module editing screen.

Site actions example: Configuring basic site settings

The **Site** menu and **Tools** menu in the Control Panel menu bar offer you some more advanced functions, ranging from user management to database maintenance. Later on you'll learn which functions are important for day to day site management. For now, we'll take a look at the **Site | Basic Configuration** settings where you can set Joomla! preferences.

Time for action – set Joomla! preferences

When browsing the Joomla! backend you may have noticed that after a certain amount of idle time Joomla! will ask you to log in again. By default, Joomla! kicks you out when you've been logged in for 15 minutes without any activity. When developing a site it can be quite annoying to have to log in every time you return to your desk with a fresh cup of coffee. Let's change this with the **Session Lifetime** setting in the Joomla! preferences.

1. From the Control Panel, navigate to **Site | Global Configuration** (you can also click on the **Global Configuration** button below the menu bar; it's a shortcut).

2. **Global Configuration** is divided into **Site** settings, **System** settings, and **Server** settings. Click on the **System** link to show the appropriate settings panel.

3. On the **System** page, you'll see **Session Settings** in the bottom-right corner. Change **Session Lifetime** to **45** minutes.

4. Click on **Save**. From now on you can leave the computer for 45 minutes before Joomla! prompts you to log in again.

What just happened?

You've just made your life as an administrator a little easier by changing one of Joomla!'s system settings. Now you can leave your computer idle for 45 minutes before Joomla! kindly kicks you out and asks you for your login name and password again.

Have a go hero – explore the configuration options

Check out the other **Global Configuration** options, but be careful. Most of the settings you should leave unchanged. Don't touch the **Server Settings** and **Database** settings (on the **Server** page) unless you know what you're doing as these contain critical data that Joomla! needs to function properly. However, you can easily change some harmless **Site** settings. Maybe you would like to change the **Site Name** (the name shown in the backend header bar) or replace the default Joomla! text in the **Metadata Description** field with a few appropriate words to let search engines know what your site's about. If you're not yet familiar with these concepts, however, that's fine. You'll learn more about the options you need later on in the book.

Looking for all the answers?

In the course of this book you'll learn much more about what the Control Panel is all about. However, we won't cover every tiny little detail of the administration interface. Luckily, Joomla! offers an exhaustive online reference to all backend menus, submenus, options, settings, and screens. In the backend, click on **Help | Joomla! Help**. There's a wealth of up-to-date information from the Joomla! help site.

Pop quiz – test your knowledge of the Joomla! way of web building

1. What's makes a CMS-based website different from a traditional, "static" website?

   a) A CMS consists of an unlimited database of web pages.

   b) A CMS doesn't use traditional coding languages, such as HTML.

   c) A CMS dynamically builds web pages by gathering content blocks from a database.

2. What's the backend of a Joomla!-powered website?

   a) It's the interface where administrators log in to change site configuration settings.

   b) It's the interface where administrators log in to build and maintain the site.

   c) It's the part of the site that's only accessible for registered users.

3. How can you rearrange the page layout of your site and move about content blocks?

   a) By moving and deleting articles.

   b) By using the Module Manager to the position and visibility of modules.

   c) By using the Article Manager to change the position and visibility of articles.

Summary

We learned a lot in this chapter about what makes building websites with Joomla! special, what the frontend of your site can look like, and how to use the backend Control Panel.

- ◆ You've learned the difference between static websites and building websites the Joomla! way. A Joomla! powered website is a collection of building blocks, dynamically constructed from the database.

- ◆ The frontend of the website—the site as your visitor experiences it—is constructed out of different building blocks. The central part of the page is called the mainbody; the surrounding blocks are called modules.

- ◆ Joomla! offers a great number of options to present information in the central content area, the mainbody. Moreover, you can combine the mainbody with almost any combination and number of modules in the header, in the footer, in the left-hand side column, and the right-hand side column.

- ◆ Every Joomla! site has a backend; a Control Panel to administer your site. When you log into the backend you can manage content, add new features, change settings, and so on. You add an article through the Article Manager, rearrange elements on the page through the Module Manager, and change site settings in the Global Configuration panel.

In the next chapter we'll get up to speed and take things much further. Now that you've experimented with Joomla! a bit, you'll create a fully functional website that perfectly meets your first client's demands—and it will be finished in an hour!

4

Web Building Basics: Creating a Site in an Hour

In the previous chapter, you have acquainted yourself with the Joomla! interface, explored the example site, and tried out Joomla!'s administration interface.

You know your way around, you've got a good idea of how things work—so now it's high time to start building a website! In this chapter, you'll build a complete site in just one hour. Imagine, you've just got a call from your first client. They have founded a club that is about to get some media attention, but they still haven't got a website they can refer to. They need a website and they need it fast. Can you help them out?

That's a perfect opportunity to put your new web building toolkit to the test. And, well, being new to Joomla!, maybe you'll need a little bit more than just one hour. However, if you start now, you're certain to meet tomorrow's deadline—and have time left to have dinner in time, take a hot bath, and grab a movie too.

In this chapter, you'll learn to:

- ◆ Remove Joomla!'s sample data to create a blank canvas for your site
- ◆ Customize the site's template
- ◆ Add content: create a framework, add articles, and add menu items
- ◆ Add new features: create a contact form and a poll

What you will be making

In the following screenshot, you see what you will be building throughout this chapter. It's based on Joomla!'s sample site, but it's perfectly tailored to the client's specifications:

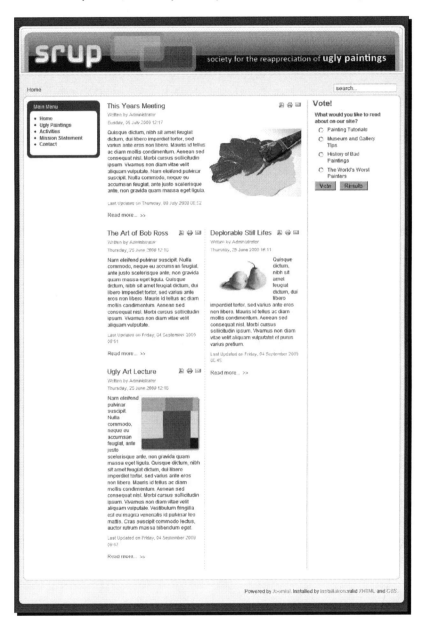

SRUP's the word

Allow me to introduce you to your first client! It's the Society for the Reappreciation of Ugly Paintings. They just love amateur paintings that mostly end up dumped in the trash heap or turn up in charity shops. According to the SRUP philosophy, those ugly paintings represent the ordinary people's artistic view on reality, and this should be treasured. Now that a big newspaper is about to write an article about SRUP, the society needs a website to broadcast their message and tell the public what they're all about. You may not be into art, but you are into the art of building websites, so you're just the one the SRUP people need.

SRUPs wish list is as follows:

◆ The look and feel of the site should fit with the logo and colors found on the society's stationery

◆ The site should present several content pages in a well organized way, providing a solid basis for further expansion

◆ The home page should show a poll, to increase visitor interaction

◆ Visitors should be invited to get in touch; there has to be a contact form

Logging in again

If you want to follow along with the exercises in this chapter, I'll assume you're logged in to the backend of your site. Remember, it only takes two steps:

1. In your browser, log in to the backend, by adding `administrator` to the URL of your website: `www.mysite.com/administrator`.

2. At the login prompt, enter your username and password and click on the **Login** button. Once you are logged in, you'll see the **Control Panel**. The Control Panel is the home page of the backend.

Cleaning up: Removing the sample data

In Chapter 2, you've installed Joomla! with the example site data. You'll only do that once, when you're new to Joomla! and want have a first look at its possibilities. Once you start building your own site, you don't need the sample data anymore. Unfortunately, there is no "Uninstall Sample Data" button. You could install Joomla! again without sample data, but it's faster to clean things up. In the next two steps we'll do just that.

Admittedly, cleaning up Joomla! may seem about as exciting as wiping clean a wall-to-wall classroom blackboard before the lesson starts. However, it's a great way of preparing yourself for your very first Joomla! site. You'll find that stripping Joomla!'s example site will give you some useful insight in the way it's constructed. Bit by bit, it will reveal the different types of content that have been used to fill the empty CMS framework.

If you have installed Joomla! with no sample data you can skip these two steps.

Step 1: Hide the unnecessary stuff

The sample data consists of two types of content. On the one hand, you have *articles* (basic content), on the other hand there are *modules* (remember, these are prefab function blocks, such as banners, forms, and additional menus).

Time for action – hiding modules

Let's start with the modules. As much of the default ones are redundant for our goal, we'll switch them off. In Joomla! lingo, switching things off is called disabling. Disabling doesn't erase these modules; you can always enable them again.

1. In the **Extensions** drop-down menu, click on **Module Manager**. The **Module Manager** displays a big list of modules that are installed: **Breadcrumbs**, **Banners**, **Footer**, and so on. In the **Enabled** column, you see whether or not the module is in use (and therefore visible in the frontend):

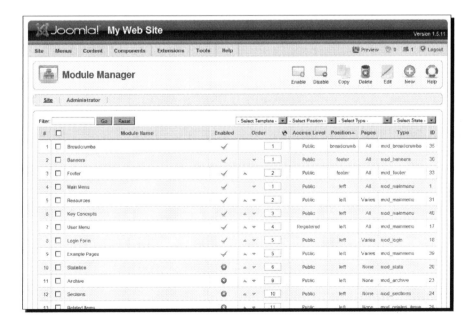

2. Click on the green check mark to the right-hand side of the **Banners** module name. The check mark changes to a cross indicating that the module is now disabled.

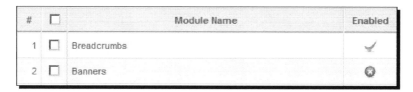

#	☐	Module Name	Enabled
1	☐	Breadcrumbs	✓
2	☐	Banners	⊗

3. Now disable all of the following modules by clicking on the **Enabled** check mark next to the module name: **Banners**, **Footer**, **Example Pages**, **Advertisement**, **Polls**, **Resources**, **Key Concepts**, **Login Form**, **Who's Online**, **Newsflash**, **Latest News**, **Popular**, **Top Menu**, and **Syndication**. If you've followed along in Chapter 3, some of the menu modules may already be disabled. Make sure you don't inadvertently enable them again!

4. To see the results click on **Preview**. Only a few modules are left, such as the main menu and the search box:

What just happened?

To be able to put together our first Joomla! site, we're getting rid of a lot of distracting extras so that we can build on a solid, simple foundation—a blank canvas perfectly suitable for the new Ugly Paintings site. That's why you have hidden a few extras that come with the example site. They're still ready for use, but you won't be needing them for now.

Step 2: Remove sample content

Let's remove the sample content now. It consists of three groups:

- ◆ Actual content: articles.
- ◆ The containers Joomla! uses to organize articles; these are called *sections* and *categories*. We'll learn more about them in the rest of this chapter.
- ◆ Menu links to these articles, sections, or categories.

Time for action – deleting articles, categories, and sections

To remove content you always start with the actual articles. That's because you cannot remove containers (categories and sections) as long as they're not empty.

1. Navigate to **Content | Article Manager**.

2. In the **# Display** drop-down menu at the bottom of the screen, select **all**. Now all of the articles are displayed in one list.

3. Select the checkbox at the top of the list (just to the right-hand side of #). This way all of the items in the column are selected:

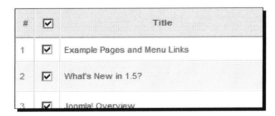

4. Click on the **Trash** button in the toolbar. Joomla! shows a message confirming that the articles have been sent to the Trash.

5. When articles are in the Trash, they're still in Joomla!'s database should you wish to restore them. However, you won't be needing these articles again. To permanently delete them navigate to **Content | Article Trash**. Select all of the items and click on **Delete**.

6. In the next screen, click on **Delete** again to confirm you want to delete all of the articles.

Now remove the sample categories and sections. These are containers for articles that no longer exist:

7. Navigate to **Content | Category Manager**. Select the top row checkbox to select all of the categories. Click on **Delete**.

8. Navigate to **Content | Section Manager**. Select the top row checkbox to select all of the categories. Click on **Delete**.

Finally, you have to empty the Main Menu. Nothing new here; this is done in a similar way:

9. Navigate to **Menus | Main Menu**. Select the top row select box to select all of the menu items. Click on **Trash**. A message is displayed that all of the items are sent to the Trash except for the default menu item, **Home**. This item can't be deleted because without at least a home link it would be impossible to make any of the site's contents visible.

10. As you won't be needing these menu links any more, you might as well permanently remove them from the **Menu Trash**. Navigate to **Menus | Menu Trash**, select all of the items, click on **Delete**, and confirm.

Now all of the content has been removed from the example site except for the **Home** link and the Search module:

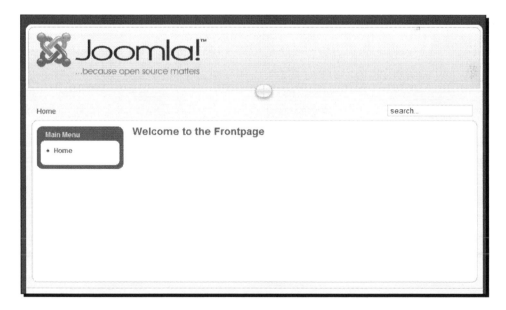

What just happened?

There it is! You have peeled the Joomla! onion. The website is stripped of its contents. You've seen how Joomla! content consists of content containers (called sections and categories) and articles (the actual content). Apart from this, menu items are used to make the content visible. In a few minutes we'll add new content in the same order that we've just used deconstructing the example site. First we'll create sections and categories, then we'll create articles assigned to those sections or categories, and finally we'll create menu links to this new content. We'll be practicing this *content containers—articles—menu links* mantra quite a lot—but don't worry, soon enough it will come natural.

Remember, installing Joomla! with sample data is only recommended when you're new to Joomla! and want to get familiar with the system by exploring its page layouts, menus, modules, and so on. When you already know Joomla!, it's much easier to start without sample data.

Have a go hero – clean up those menus

Actually, there is some more content that comes with the Joomla! installation. There are more menus! You have disabled all menu modules apart from the Main Menu, which means they're invisible on the frontend. But these menus (Top Menu, Resources, and so on) are still available in the backend, and their contents (the menu links) still exist. Although they won't be in your way when constructing a new site, they will still show up in **Menus | Menu Manager**. If you like to a have a thoroughly cleaned slate to start with, why don't you delete all unused menus? Throughout the course of this book, you'll only need the Main Menu. To delete any of the other menus, first delete the menu contents (in the **Menu Manager**, select the menu and click on **Delete**) and then delete the menu modules (in the **Module Manager**, select the menu module and click on **Delete**).

Building your site is a three step process

You've now got a blank canvas. The site is empty, there's no content, and there are just a few basic layout elements. It's high time to start building something new, cool, and attractive! We'll do this in three steps:

1. **Customize the layout**: Tweak the basic layout to fit your needs.

2. **Add content**: Design a structure for your content (using sections and categories) and add articles that fit the content framework.

3. **Add extras**: Add further functionality to your site, such as a contact form or a poll.

Step 1: Customize the layout

In Chapter 3 you've seen that the overall site layout (columns, colors, typography, and so on) is set in the site's template files. Joomla! makes it easy to edit the current template using the **Template Manager**. In this case, we'll choose a new color scheme, add a new header image, and make a few additional changes.

Customize the color scheme

The color scheme of Joomla!'s default **rhuk_milkyway** template is all too well known. There must be thousands and thousands of websites with a dark blue background, dark blue rounded menu corners, and dark blue heading texts. Corporate and professional looking as this may be, it's also about as special as a dark blue Japanese sedan in a car park full of dark blue Japanese sedans. Of course, you don't want your client to think their new website is just the same as everybody else's, so let's change things a little.

Time for action – choosing a color variation

The **rhuk_milkyway** template offers you a choice of color schemes or "color variations". Let's pick a different one:

1. Navigate to **Extensions | Template Manager** and click on **rhuk_milkyway**.

2. In the **Template: [Edit]** screen, change a few values in the **Parameters** section. Select **Color Variation: Black** and select **Background Variation: Black**.

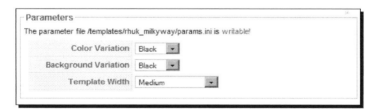

3. There are three **Template Width** options:

  ◆ **Fluid with Maximum**: The width of the template is liquid; in a big window, it will be displayed wider.

  ◆ **Medium**: The width of the template is set to 930 pixels.

  ◆ **Small**: The width of the template is set to 750 pixels.

  ◆ **Fluid**: The minimum size is 750 pixels; the width varies with the window size.

Choose **Medium**. We'll have a fixed page width of 930 pixels.

4. Click on **Preview**. You'll notice the background color has changed to a very dark grey—nothing fancy, nothing extremely exciting, but it does go nicely with the SRUP logo color. Moreover, the **Main Menu** border has changed to a stylish black:

What just happened?

By setting a few parameters in the Template Manager Edit screen you changed the width and colors of the site template. Choosing a fixed width means the size of the layout will be the same, no matter how big the users' monitor or browser window may be. A fixed width of 900+ pixels is very popular these days and is used by big sites such as www.apple.com and www.microsoft.com. It looks good on most screens and leaves some room for left-hand side and right-hand side margins. Having a fixed width gives you pixel perfect control over the size of the layout; you won't have to bother adjusting our layout or graphics for different screen sizes (such as the fixed width header graphic we're going to replace in a minute).

The **rhuk_milkyway** template lets you change the colors and the overall width of the layout. There are other templates available with their own set of parameters that allow you to choose the number of columns or set other layout options.

Time for action – preparing a new header file

As it is, our design still very much looks like any Joomla! site—and that big Joomla! logo on every page isn't helping much! You'll replace this with your client's logo. The original Joomla! logo is just 298 pixels wide and 75 pixels high. We'll create a new image that takes up the full width and height of the header; this way, we can change the site's looks distinctively with just one graphic.

1. Open up your image editing tool. In this example, we'll use Adobe Photoshop, but any image editor will do.

2. The space where we want to place our image (the full width and height of the template header) has these dimensions: 920 x 108 pixels. To leave room for a little margin, we'll create a new header file of slightly smaller dimensions: 900 x 98 pixels. Click on **New**. In the **Width** and **Height** boxes, fill in **900** and **98** pixels. Choose **Background Contents: Transparent**.

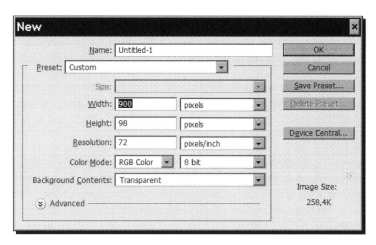

3. In Photoshop, the PNG file shows a grey and white "checkerboard" background. This indicates the background is transparent, which means the colors of the header background will shine through. This way, the logo image you create blends in nicely with the overall design.

4. Now you can create any logo you like. Let's skip the details, as these depend on the specific needs of your site and the tool you are using. For this example, I've created a nice rounded Web 2.0 style logo using two free fonts: Airstrip Four from `www.dafont.com` (see `www.dafont.com/faq.php` for installation instructions) and the Calibri Windows system font, I have also applied some Photoshop shapes and effects.

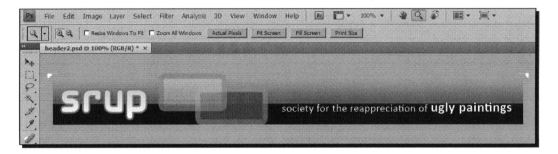

5. Save the image as a PNG file. In Photoshop, click on **Save for Web and Devices**, choose the PNG-24 file format, and save the image as `srupheader.png`. Make sure to select the **Transparency** checkbox to preserve the transparent background. Click on **Save**.

6. In the next screen, choose a location on your computer and click on **Save** again. Done!

A previous version of the Microsoft Internet Explorer browser (version 6) doesn't display PNG images correctly if they contain transparent areas. If you want to accommodate for visitors using this old browser, it's better to use an image without transparency. Another solution is to use a Joomla! extension that remedies this specific browser issue. In Chapter 10, you'll learn more on adding extensions to Joomla!. Do a Web search for "Ultimate PNG Fix Plugin" to read more about this specific PNG extension and its use.

What just happened?

The header image file to replace the default Joomla! logo is ready, but we're not done yet. To get Joomla! to display this new file, we'll upload the image file to the web server and change a few simple lines in the template code

Living without Photoshop—free alternatives

Photoshop may be a fine graphic editing tool, but it's not exactly cheap. The standard Windows graphics editor Paint can do the job—but it's capabilities are very, very basic. Fortunately, there are many excellent and free Photoshop alternatives. You can even have essential Photoshopping capabilities on your computer without installing a thing. Just browse to www.pixlr.com and start creating and editing!

If you're looking for free graphic editing software programs, do a Web search for Paint.NET or GIMP. Both are very capable programs; Paint.NET is beginner friendly and at the same time quite powerful. The **GIMP**, an acronym for **GNU Image Manipulation Program**, is arguably the most popular free Photoshop contender. It's an open-source program that features a truckload of photo retouching and image editing tools.

Time for action – display the new header image file

Let's get Joomla! to show our new header image. To do this, you'll first upload the file to your web server using FTP—which is very similar to moving or copying files on your own computer using File Explorer in Windows or the Finder on the Mac. If you've installed Joomla! yourself, you've already used FTP to put the Joomla software files on the web server (see Chapter 2 on installing Joomla!). If you're new to FTP, you can read more on the Web on using FTP software such as FileZilla (www.siteground.com/tutorials/ftp/filezilla.htm).

1. Using your FTP program, connect to your web server and find the root directory where Joomla! is installed. Browse to the /templates/rhuk_milkyway/images directory. This is the directory that contains the images files for the default Joomla! template, rhuk_milkyway. Upload the srupheader.png file you just created to this folder.

Next, we'll take a peek under the Joomla! hood and change a rule in the template files to point to the new image file. Yes, you're going to change a few lines of code—but don't worry, it's really straightforward and we're going to explain this code thing in a minute.

2. In the Joomla! Control Panel, choose **Extensions | Template Manager**. In the **Template Name** column, click on the name of the default template, **rhuk_milkyway**.

3. Click on the **Edit CSS** button, select template.css and click on **Edit**. The **Template Manager** editor screen opens. Scroll down to find the code that starts with div#logo. This is the code that tells Joomla! where the logo is positioned on the screen and what image file should be used.

4. Change the `background: url` code to refer to the new image file. This code should now read: background: url(../images/srupheader.png) 0 0 no-repeat;

5. Change the `width` and `height` values to reflect the size of the new image. To shift the image a little to the left-hand side, decrease the `margin-left` value. The three lines of `div#logo` should now read:

```
width: 900px;
height: 98px;
margin-left: 25px;
```

6. Click on the **Save** button. Click on **Preview** to see the results on the frontend. If you still see the Joomla! logo press *F5* to force your browser to refresh (reload the page).

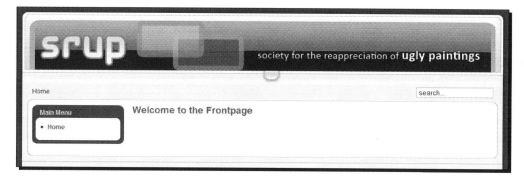

What just happened?

The new look for your site is beginning to take shape. You have updated the CSS stylesheet of the current Joomla! template to point to your new header file. You've replaced the original logo image with a new image that takes up all of the header screen space.

CSS ... stylesheets? Come again?

You've just changed some code in one of the Joomla! template files. Specifically, you've opened up the CSS file. Editing the CSS file of a Joomla! template is a quick way to change the appearance of your site. But just what is it, this CSS thing?

◆ You probably know web pages are documents containing HTML code. HTML tells the web browser what content it should display and roughly where this content is placed on the web page.

◆ These HTML documents can be linked to **Cascading Style Sheets (CSS)** files. These CSS files tell the web browser how the data in the HTML file should be displayed. CSS is a relatively simple set of rules that define the web pages' colors, fonts, page layout, and more.

As CSS instructions are stored in a separate file, these layout instructions can be linked to (and used by) any number of HTML documents. In other words—changing one line in a CSS file can change the appearance of a number of web pages using that CSS file. You've just seen an example of this when you made all pages on the site display a new logo image by editing the `template.css` file.

Joomla's built-in CSS editor screen makes it easy to quickly tweak the current template's layout details; however, you do need to have some knowledge of CSS for this. If you're new to CSS you can find a wealth of information on the Web. Just google the phrase "introduction to CSS" or "CSS tutorial" and you'll be presented with some great resources. To get a quick introduction, have a look at `www.yourhtmlsource.com/stylesheets/introduction.html`.

We'll be exploring CSS in more detail in Chapter 11.

One last thing: Clean up a little whatchamacallit

It's time for one last template customization job. You may have noticed a little... well, a little whatchamacallit in the center of the design, just below the header:

These are two half spheres stuck together. It's what remains of the Top Menu. When the Top Menu is enabled, these two spheres are displayed to the left-hand side and right-hand side of the menu links. Now that you have vigorously removed the contents of the site and disabled the Top Menu module, the template design leaves a few unwanted traces.

Time for action – remove the whatsis

We won't use the top menu on our site, so we want to remove all traces of it. To do this, we'll have to delete a few lines in the template stylesheet:

1. Navigate to **Extensions | Template Manager** and click on **rhuk_milkyway**. Click on the **Edit CSS** button and select the CSS file `template.css`. Click on the **Edit** button.

2. Find the CSS code that starts with `/* horizontal pill menu *//`.

3. Now, select all code of the `horizontal pill menu` styling: from the `table.pill` style to the style `pill # menu a # active_menu-nav`.

4. This last style definition ends with `background-position: 0 0;}`.

5. Because we will never use the horizontal menu in this site, we will remove these styles. Press the *Delete* key.

6. Click on **Save** and then click on **Preview**. The header looks nice and clean.

What just happened?

You've changed the template stylesheet to remove some unnecessary formatting. Again, you've experienced how easy it is to use the built-in CSS editor to tweak the current template's layout .

Have a go hero – explore layout settings

As you've seen, there are two ways to influence the look and feel of your current template. The first way is tweaking the template parameters; the second is editing the template stylesheet. Have a go and experiment a little with the built-in template parameters. Get a feel for the effects that the different parameters have by trying out some width settings and color combinations. Pick your flavor, click on **Apply,** and click on **Preview** to see the output on the frontend.

You'll notice that template parameters only allow you to change a limited set of options. It's far more powerful to take a look under the hood and edit the template CSS files in the Joomla! editor. That way, your layout options are only limited by your CSS skills. Take a scroll through the template editor CSS files to get a feel for what coding in CSS is like—you'll notice that CSS rules are, for the most part, written in plain English and don't look at all difficult to understand.

Step 2: Add content

The template now looks OK, but the site's still empty. It's high time to actually populate it with some articles! In the previous chapter, you've already made one simple article that fit neatly into the Joomla! example site. However, when you create your own site you'll want to choose a more structured approach.

Create a foundation first: Make sections and categories

If you have some experience in designing static websites, you've probably created new pages in two steps. You start making a new HTML document—the page—and then added a link to that page, making sure your new content can be found.

In Joomla!, you have to take a little preparatory action. Before you make new pages, you create containers for your content. These containers are called sections (the top level) and categories (the second level). Categories hold articles. You have seen sections and categories in action in the sample site you explored in the previous chapter (and you've deleted them later on). We won't go into the specifics of organizing content just now, as we'll be exploring the ins and outs of sections and categories in the next chapter. For now, let's experiment a little and see how this thing works.

As you've got a tight deadline to meet, we'll follow the three content creation steps the quick and dirty way. For this basic site, one section split up into two categories will do.

Time for action – create a section and some categories

Your client wants to publish a range of articles on the club activities on their new site; that's what they're all about. Specifically, they want articles on lectures and meetings.

How can we categorize these articles the Joomla! way? Let's create an Activities section and add two categories in that section: Lectures and Meetings.

1. Navigate to **Content | Section Manager**. Click on the **New** button.

2. In the **Title** field, type **Activities**. Don't worry about the other fields; you can leave them empty for now. Click on **Save**. You have created a section.

3. Navigate to **Content | Category Manager**. Click on the **New** button.

4. In the **Title** field, type **Lectures**. As there is only one section, the category is automatically added to this section. Click on **Save**. You've created a category in the **Activities** section.

5. Adding more categories is done in a similar way. In the **Category Manager**, click on **New** again to add a **Meetings** category. Click on **Save**.

The **Category Manager** shows the results (two new categories), all in one section:

What just happened?

In Joomla!, you create content groups before you can actually start adding articles and menu links. Sections are the main, high-level way to organize your site; categories are the second level. When you add sections and categories in the backend you'll notice nothing changes on the frontend. Sections and categories aren't automatically shown on the site. To get them to display we'll create a menu link pointing to this section and category content later.

By defining a section and some categories you've now got a foundation to add any amount of content on these two main subjects. In later chapters, we'll expand this structure.

Add articles to the categories

Now we come to the core of content management and actually start creating content! We'll make some articles, apply the appropriate formatting, and add images.

Time for action – create an article

First, let's create an article in the **Lectures** category:

1. Navigate to **Content | Article Manager**. Click on **New**. The **Article: [New]** screen opens.

2. In the **Title** box, type the title of the article (in this example **Bad Abstract Paintings**). You can leave the **Alias** field blank.

3. In the **Section** drop-down box, select **Activities**. In the **Category** drop-down box, select **Lectures**. Now you see why you needed to create a section and a category before. Without these you cannot assign the article to the appropriate "containers" within in your overall site structure.

4. In the editor screen, write the article. In this example, we'll just use dummy text. It's quite easy to copy and paste any amount of fake paragraph text from www.lipsum.com.

5. To divide the article text into an intro text and the main article text, position the cursor in the first line below the first paragraph. Click on the **Read more...** button at the bottom of the editor screen. A red dotted line appears indicating the separation between intro text and main article text.

6. Finally, we'll add an image to the article. Click on the **Image** button at the bottom of the editor screen. A pop-up screen with thumbnails of the available images in Joomla!'s default image folder appears. Select one of these images by clicking on its thumbnail.

7. In the **Align** drop-down box, click on **Right**. Click on **Insert**. The pop-up window closes.

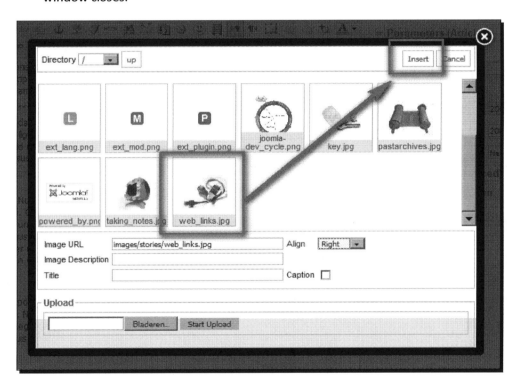

This is what the **Article: [Edit]** screen will look like once you've completed inserting all of the article data:

8. Click on **Apply** to save changes to the article and click on the **Preview** button in the article editor toolbar. A pop-up screen opens. This will give you a rough impression of how the formatted article will look. However, it doesn't reflect the frontend formatting reliably:

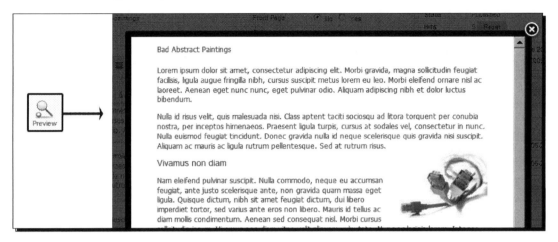

9. Now, click on the other **Preview** button (the one in the Info Bar in the top right screen area). This will show the frontend of the site. Try not to show your disappointment. There is no sign of your new article! That's because you have to take one last step and add a menu link.

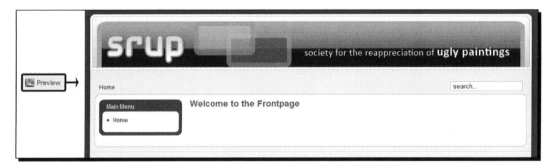

What just happened?

You've created a full-blown article, consisting of text and an image. Moreover, you've divided the article text into an intro text and the main article text. This way Joomla! will be able to separately display the intro, with a **Read more** link to the full article. In the editor, the separation is indicated by a red dotted line.

You've seen this division at work on the sample site home page that contains several short intro texts. Only when a visitor clicks on the accompanying **Read More** link they are taken to a page with the full article text.

Have a go hero – add your own images to articles

To the article you just created, you added an image from Joomla!'s default image set. For testing purposes that's okay, but in real life you'll want to add your own imagery. To do this, click on the **Image** button at the bottom of the article editor screen. In the pop-up screen, you'll see an **Upload** box. Click on **Browse files** to find an image file on your hard drive. Select the image file and click on **Start Upload**. A thumbnail of the uploaded image will appear among the other thumbnails (you may have to scroll down if there are a lot of pictures). Click on the desired thumbnail. Choose the appropriate **Align** setting and click on **Insert**. The pop-up window closes; your picture is inserted.

Making content visible: Create a menu link

The article you've just created is ready and it's stored in Joomla!'s database—but it's still invisible on the frontend of the site. That's because there's no link pointing to it. The **Main Menu** is empty, except for the **Home** link.

Time for action – add a menu link

Let's finish the three steps of content creation and add a link to your article:

1. Navigate to **Menus | Main Menu**. Click on the **New** button.

2. In the **Select Menu Item Type** box, click on **Articles | Section Blog Layout**. This menu link type tells Joomla! to display intro texts and Read More hyperlinks to all section content. You'll see what that looks like in a minute.

3. In the **Title** field, type **Activities**.

4. In **Parameters (Basic)**, select the appropriate **Section: Activities**. Click on **Save**.

What just happened?

Creating just one link to the **Activities** section changes a lot on the frontend. The site now looks as follows:

The home page is still empty, but the menu does contain a new link, **Activities**.

When the visitor clicks on the **Activities** link they are shown a Section Blog Layout page. This is an overview page of all contents of the **Activities** section. The overview consists of intro texts and Read more links to the full articles.

For now, there's just one article intro text. When you add new articles to the section Joomla! will automatically display them on this overview page too.

When the visitor clicks on the **Read more** link he is taken to the full article. The breadcrumb trail just above the article reflects the sections and categories structure that you have created: **Home | Activities | Lectures | Bad Abstract Paintings**.

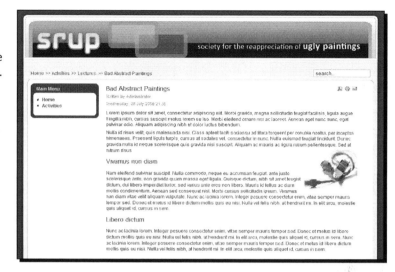

Have a go hero – create more articles

For the example site you'll need some more articles. Add a few dummy articles to each of the new categories. To do this repeat the steps you just took in *Time for action - create an article*. You can create articles using the titles displayed in the following screenshot. In this example, three articles have been added to each of the categories:

#		Title	Published	Front Page	Order			Access Level	Section	Category
1		Bad Abstract Paintings	✓	⊗		▽	1	Public	SRUP Activities	Lectures
2		Ugly Art Lecture	✓	⊗	▲	▽	2	Public	SRUP Activities	Lectures
3		Deplorable Still Lifes	✓	⊗	▲		3	Public	SRUP Activities	Lectures
4		The Art of Bob Ross	✓	⊗		▽	1	Public	SRUP Activities	Meetings
5		This Years Meeting	✓	⊗	▲	▽	2	Public	SRUP Activities	Meetings
6		Hideous Portraits Exhibition	✓	⊗	▲		3	Public	SRUP Activities	Meetings

As you can see, the **Article Manager** displays an overview of the entire site contents. In the **Title** column all of the articles are shown; at the far right you'll see the sections and categories these articles are assigned to.

A quick way to add new articles is using the **Copy** button in the **Article Manager**. Just select the article you want to use as a base for a new article and click on **Copy**. Follow the screen instructions to add a copy of the article to any category. Open the copied article (it will have the exact same title as the original) and change its title and as much as needed of its contents.

Now that's the all-important power of menus

The previous example illustrates the power of Joomla! menu links. Just by adding a menu link you make content accessible in several ways. Whatever you add to the two categories you've set up, no new menu links are needed. Any new content will show up through the **Activities** section link that you have already created.

It's clear that Joomla! menu links are very special. They don't just point to existing pages; rather, they determine what page will be displayed. Menu link settings tell Joomla! exactly what to fetch from the database and how to display it. That's why you see such an impressive list of Menu Item Types when you add a new link to a menu. In fact, these Menu Item Types represent different preset ways to display all kinds of content. In the previous example, you have used the **Menu Item Type** that displays articles in a **Section Blog Layout**. This makes Joomla! display bits of articles in a section in a "blog style"; that is, as a series of short intro texts on one page. If you would have created a direct menu link to the new article using an **Article Layout**, the menu link would have pointed to the same content in a different presentation: the full article page.

In Chapter 8 we'll dive deeper into the art of creating menu items and the effects that different Menu Item Types and their settings have on the final results, a broad range of web page types.

Add some individual content pages: Uncategorized articles

For now, your client would like to have just a few more content pages on their first website. Let's say they'd like a page introducing their arty subject matter and a page on their mission statement. As there's no need just yet for more content, it would be overkill to create categories to accommodate for these two articles. Luckily, Joomla! allows you to add uncategorized articles. They're ordinary articles except for one thing; when adding them, you don't assign them to any category.

Time for action – add uncategorized articles

Let's create a Mission Statement page by adding an uncategorized article.

1. Navigate to **Content | Article Manager**. Click on **New**.

2. In the **Title** box, enter **Mission Statement**.

3. In the text editor area, add the **Mission Statement** text and add an image, if you like. For this example, we've entered the following text:

We all know the works of great art throughout the centuries. But what about ordinary people's art? What did amateur artists create? Much of their creative output has been discarded, thrown away because of its lack of artistic value. Let's not let that happen to today's amateur paintings. Let's preserve the ordinary man's artistic view on reality.

The beauty in ugliness

The Society for the Reappreciation of Ugly Paintings seeks to find and promote the beauty that's hidden behind superficial ugliness. Tour our website to discover that beauty, too!

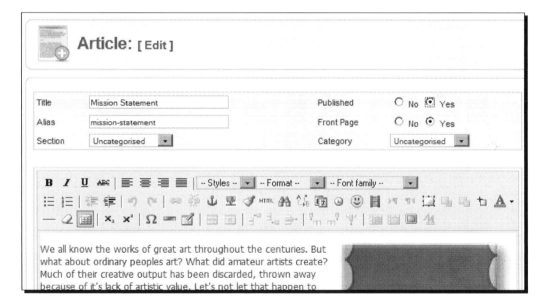

4. You can add an image to the text if you like; click the **Image** button at the bottom of the editor screen; select and insert an image.

5. Click on **Save**.

The uncategorized article is finished—we just need a menu link to make it visible.

6. Navigate to **Menus | Main Menu**. Click on **New**.

7. In the **Menu Item: [New]** screen, we'll create a link to a single article. Let's select the appropriate **Menu Item Type**; click on **Internal Link | Article | Article Layout**.

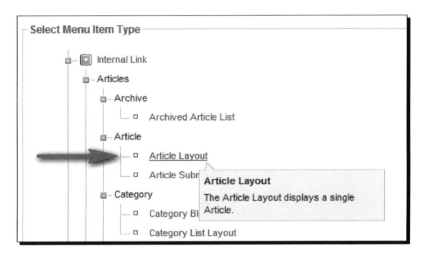

8. In the **Title** box, enter **Mission Statement**.

9. In **Parameters (Basic)** section, click on **Select** to choose the article this menu link will link to. In the pop-up box, select the **Mission Statement** article. The pop-up window closes.

10. Click on **Save**. Click on **Preview** to admire the results. The menu now displays a new link to the **Mission Statement** article.

Your first uncategorized article is ready. Add the second uncategorized article by repeating the steps you took above. Call the new article **Introducing Ugly Paintings** and create a menu link **Ugly Paintings** pointing to this article.

What just happened?

Uncategorized articles are a perfect solution to place content on your site that doesn't fit the categories structure. You've added two articles and menu links. On the frontend of your website, the output is as follows:

Two new menu links are displayed as the last item in the **Main Menu**.

Clicking on the **Mission Statement** link or the **Ugly Paintings** link reveals a single article page.

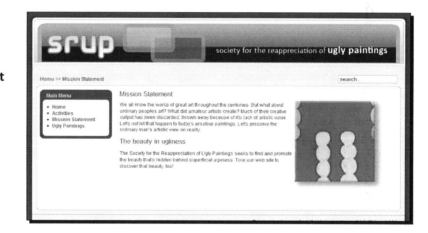

Have a go hero – clean up the Main Menu

You'll have noticed that Main Menu items are shown in the order that you've created them. The last two menu items you've just added, are displayed at the bottom of the menu. You can change the order of items in the main menu by navigating to **Menus | Main Menu** and clicking on the arrows in the **Order** column to move things up or down. Try this out now. For example, try to move the **Ugly Paintings** article link to the second position:

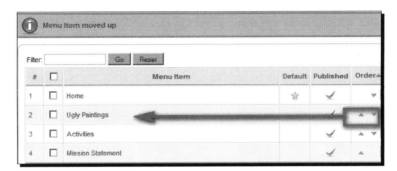

Put some content on the home page—at last!

Now that you've stuffed your site with content, there's one essential page to take care of. As we haven't added anything to the home page yet, its main content area is still empty.

It may seem strange that you do not *start* with the home page when adding content; after all, it's the official entrance to the site. However, you do need to have the actual content—articles—before you can start publishing anything on your home page. After all, the home page usually is a selection of content items—teasers, images, or hyperlinks—drawn from the rest of the site.

Add items to the home page

How do you control which pieces of content are shown on the home page? When you write a new article (**Content | Article Manager | New**), or edit an existing article in the Article Manager, you can choose whether you want the article to be displayed on the home page. In the **Article : [Edit]** screen, click on the **Front Page : Yes** radio button.

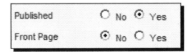

Another way to quickly add items to the home page (or remove them) is to use the Article Manager overview screen (**Content | Article Manager**). A check mark in the **Front Page** column means the article is displayed on the home page. Clicking on the check mark changes it to a cross. This indicates the article will not be displayed on the home page. We'll try this out right now.

Time for action – adding items to the home page

Let's add some stuff to the home page through the **Article Manager**.

1. Navigate to **Content | Article Manager**.

2. In the **Front Page** column, click on the red cross of four articles: **Deplorable Still Lifes, Ugly Art Lecture, The Art of Bob Ross**, and **This Years Meeting.** The red cross turns into a green check mark. The results are shown in the following screenshot. Four articles are set to show on the Front Page:

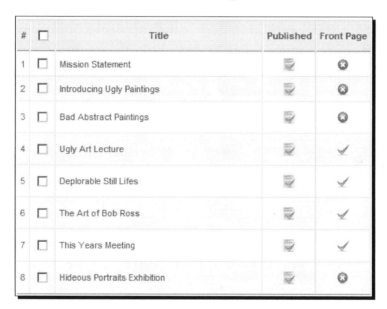

#	□	Title	Published	Front Page
1	□	Mission Statement	✓	⊗
2	□	Introducing Ugly Paintings	✓	⊗
3	□	Bad Abstract Paintings	✓	⊗
4	□	Ugly Art Lecture	✓	✓
5	□	Deplorable Still Lifes	✓	✓
6	□	The Art of Bob Ross	✓	✓
7	□	This Years Meeting	✓	✓
8	□	Hideous Portraits Exhibition	✓	⊗

3. Click on **Preview**. You've got a home page filled with content! Four articles are displayed on the home page as intro texts with Read more links:

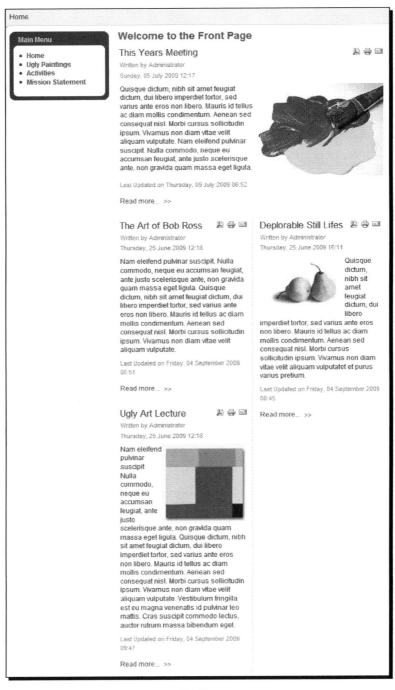

What just happened?

By clicking on the icon in the **Front Page** column in the **Article Manager** you have added four articles to the home page. On the frontend, these four articles are now shown in the default Joomla! Front Page layout; the first intro text is displayed in the full mainbody width, the intro texts below that are presented in two columns. We'll leave this for now—but rest assured, you'll learn how to tweak these display options to your heart's content in the later chapters.

Remove the "Welcome to the Front Page" heading

By default, a Joomla! home page shows the headline "Welcome to the Front Page". We don't want to keep that message. To remove it, we'll have to tweak the settings of the **Home** link in the **Main Menu**:

1. Navigate to **Menus | Main Menu**.
2. Click on **Home**.
3. In the **Parameters (System)** section, delete the text in the **Page Title** box.
4. Click on **Save**. The **Page Title** has now been removed.

It's not enough to just leave the welcome message and change **Show Page Title** to **No**. In that case, the page title would effectively disappear from your home page. However, it would still show in the browser Title Bar.

The Front Page is not the home page (or is it?)

Are you in for a little confusion on Joomla! jargon? You'll notice Joomla! uses the word Front Page instead of home page. Technically, these two are not the same:

- The home page is the full page the user sees when clicking on **Home** in the Main Menu; it's the top level page of your site.

- In Joomla!, the **Front Page** is the main content area (the mainbody) within the home page. The home page can feature other items—modules—around the mainbody.

In other words, there is more to the home page than just the Front Page in the form of modules. As modules aren't part of the Front Page, you cannot control them through the Front Page settings. You'll use the settings of the modules themselves to control whether they appear on the home page. We'll see an example of that when we add a Poll module later in this chapter.

Step 3: Add extras through components and extensions

You've just taken a few giant leaps! You have customized the layout of your new site, framed a structure, and have created and published the contents to match. If this were a static HTML site, this would be about it. This would be all there was to a website. In Joomla!, however, the fun has just begun. You can now add functional or even just plain cool extras. For this, you'll use Joomla!'s components and extensions—that's where the Joomla!'s real magic power lies.

Components and extensions, what's the difference?

To manage Joomla!'s extended functionality, you'll find yourself working with both the **Components** and the **Extensions** menu in the backend. The main difference between these two is that components are more powerful and more complex; they're applications within the Joomla! application. Modules are smaller add-ons that can contain all sorts of dynamic information. Sometimes, components and modules are designed to work together.

So, in spite of the differences between components and extensions, behind the scenes, they generally serve the same purpose. Both enhance your site's functionality.

For now, we'll be using components and extensions that are included in the default Joomla! setup. Later, you'll probably want to add other extensions. There are thousands of them available on the Web, providing whatever functionality you might want to add to your site. You'll learn more about adding extensions in Chapter 10.

Add a contact form

Let's take care of one of the last items on your client's wish list and enable site visitors to get in touch through a contact form. Adding this form will take two steps. First, we'll create a contact; after that, we'll create a menu link that displays a contact form.

Time for action – create a contact

Let's add a contact, that is, someone whose (mail) address and other contact details can be displayed on the form page and who will receive the form data in their mailbox.

1. Navigate to **Components | Contacts**. The **Contact Manager** opens. Click on **New**.

2. In the **Contact : [New]** screen, enter the details for the contact. In the **Name** box, enter **SRUP Staff**.

3. In the **Category** drop-down list, select **Contacts**.

4. In the **Information** section, enter the contact information details you want to display. In this case, just fill out the **E-mail** box and the **Telephone** box. It is important to specify a valid e-mail address, because this is where the form data will be sent to.

5. None of the other items in the **Information** section are mandatory. However, you should add some text in the **Miscellaneous information** box. This will be displayed as an introductory text on the form page. You might want to add text such as:

Would you like to know more? Call us or fill out the form below. We'll get in touch as soon as possible.

6. In the **Contact Parameters** section you can specify whether you want to show or hide specific contact details on the contact form page. In this case, we want to display only **Name**, **Telephone**, and **Miscellaneous Information**. You could, of course, display more contact details to offer visitors various ways to respond.

7. In the **E-mail Parameters** section, it's important that **E-mail form** is set to **Show**. This will add the contact form to the contact information page—just like we want to.

8. Click on **Save**.

What just happened?

To be able to create a contact form, you have to first creat a contact. Using the Joomla! Contact Component, you can build a comprehensive system of contacts organized by contact categories. For our goal, just one contact name and e-mail address will suffice.

Time for action – create a Contact Form menu link

Now that a contact exists you can add a link to a contact form to the main menu:

1. Navigate to **Menus | Main Menu**.

2. Click on **New**.

3. In the **Select Menu Item Type** list, select **Contacts | Standard Contact Layout**.

4. Enter a **Title** for the menu item (for example, **Contact**).

5. In the **Parameters-Basic** section, in the **Select Contact** drop-down box select the contact you just created: **SRUP Staff**.

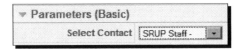

6. In the **Parameters (System)** section, add a **Page Title** (for example, **Get in touch**). This will be displayed at the top of the form.

7. Click on **Save**. The site now has a **Contact** menu link that displays a contact form:

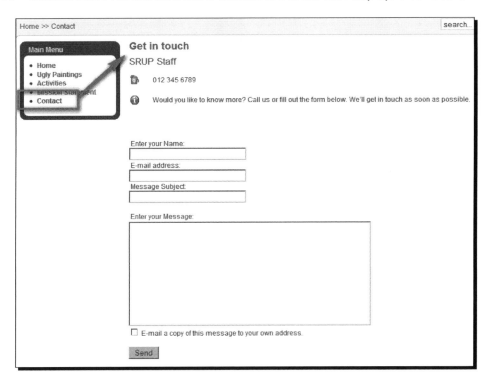

What just happened?

You have used the Contacts Component to create a contact and added a menu link to a contact form. Again you have experienced how powerful menu links are in Joomla!. Just by selecting the **Menu Item Type: Standard Contact Layout** you have created a menu link that takes the visitor to a contact form page.

Add a Poll

The SRUP people would like to enable a bit of user interaction on their site. They suggest adding a poll, a simple survey of one multiple-choice question. In Joomla!, the polling functionality is built-in.

Time for action – create a Poll

First, let's create the Poll question and the set of possible answers:

Navigate to **Components | Polls**. In the **Poll Manager** screen, click on **New**.

1. Click on **Published: Yes** to make sure the poll will be displayed in the frontend.

2. Leave **Lag** unchanged. A visitor may vote only once a day (the standard Lag of 86,400 seconds, i.e., 24 hours).

3. In the **Poll: [Edit]** screen, enter the details of the survey. In the **Title** box, enter **What would you like to read about on our site?**

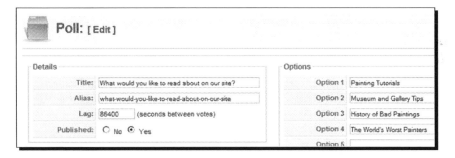

4. In the **Options** section, add four possible answers: **Painting Tutorials, Museum and Gallery Tips, History of Bad Paintings,**and **The World's Worst Painters.**

5. Click on **Save**.

Time for action – display the Poll

The Poll component uses the Poll module. This module tells Joomla! on what pages the Poll should appear and on what position it should be displayed:

1. Navigate to **Extensions| Module Manager**. Click on **New**.

2. In the **Module: [New]** screen, click on the **Poll** module. Click on **Next**.

3. In the **Title** box, type **Vote!**.

4. Click on **Show Title: Yes**.

5. Select **Position: right**. The survey will appear in the right-hand side column.

6. In the Menu Assignment section, click on **Select Menu Item(s) from the List**. Select **mainmenu: Home**. You can have the survey appear on any page; in this case, it will appear only on the home page.

7. In the **Module Parameters** section, select the poll you've created.

8. Click on **Save** and click on **Preview**. The Poll is displayed on the frontend:

What just happened?

Your site now shows a simple poll on the home page. The site visitor can select one option, click on the **Vote** button, and view the results. The results are shown in the main content screen.

Wrapping up: Change site settings

The one-hour website is finished. However, there are a few adjustments to be made in the backend.

Time for action – change site configuration

The site configuration still shows some default values that don't match the new site contents. Let's enter the appropriate site name and add site metadata.

1. Navigate to **Site | Global Configuration**.

2. In the **Site Settings** section, enter the **Site Name: SRUP - Ugly Paintings Society**. This is the site information that will be shown on in the Title Bar of the visitors web browser:

> **SRUP - Ugly Paintings Society - Mozilla Firefox**

3. In the **Metadata** section, change the text of **Metadata Settings**. Metadata are important for search engines—but if you leave the default text unchanged, search engines will find information on Joomla! instead of information on SRUP. In the **Global Site Meta Description**, enter: **SRUP is an international Society For the Reappreciation of Ugly Paintings**.

4. In the **Global Site Meta Keywords**, enter a few keywords that characterize the site's contents: **ugly paintings**, **bad painting**, **bad art**, **SRUP**.

What just happened?

By entering a few lines in the **Global Configuration** screen we've made sure the right site name shows up in the visitors' web browser and search engines pick up the right information about the site's contents.

Pop quiz – test your basic Joomla! knowledge

1. What can you use the built-in Joomla! CSS editor for?

   a) To add some content containers

   b) To change the appearance of your site

   c) To change menu settings

2. In what order do you add articles and menu links?

   a) Create menu links first, then add articles

   b) Add articles first, then create menu links

   c) You can choose whatever order you like

3. What do you use components and extensions for?

   a) Adding extras, such as newsletters or contact forms

   b) Adding content that only registered users can see

   c) To quickly add new content

Summary

You may not be aware of it, but you did actually do an incredible job. Your first Joomla! website is up and running!

♦ You've seen that building your site is a three-step process. First you customize the layout, then you add content, and then you add further functionality (such as a contact form or a poll) to your site.

♦ You can personalize the looks of the site by editing the template files. If you know just a little CSS, you can edit the template files directly in the Template Manager editor screen.

♦ Before you create content pages you create the containers they belong in. These containers are called sections (the top level) and categories (the second level). Create uncategorized articles if you need some content pages that don't fit any category.

♦ To make any content visible on your site there has to be a menu link pointing to it.

♦ You add items to the home page by changing their Front Page setting. In the Front Page Manager you can change the order in which these items are presented on the home page.

♦ You can add extra functionality through components and extensions. An example of this is the Contacts component that allows you to add contact details and contact forms.

In this chapter, we followed the fast and simple approach and used only the basic capabilities of the system, leaving most settings at their default values. Building on this, it is possible to create much bigger, complex, sophisticated, and cool sites. The next chapters will cover the subjects we've touched upon in more detail. In Chapter 5, we'll look specifically at the site's structure; how can you organize the content of your site, whether it's a ten page personal website or a big corporate site? The challenge is to make your site's organization user friendly, expandable, and keep it easily manageable.

5
Small Sites, Big Sites: Organizing your Content Effectively

In the last chapter, you saw that creating a website in Joomla! revolves around three major tasks: designing a layout, creating content, and adding extras. The central part is, of course, creating content. You can have a Joomla! site using a simple default template, you can have a site without adding extra functionality, but you can't have a site without content. That's why, in the next few chapters, we'll concentrate on managing and creating content. In later chapters, you'll work on the layout and add extras.

In this chapter you'll:

◆ Understand how to translate a basic site map to a workable blueprint for a Joomla!-based site

◆ Design a clear, scalable framework for your content, grouping your content with sections and categories

◆ Use uncategorized pages to build sites that don't require a multi-level content

Building on the example site

The SRUP site you developed in Chapter 4 is a great little site, perfectly suited for your client's initial purposes to their first Web presence. Now it's time to make room for growth. Your client has a big pile of information on ugly art that they want to present to the public. You are asked to design a site framework that makes it easy to add more content, while at the same time keeps it easy for visitors to quickly find their way through the site.

Can you do that? You most certainly can! Joomla! allows you to build sites of all sorts and sizes, whether they consist of just a few pages or thousands of them. If you plan ahead and start with a sound basic structure, you'll be rewarded with a site that's easy to maintain and extend. In this chapter, we'll review the site you've just built and look at the different ways the content can be structured—and rearranged, if need be.

Grouping content: A crash course in site organization

To lay the groundwork for your site, you won't use Joomla!. The back of a napkin will do fine. Draw up a site map to lay out the primary content chunks and their relationships. View your site from a user's perspective. What do you think your visitors will primarily look for, and how can you help them find things fast and easily?

Designing a site map

To create a site map, first collect all information you plan on having on your website and organize it into a simple and logical format. Let's have a look again at the SRUP website you built in the last chapter. The following is the basic outline of the site you've created up to now:

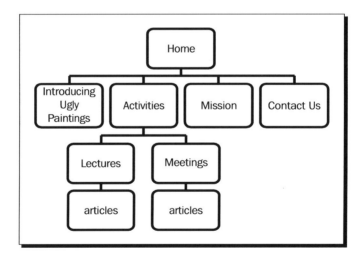

As site maps come, this is a very basic one. For the most part, it's just one level deep. **Introducing Ugly Paintings** and **Mission** are basic web pages (articles). **Activities** is a section that allows the visitor to browse two other categories. **Contact Us** is a contact form page. This structure was good enough for a basic website, but it won't do if SRUP wants to expand their site.

Time for action – create a future proof site map

Let's make some room for growth. Imagine your client's planning to add an indefinite amount of new content, so there's a need for additional content containers. They have come up with the following list of subjects they want to add to their site:

- ◆ News items
- ◆ A few pages to introduce the founding members of SRUP
- ◆ Reviews on ugly art
- ◆ Facts on ugly paintings (history, little known facts, and so on)

What's the best way to organize things? Let's figure out which content fits which type of container.

Step 1: You'll probably want to create a separate **News** section. News should be a top level item, a part of the site's main menu.

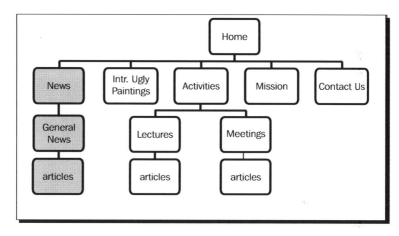

Step 2: The information on the SRUP founders fits in a new section **About SRUP**.

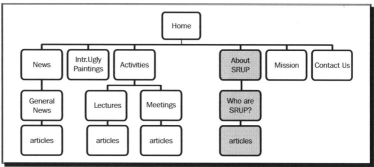

Step 3: Both **Reviews** and **Facts** can be categories in a new general section on **Ugly Paintings**. The existing article **Introducing Ugly Paintings** could be moved here (or dropped).

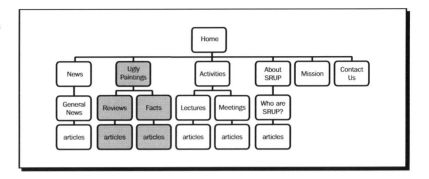

What just happened?

You've laid a solid foundation for your site—on paper. Before you actually start using Joomla! to create sections and categories, create a structure for the content that you have in mind. Basically, no matter how big or small your website is, you'll organize it just like the example you've just seen. You'll work from top to bottom, from the primary level to the lower levels, defining content groups and their relations. Bear in mind, though, that there will certainly be more than one way to organize your information. Choose an organization that makes sense to you and your visitors, and try to keep things lean and clean. A complex structure will make it harder to maintain the content, and eventually—when building menus—it will make it harder to design clear and simple navigation paths for your visitors.

Tips on choosing sections

- It can be useful to choose sections based on the main intentions people have when they come to the site. What are they here for? Is it to *Browse Products* or to *Join a Workshop*?

- Common choices for sections are: *Products, Catalog, Company, Portfolio, About Us, Jobs, News,* and *Downloads.*

- Try not to have more than five to seven sections. Once you have more than that, readers won't be able to hold them all in their heads at once when they have to choose which one to browse.

Transferring your site map to Joomla!

Let's have a closer look at our new site map and identify the Joomla! elements. This—and any—Joomla! site is likely to consist of five types of content.

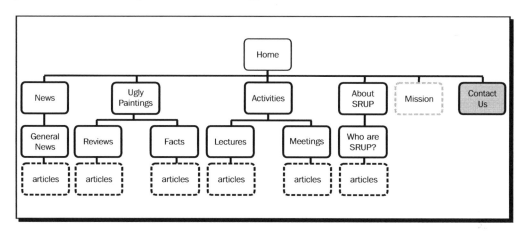

The following are the content types in our SRUP site map:

Obviously, the top level item will be the **home page**.

The main content groups we can identify as **sections and categories**. This small site has four sections, three of which contain two categories.

Each of the categories hold actual content; this is what will end up in Joomla! as articles.

In this site map, there is one article that doesn't really belong in any category: the Mission Statement page. Every site will have one or two of those independent articles. In Joomla!, you can add these as uncategorized articles. You've seen some examples of this type of articles when building your first site in the last chapter.

Finally, there's one item that represents a very different type of content. In the site map above, a grey background indicates an item containing special functionality. In this case this is a contact form. Other examples are guest books, order forms, and photo galleries.

Basically, that's all there is to a Joomla! site. When you've got your site outlined like this, you won't meet any surprises while building it. You can transform any amount of content and functionality into a website, step by step.

How do you turn a site map into a website?

If you've got your site blueprint laid out, you probably want to start building! Now, what should be the first step? What's the best, and fastest, way to get from that site map on the back of your napkin to a real-life Joomla! site? In this book, we'll work in this order:

1. **Organize**: Create content containers.

    You've seen that much of the site map we just created consists of content containers: sections and categories. In this chapter, we'll focus on these containers. We'll create all necessary containers for our example site.

2. **Add content**: Fill the containers with articles.

    Next, we'll add articles to the sections and categories. Articles are the "classic content" that most web pages are made of. We should also check for articles that do not belong in any category. Instead of assigning them to a section and a category, we'll add them as Uncategorized content. For our example site, we'll work on article contents in the next chapter.

3. **Put your contents on display**: Create the home page and content overview pages.

    Next, you'll want to guide and invite visitors. You can achieve this using two special types of pages in the site map, the home page and Joomla!'s section/category overview pages ("secondary home pages"). You'll focus on deploying these page types in Chapter 7.

4. **Make everything findable**: Create menus.

    The top level items in your site map will probably end up as menu items on the site. To open up your site to the world you'll create and customize menus helping visitors to easily navigate your content. This is the subject of Chapter 8.

And what about the special content stuff?
You'll notice that in the above list we've summed up all sorts of "classic content", such as articles, home pages, overview pages, and menus linking it all. We haven't yet mentioned one essential part of the site map, the special goodies. On a dynamic website you can have more than just plain old articles. You can add picture galleries, forms, product catalogues, site maps, and much, much more. It's important to identify those special pages from the beginning, but you'll add them later using Joomla!'s components and extensions. That's why we'll first concentrate on building a rock-solid foundation; later we'll add all of the desired extras.

Let's start with step one now, and get our site organized!

Creating content containers: Sections and categories

In the previous chapter you have already had a foretaste of how easy it is to create sections and categories. To create a section, navigate to **Content | Section Manager | New**.

To make a new category, you'll use the **Category Manager** instead. Just add a title for your new section or category and click on **Save**. You've created a perfectly workable section or category with the default settings (or parameters as Joomla! likes to call them).

Time for action – create a new section and a category

Your client was happy with the initial site structure you designed, but now their website is evolving, there's a need for more content containers. Let's add a news section first:

1. Navigate to **Content | Section Manager** and click on **New**.

2. In the **Section: [New]** screen, fill out the **Title** field. In this example, type **News**:

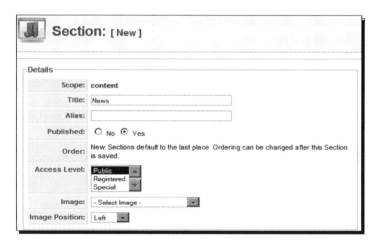

3. Leave the other values unchanged; click on **Save**. You're taken to the **Section Manager**. The **News** section is now shown in the section list.

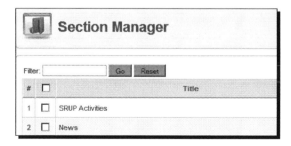

Now, add a category to the new section. We'll call this category **General News**:

> **4.** Navigate to **Content | Category Manager** and click on **New**.
>
> **5.** In the **Title** field, type **General News**.
>
> **6.** In the **Section** field, select **News**.
>
> **7.** Click on **Save**. You're done!

What just happened?

You have added a **News** section with one category: **General News**. Remember, a section needs at least one category. For now, this **General News** category will do. Should the client wish to have more specific news categories later, these can easily be added.

It's quite OK to have sections with single categories. In the backend they serve as a functional (and mandatory) container for content, in the frontend the user won't have to click his way through redundant links. On clicking the **News** link, he'll be shown all of the news content in one go. Basically this means it's possible to add content to a Joomla! section without having to create several categories when they're not really needed.

Have a go hero – add some articles

The News category you just added is still empty. Add some dummy content to it by repeating the steps you took in the last chapter (see Chapter 4). In short, navigate to **Content | Article Manager** and click on **New**. Add a **Title,** and in the **Section** drop-down box select **News**. In the **Category** drop-down box, **General News** will be selected (it's the only option). Add some dummy content. Add a **Read More** link after the first paragraph to enable Joomla! to separately show the introductory text and the body text. Click on **Save** and you're done.

In this example, we've added three news articles to our new section:

3	☐	SRUP Magazine looking for authors		⊘	▼	1	Public	News	General News
4	☐	New Ugly Paintings Discovered		⊘	▲ ▼	2	Public	News	General News
5	☐	Bob Ross Exhibition Announced		⊘	▲	3	Public	News	General News

Displaying sections and categories on your website

Sections and categories are content containers; they tell Joomla! how to group things in the backend. Now, how do you get the content in those containers to show up on your website? You've already seen in Chapter 4 that you add a menu link to do this. Let's add a new menu link now to present the contents of the section we just created to our visitors.

Time for action – create a link to point to a section

Creating a menu link to point to a section or category takes these four steps:

1. Navigate to **Menus** | **Main Menu** and click on **New**.

2. In the **Select Menu Item Type** section, select **Articles | Section Blog Layout**.

3. In the **Menu Item : [New]** screen, add a **Title** (i.e., News). In the **Parameters (Basic)**, select the **News** section in the **Section** drop-down list.

4. Click on **Save**.

As you can see in the following screenshot, **News** now shows up as the last item in the **Menu Item Manager**. The order in which Menu Items are presented here is the same order they'll have in the **Main Menu** on your website. If you would like to move the **News** link up in the **Main Menu**, just click on the arrows in the **Order** column as desired. In this example, we'll leave the order unchanged.

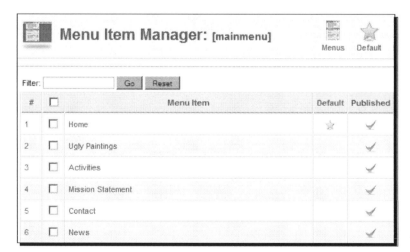

5. Click on **Preview** to check out what's changed on the frontend:

On the home page, there's a new link added to the **Main Menu: News**

On clicking this, the visitor will see an overview of the **News** section.

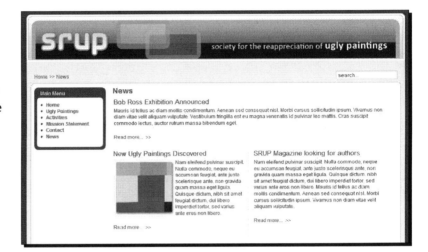

How are sections and categories displayed?

The format of the section overview page you just created on the frontend of your site is called a Section Blog Layout. There is, however, much more to section and categories content presentation than just the Section Blog Layout. You can choose to display section contents in different formats. Moreover, you can have your menu link point directly to a specific category (instead of its parent section). For now, presenting the contents of your section and the underlying categories through the Section Blog Layout format will do just fine; you'll learn about the other ways of displaying section/category contents in Chapter 7.

Have a go hero – create some new sections and categories

Let's have a look at the SRUP site map again. To completely transfer the structure we designed on our napkin to the Joomla! backend we should add two more sections: **Ugly Paintings** and **About SRUP**. In the following design you can see which categories these sections should hold:

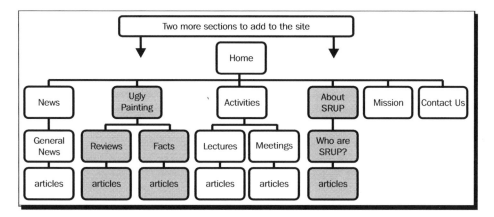

Add sections and categories

You can now add these sections/categories by repeating the steps you took previously:

◆ To create sections, navigate to **Content | Section Manager | New**

◆ To create categories, navigate to **Content | Category Manager | New**

Add links

Although the sections and categories are still empty (they hold no articles yet), it's a good idea to already add menu links to point to the new sections.

◆ To add menu links, navigate to **Menus | Main Menu** and click on **New**. Add two section links: a link to the Ugly Paintings section (call this link **Ugly Paintings**) and a link to the About SRUP section (let's call it, well, yes, **About SRUP**).

Remove an unneeded article

There's just one little bit of unfinished business remaining. Once you've created a new section on Ugly Paintings you should remove all traces of its predecessor, the Uncategorized article called *Introducing Ugly Paintings*. There's no need for it anymore; we'll replace it with the new section content. Let's trash both the article and the old menu link pointing to it:

◆ Navigate to the **Article Manager**, select the article and click on the **Trash** button in the toolbar.

◆ To remove the redundant menu link **Introducing Ugly Paintings** from the **Main Menu**, just navigate to **Menus | Main Menu**, select the link and click on the **Trash** button in the toolbar.

And what about the articles?
By adding some new sections and categories, you've made room for growth. We'll leave these containers empty for now; in the next chapters, we'll add articles to them.

Refining your site structure

It's a fact of life: you probably won't get your site structure right in one go unless you've got a really simple, really static site. It that a bad thing? No, it isn't—because websites evolve and Joomla! makes it easy to go ahead with a provisional structure and change things when needed. Maybe because new content has become available that has to go into a new section. Or maybe because when you're actually adding content, you learn that your well-organized site isn't altogether logical after all. That's fine; keeping a close eye on the structure of your website is a continuous process. And luckily, sections and categories, once defined, are not set in stone. You've seen how easy it is to add new ones, and it's equally simple to move content from one category to another.

Time for action – move content from one category to another

The **Activities** section contains some articles that you might want to move to the News section. Let's clean up the **Activities - Meetings** category and move anything topical into the **News - General News** category:

1. Navigate to **Content | Article Manager**. From the list, select the items you want to move from the **Meetings** category to the **General News** category. In this example, we've selected two articles:

2. Click on **Move** on the toolbar. You'll be taken to the **Move Articles** screen:

3. In the **Move to Section/Category** list, select **News/General News**. At the far right-hand side, you can check which articles are being moved.

4. Click on **Save**. In the **Article Manager** screen, the three articles are now part of the News section. You can check this by clicking on the **News** link on the frontend Main Menu.

What just happened?

You've stood the real life challenge of content management! Now, you're not only able to create a sound content structure for your website, but you also know how to improve on it. By adding a new container for all news items and moving existing news content there you've now made room for growth on the SRUP site.

Have a go hero – moving entire categories

Sometimes you might want to move an entire category and all its contents to another section. Try this out for yourself—it's not much different from moving articles. Imagine you'd like to move the Reviews category from the Ugly Paintings section to another section. In the **Category Manager**, select the category you want to move and click on the **Move** button. Select the section you want to move things to, and click on **Save**. It's just as straightforward to move the entire category—including all of its article contents—back again. This flexibility is great when you're setting up or rearranging your site.

Renaming sections or categories

As we've just seen, Joomla! allows you to easily rearrange your site structure and its contents. You can also *rename* sections and categories that already contain articles; no content will be lost.

Time for action – rename a section

On your client's website there's an **Activities** section. Your client wants to make it clear this section is not about activities organized by other art societies—it's only about SRUP. Could you please change the name of the section to **SRUP Activities**? It's a breeze.

1. Navigate to **Content | Section Manager** and click on the title of the **Activities** section to open it for editing.

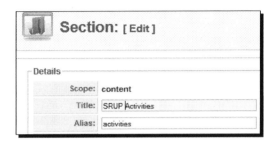

2. In the **Section: [Edit]** screen, change the **Title** to **SRUP Activities**.

3. In the **Alias:** field, remove the existing alias (remember, the Alias is Joomla!'s internal name for the article used when creating user-friendly URLs). Leave this box blank; Joomla! will fill it with **srup-activities** when you apply or save your changes. You can check that now by clicking on **Apply**. You'll notice the **Alias** box is filled out automatically.

4. Click on **Save**.

What just happened?

By changing a section or category name, all of Joomla!'s internal references to the name are updated automatically. All articles and categories in the renamed section will reflect the changes you made. In the **Article Manager**, for example, all items that belonged to the **Activities** section are now updated to show they are in the **SRUP Activities** section. No manual labor here—and more importantly, nothing is lost!

On the frontend, the new section name shows up on the section overview page when the user clicks on the **Activities** link:

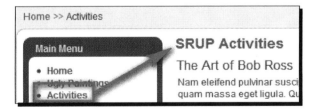

Have a go hero – name and rename!

Using appropriate, short, and descriptive labels for sections and categories (and for the menu links pointing to them) is really essential. After all, these are the words that guide your visitors to the content you want them to discover. It's a good idea to tweak these labels until you're perfectly happy with them. To modify the names of categories, navigate to the **Category Manager**; it's similar to changing section names. Maybe you would like to change menu link labels too, as these don't automatically change with the category or section name. Try to find short and appropriate menu link labels. To change menu link labels, navigate to the Main Menu, select any of the menu items and change what's in the **Title** field (that is, SRUP Activities).

When changing Titles (of Sections/Categories/Menu Link Items) make sure to clear the contents of the **Alias** box. Joomla! will automatically create an Alias for the new Title.

Changing section and category settings

You've already created a good deal of sections and categories without altering any of the default settings. In some cases, however, you might want some more control over the section or category you're editing. In the table below you can see the options that are available in the **Section/Category: [New]** or **Section/Category: [Edit]** screen.

Basically, you can customize these settings for two purposes:

♦ To determine whether a section or category is visible (and which user groups can see it)

♦ To add a short descriptive text whenever the section or category contents are displayed

We'll cover both the Section and Category edit screen in the overview next, as all settings and options are identical. The only difference is that when adding a category, Joomla! wants you to specify the section that holds the new category.

This is what the **Section: [New]** and the **Category: [New]** screen look like:

 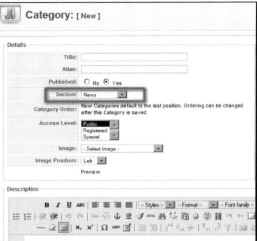

Adding or editing sections and categories: An overview of the settings

Title:
The section or category title as it will be displayed. You can use lowercase, uppercase, and spaces.

Alias:
Leave the **Alias:** box blank. The Alias is the internal name of the item. When you save the section, Joomla! will automatically fill in the section name in lowercase letters without spaces or special characters. If the the **Title** is **About SRUP**, the alias will be **about-srup**. The Alias will be shown in the page URL (www.example.com/about-srup.html) when you activate Joomla!'s special search engine friendly URLs (see Chapter 12 on attracting search engine traffic).

Published:
Select **Yes** to show the section, **No** if you want to hide it for your visitors. The latter can be useful when your site is live and you're preparing a new section. That way, your site visitors won't know the section is there until you publish it. When you have finished the section, click on **Published: Yes**.

Section:
This drop-down select box appears in the Category screen only. Select the **Section** it belongs to.

Order:
The **Order** setting determines the place of this item in the list of sections in the **Section Manager** or the list of categories in the **Category Manager**. Setting a specific order is only relevant when a list of sections or categories is displayed as a list of hyperlinks. You can't change the **Order** value until you have saved the section.

Adding or editing sections and categories: An overview of the settings

Access Level:	Select an option in the **Access level** to determine who has access to this section: all users (**Public**), registered users (**Registered**), or users with administrator permissions (**Special**). The default value, **Public**, should be okay. When you start working with different user types on your site you can change settings (see Chapter 9 on user access levels).
Image: **Image Position:** **Description:**	These last three options affect how overview pages of section or category contents are displayed. At the top of these pages an image and a short description can be shown. If you want to select an **Image** it has to be in the default Joomla! images folder: `images/stories`. The **Image Position** determines where the image is displayed, relative to the description text. In the **Description** text editor area, you can enter and format a short descriptive text introducing the subject of the section or category. Section and Category descriptions can be displayed at the top of pages showing content overviews.

For more on Images and Descriptions, see Chapter 7 on section and category overview pages.

Building a site without sections or categories

In the previous chapter, you've already seen some examples of uncategorized articles. When organizing your site content you might end up with articles that do not belong in any category. These you can add as Uncategorized articles. Usually, uncategorized articles contain static content, such as a mission statement or some legal information. Uncategorized pages are the odd ones out in a site that's for the main part organized through sections and categories. If you've got more than a handful of uncategorized pages, that might be a reason to rethink your content organization.

What sites can you build with uncategorized content only?

Sometimes, Joomla!'s powerful multi-level site organization capabilities are just too much. Very small sites—"brochure sites" of some five to ten pages—without secondary page levels, can consist of uncategorized articles only.

Let's say your local yoga teacher asks you to develop a website. She probably wouldn't need much more content than shown in the following diagram:

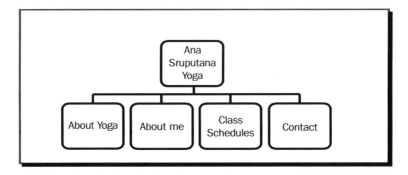

In this case, there are no layers of content below the menu link level. There will probably be five menu links: Home, About Yoga, About Me, Class Schedules, and Contact. Three of these will each point to an article (About Yoga, About Me, and Class Schedules). The Contact Page could also be a plain article, but let's assume this is—just like we've seen before—a contact form generated by Joomla!'s Contacts component. This is how we could translate the above site map in Joomla! terms:

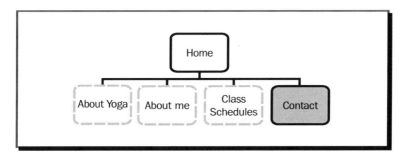

The boxes with grey dotted outlines represent uncategorized articles; the box with a grey background represents a special functionality page (in this case a contact form).

This same simple one-level structure would be appropriate for all kinds of small sites with a dedicated subject matter, i.e. a portfolio site for a one man company or an event site. A copy writing company would have a Joomla! site structure similar to the following:

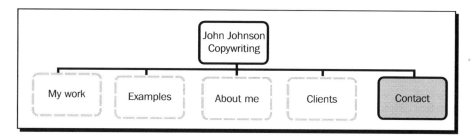

For an event site—such as a site for a congress or seminar—a structure like the one shown in the following diagram would be fine:

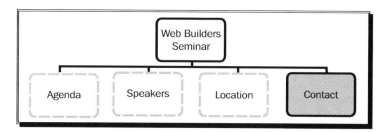

Although you'll leave much of the built-in functionality for managing big, content-rich sites untouched, it's still worthwhile to use Joomla! for sites like these. All the other advantages of Joomla! still hold, such as the ability to add any extra functionality you like. If your client wants a registration form for his seminar site, or a photo gallery for his portfolio site, you can add these using Joomla! extensions. And, of course, your client will be able to manage and update content easily.

How do you go about building a small site?

Creating a small site like the examples previously shown simply means you'll skip a few steps, as there's no need to create any sections or categories. These are the actions it takes:

1. Create the uncategorized content pages you need.
2. Add menu links to the **Main Menu**. In this case, you'll link directly to articles instead of sections or categories.

An example is as follows, a three page site based on a "clean" Joomla! installation (without sample data). Creating the basic setup of a tiny site like this takes just a few minutes.

In this example, in our new and empty Joomla! site we've created three uncategorized articles. We've set them all to display on the Front Page, too.

For each of the articles, we've added a menu link in the **Main Menu** (via **Menus | Main Menu | New**).

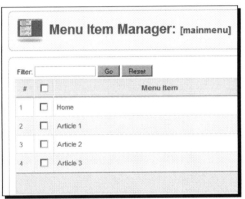

This is what the visitor sees. The **Main Menu** contains three links; the **Front Page** shows intro texts to the three articles with **Read more** links.

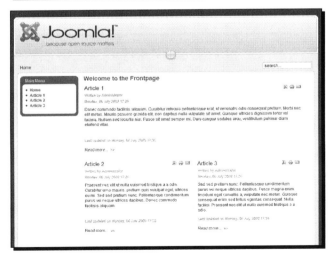

When the visitor clicks on a link, the full article is shown.

That's all there is to setting up a tiny one-level website in Joomla!. You can write a few articles, and create links pointing to them. After that, you can focus on the extras you want to add (see Chapter 10 on extending Joomla!) and the design (see Chapter 11 on using templates).

Downsize the home page, too

For a very small site, you can still build the home page with Joomla!'s default Front Page tools. Just select a few articles to display (fully, or only as intro text) on the Front Page. However, you may want something simpler for this type of site. You might want to consider showing just one article as your own, customized home page content. You'll read more about this technique in Chapter 6 on home page display options.

Have a go hero – organize a site!

Imagine you've been asked to build an informative website for a small company you know. How would you go about this? Think of what you want to achieve, create an outline of the main and secondary sections, and translate this outline to Joomla!. What would be your sections and categories, where would you put uncategorized articles?

And how about creating a small website about yourself? Using the site structuring skills you've acquired in this chapter, go ahead and create a great structure that would be both realizable in Joomla! and appeal to your visitors.

Pop quiz – test your site organization knowledge

1. What's the best order in which to build Joomla!-based sites?

    a. Start with extensions, add content, add menu links, add content containers.

    b. Start with menu links, add content containers, add content, add extensions.

    c. Start with content containers, add content, add menu links, add extensions.

2. What can you use uncategorized articles for?

    a. To display articles that have not yet been authorized.

    b. To display articles that do not belong to categories.

    c. To display articles that belong to a section, but not to a category.

3. How can you get categories to display in the frontend?

    a. Categories are backend stuff; they're only displayed in the Category Manager.

    b. A category can be displayed by adding a specific menu link that points to a category overview page.

    c. Categories are automatically displayed on overview pages when added to the Category Manager.

Summary

In Chapter 3, you've learned that Joomla! retrieves content from a database, block by block. Together these blocks form a web page. That's why you start building a site creating categories; you actually build a well-organized content database. In this chapter, we've learned what it takes to create content categories and to build a future proof framework for site content.

Specifically, you've learned:

◆ Every website, big or small, requires planning. It all starts with creating a logical site map reflecting the structure of the content you have in mind. Keep it lean and clean. Bear in mind that visitors will want to get to the content they're looking for as fast as possible.

◆ To transfer your hand drawn site map to a working Joomla! site, first identify the different Joomla! content elements in it. This will help you build the site step by step.

◆ The main content containers are sections and categories. You'll create these first. Sections hold at least one category, categories hold articles.

- ◆ To show section and category contents on the site, you add menu links pointing to sections or categories.

- ◆ At any time, you can rearrange and rename sections and categories or move their contents.

- ◆ Small sites, with just a few content pages, can consist of uncategorized articles only.

In the next chapter, we'll jump from organization to creating content. We'll fill the containers we've just set up with different types of articles.

6
Creating Killer Content: Adding and Editing Articles

Once you have created a framework of sections and categories, things can move pretty fast. There's nothing to stop you from creating a content-rich site—whether you want to add a dozen, hundreds, or even thousands of pages. In this chapter we'll focus on adding and editing articles, the type of content that's essential to most sites. Later, you might want to add other types of content (such as image galleries or forums); we'll deal with those in Chapter 10.

When creating the example site in Chapter 4, you've already seen how you can create a new article using the default settings. You've left all of the extra function buttons and parameters alone. But in real life, you'll probably want more control. You want to make your content look great, add pictures, and specify exactly how to display things and what details to display. Joomla! allows you to you edit articles and tweak article settings to fit your needs exactly.

In this chapter you'll learn:

- ◆ Creating, editing, and formatting articles
- ◆ Split an article into intro text and body text
- ◆ Dealing with long articles: splitting them into a series of pages
- ◆ Adjusting general article settings

So let's get it started!

Articles, content pages, what's the difference?

You might be tempted to think an article is the same as page. Strictly, it isn't. You've read before that Joomla! doesn't think in terms of pages. Joomla! figures any web page is constructed of a whole lot of database-driven bits and pieces—and almost any combination of those bits and pieces can turn up on the visitor's browser as a web page.

Although the article will certainly be at the center of a content page, there's bound to be much more to that page. Around the article there will be all kinds of other dynamic content—yes, those bits and pieces again. Be that as it may, for the sake of simplicity we'll just use the word page (or content page) for articles now and then. As long as we're aware that content pages may contain more than articles, that's OK, isn't it? Don't tell Joomla!; it will be our secret.

Creating and editing articles: Beyond the basics

Over the last few chapters, you practiced adding and editing articles. Let's recap the steps involved:

◆ To create a new article, navigate to **Content | Article Manager** and click on **New**.

◆ To edit an existing article, navigate to **Content | Article Manager**. Click on the title of the article to open it in the **Article: [Edit]** screen.

Another way to achieve the same results is to select the article (select the checkbox on the left-hand side of the article title) and click on the **Edit** button in the toolbar. The **Article: [New]** and **Article: [Edit]** are identical. You're already familiar with some of the most important functions; in this chapter, we'll boldly go to sections we haven't explored yet.

The Article Editor is shown in the following screenshot:

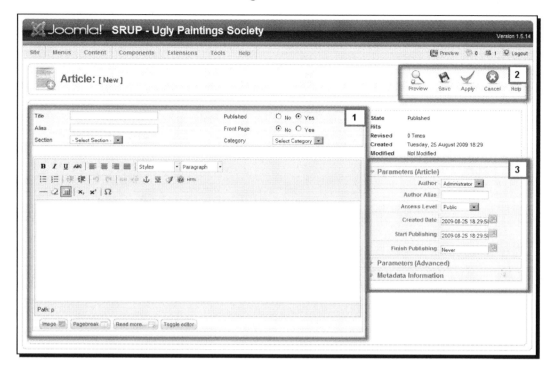

The article editing screen consists of three sections:

1. The actual text editing area offers you a simple word processor like interface for entering and formatting text. Above the actual article text you add the **Title**, select the appropriate **Section** and **Category**, and so on.

2. The toolbar buttons allow you to preview the article, save or apply changes, or cancel changes.

3. The **Parameters** allow you to set up the article to display and behave just as you need it to. You'll learn more about them in the *Adjusting article settings* section later in this chapter.

Let's now explore the power of the Joomla! article editor. We'll find out how we can tweak articles to get them to display exactly as we want them to.

Making it look good: Formatting article text

Your client, the SRUP society, wants to add some new content to their site explaining the characteristic qualities of ugly art. You've been sent a text file and have been asked to turn the contents into a new page. Can you please create a new article and make it look good?

Time for action – add styling to article text

Let's create a new article and see how we can format it adequately.

1. Navigate to **Content | Article Manager** and click on **New**.

2. In the **Title** box, enter **Just What is Ugly Art**? This is the type of factual content that fits the Facts category, so let's select the **Ugly Paintings** section and the **Facts** category:

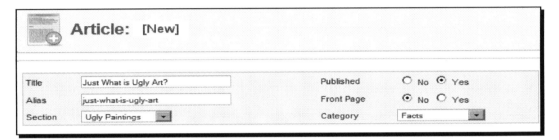

3. By default, **Published** is set to **Yes**. Let's set it to **No**. This way the article will remain invisible to your site visitors until you're finished with it (and publish it).

4. We don't want this article to show up on our home page so leave **Front Page** set to **No**.

5. In the text editor screen, add some article text. If you want to copy text from a word processor document, first strip out all of the formatting. That way you avoid invisible word processor tags messing up your article text. To do this, open the Notepad application on your PC (or TextEdit on a Mac) and paste the text from the word processor into the Notepad or TextEdit document. This will give you a clean text-only file that you can copy and paste into the Joomla! editor window. Right-click and select **Paste** from the pop-up menu.

6. In this example we've added five paragraphs: a short introductory text and four separate paragraphs. Type a subheading above each of the four paragraphs. In the example we've used the subheadings **Abstract Chaos**, **Poor Anatomy**, **Too much detail**, and **Hideous Colors**.

7. Let's use the text editor tools to change the basic formatting of the text. Select the subheading **Abstract Chaos**. Click on the **Format** drop-down box and select the pre-defined **Heading 3** format as shown in the following screenshot:

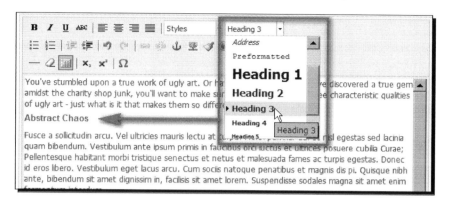

In the previous screenshot, the Heading 3 format is applied to an article subheading. As the main article titles in Joomla! usually have a Heading 2 format, the Heading 3 format is suited for the next level (the subheadings within an article).

Want more formatting control?
The font style of the heading is now set to the Heading 3 format. What this actually looks like depends on the CSS stylesheet of the template you're using. In the default Joomla! template we're using, the Heading 3 style is pre-formatted as a blue Arial font. When you install a different template, your headings and all other CSS-defined layout can look completely different. And if you really want to get creative and create a mouthwatering article layout, you'll want to change the template CSS styles yourself and adapt them to your needs. Don't worry, we'll get to the ins and outs of templates and styling in Chapter 11.

8. Select the other subheadings and apply the **Heading 3** style to those too.

9. Click on **Save**. To preview the article, click on the **Preview** button in the toolbar (that's not the **Preview** link in the top of the screen!). It looks like this:

10. Clicking on this button displays a pop-up screen:

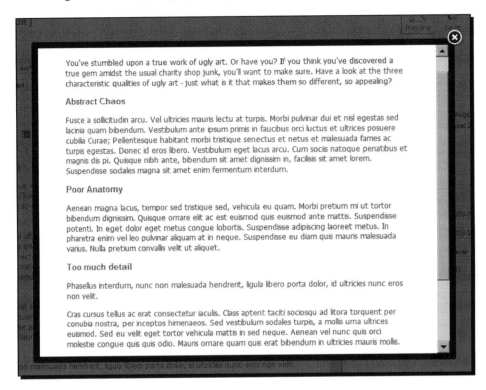

This preview screen gives you a rough impression of what the article will look like. However, like the site preview link this button doesn't take you to the frontend. The quick preview comes in handy when you want to check an article that isn't visible on the frontend (because it isn't published yet or because there is no menu link pointing to it).

What just happened?

You've created a new article in the Ugly Paintings Facts category and formatted some text using the word processor like interface of the text editor. While preparing your text, you can set it to be invisible (unpublished); later on, you'll publish the finished text in one click.

Have a go hero – change the formatting

Feel free to play around and explore the different text formatting options. Check out how to apply indenting, bulleted lists, and so on. You may want to select the first paragraph and apply bold styling to really make it stand out as the leading paragraph. Applying styles to the selected text works like you're used to in word processing software.

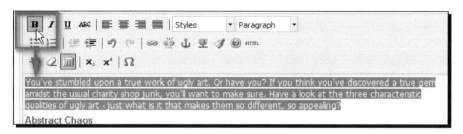

Make sure to check out the **HTML** button (just below the **Paragraph** drop-down menu). Clicking on it opens up a pop-up screen showing the HTML code of the article text:

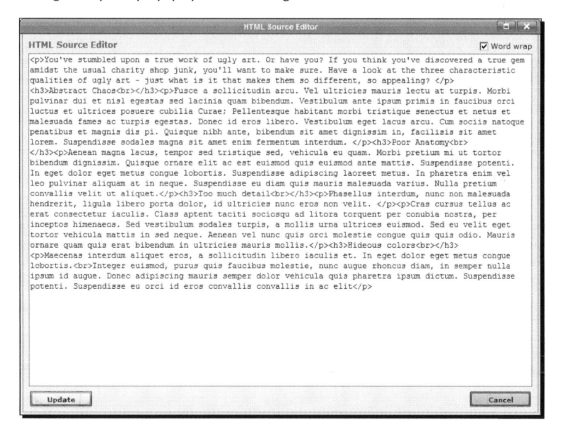

This can be particularly useful if you know your way around HTML; sometimes you might want to directly edit the HTML code or check it for unwanted tags. You can close the HTML editor window by clicking on **Update** (to apply changes) or **Cancel**.

Extending the text editor

Joomla! ships with the text editor you've just used. It's actually an extension called Tiny MCE. If you would like to have some advanced text editing controls, you can set Tiny MCE to its "Extended" view. Just navigate to **Extensions | Plugin Manager** and click on **Editor - TinyMCE 2.0** to edit the settings.

In the Plugin Parameters section, select **Functionality: Extended**. This will add some useful buttons to the editor screen, such as a "Paste from Word" button that lets you copy text from a Word document while automatically stripping all Word formatting that's not needed on a web page. The extended text editor toolbar looks similar to the following screenshot:

If you still find Tiny MCE's capabilities too limited, you can easily replace it by another (free) text editor. A very popular one is **Joomla! Content Editor (JCE)**. You'll read more about replacing the default text editor in Chapter 10.

Adding images to articles

You've just created an all-text page on paintings that's not really what makes your visually oriented art loving visitors tick. Let's show them what it's all about and add some images!

Time for action – upload images

Imagine you've been sent some image files by mail and you've copied them to your hard drive. To add them to an article, you'll first use Joomla!'s Media Manager to upload the image files to the web server.

1. Navigate to **Site | Media Manager**. The **Media Manager** will open the `images` folder. However, article images are by default stored in a subfolder called `stories`. Navigate to this folder by clicking on the **stories** folder icon.

2. In the **Files** section, type the name of the new subfolder. In this example, we've entered **paintings**. Click on the **Create Folder** button.

3. Click on the icon of the new **paintings** folder.

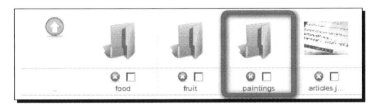

4. You'll be shown an empty folder. Add a new image by clicking on the **Browse** button below the **Files** section.

5. In the **Upload File** pop-up screen, select an image from your computer's hard drive, click on **Open,** and then click on **Start Upload**.

6. Repeat Steps 4 and 5 until you've got about five pictures. The **Files** section of the **Media Manager** now shows thumbnails of the uploaded pictures:

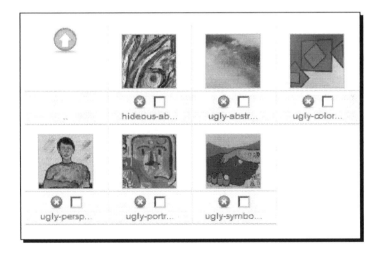

What just happened?

You've uploaded a set of pictures ready to be inserted into any article. By default, Joomla! will look for images that you can insert into articles in the /images/stories directory. That's why you have to create subfolders in stories if you want to keep different groups of images organized (for example, Paintings, Staff, and Meetings). This way, you won't end up with all image files piled up in one big default image folder.

If you'd like to use another folder as the default base directory, navigate to **Site | Global Configuration | System**. In the **Media Settings** section, change the **Path to Image Folder**. For example, entering /images as the default path will make Joomla! look in this folder when you insert article images.

When uploading image files, you'll have noticed that Joomla!'s Media Manager doesn't allow you to upload more than one file at a time. It has some more limitations; although you can add and delete files, you can't move them from one folder to another. Because of this, many Joomla! users prefer to use an FTP program to upload files and manage the media folders on the web server. There are also many extensions available that enhance Joomla!'s image management capabilities (such as the Joomla! Flash Uploader extension). The Joomla! Content Editor (see Chapter 10) is a powerful replacement for the default text editor, which also makes uploading and inserting images much easier.

Time for action – inserting and aligning images

Now, let's insert the images you've just uploaded into the article text:

1. Navigate to **Content | Article Manager** and open the article, **Just What is Ugly Art?**, to edit it (by clicking on the article title).

2. Let's place an image in each of the article paragraphs. Place the cursor at the beginning of the first paragraph below the introduction text, just after the first subheading.

> three characteristic qualities of ugly art - just what is it that makes them so different, so appealing?
>
> Abstract Chaos
>
> Fusce a sollicitudin arcu. Vel ultricies mauris lectu at turpis. Morbi pulvinar dui et nisl egestas sed lacinia quam bibendum. Vestibulum ante ipsum primis in faucibus orci luctus et ultrices posuere cubilia Curae; Pellentesque habitant morbi tristique senectus et netus et malesuada fames ac turpis egestas. Donec id

3. Click on the **Image** button at the bottom of the text editor screen:

4. A pop-up screen opens displaying the contents of the images root directory. In the top left-hand corner of the pop-up screen, select the appropriate subdirectory: paintings (another way to select this directory is by clicking on the **paintings** folder icon).

5. Select the image you want to insert:

6. In the **Image URL** box, Joomla! automatically adds the appropriate URL. The other details you can add or set yourself are as follows:

- ❏ In the **Image Description** box type a description. This text isn't displayed, but it informs search engines what the picture is about. It will also show up when the visitor uses a non-visual web browser.

- ❏ In the **Title** box enter a title. This is shown only when the web visitor hovers the mouse pointer on the image. Select the **Caption** checkbox if you want to have Joomla! display the title text as a caption just below the image.

- ❏ In the **Align** drop-down box you can choose how the image will be aligned: to the left, to the right, or centered. In the upcoming screenshot, you can see the effects of right and left alignment of pictures.

7. Place the cursor in another paragraph and repeat Steps 4 to 6. Do this until every paragraph of the article body text contains a picture.

8. Click on **Apply** and then click on **Preview** to get a first impression of the output. In the pop-up screen, scroll down to see all of the images that have been inserted. In the following example, some are aligned right relative to the text, some are aligned left:

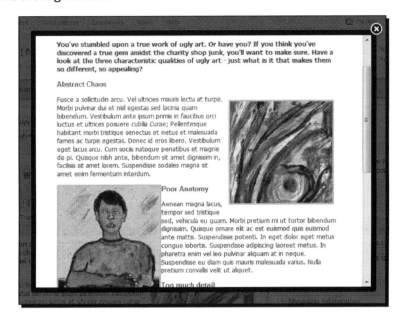

What just happened?

Adding pictures to articles is a pretty straightforward process. You upload the desired image files and use the **Image** button to tell Joomla! where you want them displayed.

Have a go hero – adjust the image settings

After you've inserted an image, you may want to adjust the display settings. To create some gutter space between the images and the surrounding text, click on the **Insert/edit image** icon (a picture of a tree) in the text editor toolbar.

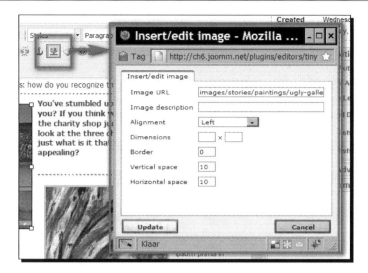

Now you can set a value for **Vertical space** or **Horizontal space** (in pixels). This will create some whitespace around the image, making it stand apart from the article text. Click on **Update** to apply the changes (yes, you're right; they'd better label this button **Apply**).

The **Insert/edit image** button in the editor isn't really suited for inserting images. After clicking on this button, you can't browse to the image file, but have to know its exact location (URL). That's why there's a separate **Image** button below the text editor screen that's better equipped for inserting images.

Changing the way the article displays

The article editor screen gives you much more power than just formatting text and adding pictures. You can also control how the article should be displayed: as one individual article, split into two parts, or even split in as many parts (subpages), as you like. Let's find out how we can enhance articles with these options.

One lump or two? Split the article in an intro text and main text

So far, we haven't added any instructions in our article to change the way it displays. Let's have a look at the frontend to see how it's displayed by default. To see how our new article looks at the frontend, on the frontend **Main Menu**, click on the **Ugly Paintings** link.

Remember, you created a link to the Ugly Paintings section in Chapter 5. This menu link (of the **Section Blog Layout** type) displays an overview of anything you add to the given section or category. As you've now put some content in this section, on clicking the **Ugly Paintings** menu link you should now see the page shown in the following screenshot:

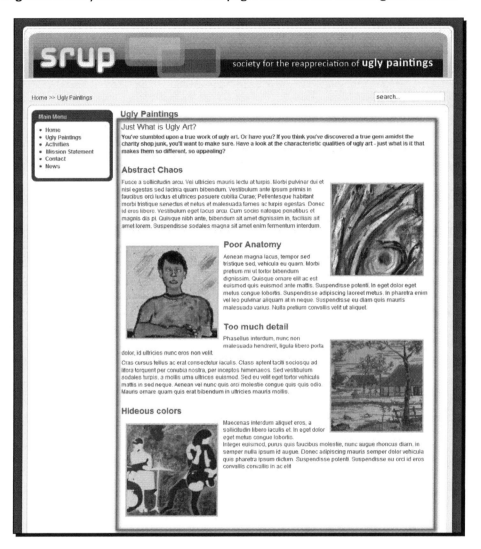

Oops! Here's the good news, the article is visible and it looks just like you've formatted it. However, there's some bad news too. The full five paragraph article shows up on the **Ugly Paintings** section overview page. This is not how we want our article to display, if we were to add more articles to this same section, they would all be fully displayed on a huge overview page. To get Joomla! to show just a short teaser text here, we'll now split the article, separating the intro text and the full article body text.

Time for action – creating an intro text

In the articles you created in earlier chapters, you've already seen it's good to add a separate intro text to an article. Now you know why; if you don't, the article can only be displayed fully on overview pages such as the section overview you just saw. Let's fix things by adding an intro text to our new article.

1. Navigate to **Content | Article Manager** and open the article that you just created (**Just What are Ugly Paintings?**) to edit it.

2. In the text editor screen, add a new first line. In this example, we've entered **The Characteristics of True Ugliness: how do you recognize them**?

3. Place the cursor just after this first line to indicate that you want Joomla! to split the article here, and create a Read More link to point to the full article, click on the **Read More ...** button at the bottom of the editor screen. A red dotted line appears:

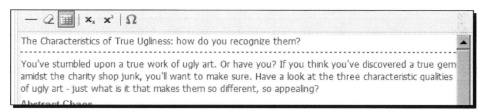

4. In the **Parameters (Advanced)** panel, set **Intro Text** to **Hide**. This means the intro text (in this case the short teaser text we just created) will be hidden when the full article is shown. It will be shown on overview pages.

5. Click on **Apply** and then click on **Preview** to see the output on the frontend. You'll be taken to the frontend home page. In the Main Menu, click on the **Ugly Paintings** link.

Mission accomplished! Now, only the intro text and **Read more** link of the new article appear on the section overview page:

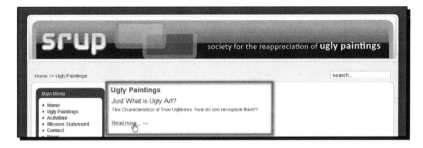

More teaser texts will be added to the overview when you add more articles to the section.

The full five paragraph article is shown (without the teaser text) when the visitor clicks on the **Read more** link:

What just happened?

In principle, any article in Joomla! can consist of one continuous text. Especially when writing short articles (think of blog posts), one lump of text can suffice. But in many cases you'll want to split articles into an introductory text (a teaser text, in newspaper terms) and the actual article body text, allowing Joomla! to publish the two parts on separate pages.

Creating multi-page articles

Suppose you have a long article with several subheadings, each covering various sub-topics that all have something to do with each other. Sometimes, you may find such an article is too long. It doesn't fit the content screen, you don't want the visitor to have to scroll all that much.

There's a tedious solution to this. It involves manually splitting the article by creating several individual short articles. But luckily, there's also a quick way out. By adding page breaks in a single article, Joomla! will display this single article in the frontend as a series of separate pages, automatically adding navigation links and a table of contents.

Time for action – using page breaks to split up an article

Let's say your client doesn't like the one page article on ugly paintings. Instead of having one article with several subheadings, they'd rather see some short pages that explain things step by step. To do this, we'll edit the existing article:

1. Navigate to **Content | Article Manager** and open the **Just What is Ugly Art?** article to edit it.

2. Select the page break locations. This is where Joomla! will split the article into separate pages. In this example, we'll replace every subheading by a page break. Select the first subheading (**Abstract Chaos**) and delete it. Now click on the **Page Break** button at the bottom of the editor screen. A pop-up screen shows:

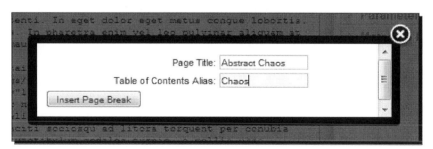

3. In the pop-up screen, enter the **Page Title** and **Table of Contents Alias**.

- ❏ **Page Title**: Enter a title for the new page. It will be displayed next to the article title, separated by a dash:
  Just What are Ugly Paintings? – Abstract Chaos.

- ❏ **Table of Contents Alias**: This is the link text that will appear in the Table of Contents of the multi-page article. The Alias and the Page Title can be the same, however, it's best to keep the Alias text as short as possible.

4. Click on **Insert Page Break**. The pop-up screen closes and a grey dotted line is inserted to indicate the location of the page break.

5. Repeat Steps 2 to 4 for each page break required and save the article. Click on **Preview** to have a look at the frontend results. In the frontend **Main Menu**, click on **Ugly Paintings** and locate the intro text of the **Just what is Ugly Art?** article. Click on the **Read More** link.

Now, instead of one article Joomla! has created a series of interlinked article pages. The first page the visitor sees is the first (sub) page. Pages include **<< Prev – Next >>** links to the previous and next page; the Table of Content's Aliases you've entered when creating page breaks now show up as hyperlinks in the **Article Index** (a table of contents featured on every sub page):

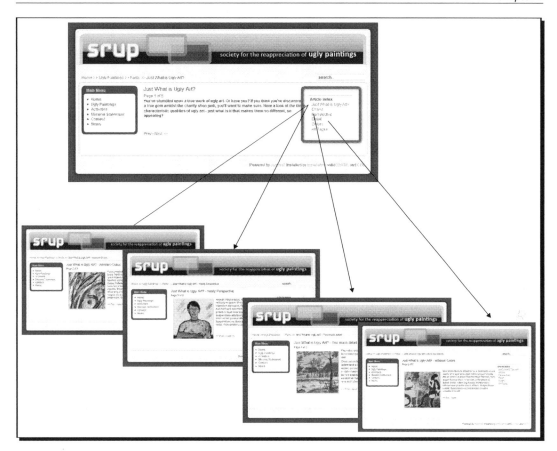

What just happened?

Joomla! lets you add page breaks to spread the content of a single article over multiple pages. To allow the visitor to move back and forth, a Table of Contents section and Previous and Next navigation is automatically added to multi-page articles.

Use it wisely

Working with page breaks gives you an extra level of content below the article level. You shouldn't, however, overuse this feature. Usually, visitors don't like clicking multiple links to read an article. It's best to reserve multi-page navigation for articles that easily break into logical chunks, such as step-by-step tutorials or portfolio pages showing different clients and projects.

Alternative page display techniques: Tabs and accordions

There are many creative ways to put a lot of content on a single page, without displaying it all simultaneously. One of these is using *tabs*. Initially the visitor only sees the contents of the first tab panel. When they click on another tab, the corresponding content panel becomes visible instead.

Another commonly used trick is called the *accordion*. This allows you to provide multiple content panels and display them one at a time. Panels slide out and slide in on a mouse click.

You can create both tabbed pages and accordions using Joomla! extensions. In Chapter 10 you'll learn how to install and apply them.

Tweaking the details: Changing article settings

When editing an article, you can set a wide array of parameters. These allow you to control exactly which article details are shown, when the article will be published, and so on. It's a good idea to explore the options to make sure what combination of setting fits your needs best. The following is an overview of the settings you can choose per article:

Parameters (Article)

Author, Author Alias	The default Author name is Administrator. If you want another name to appear with the article, you can enter an Alias. This name will appear as the author name (provided that the Author name is set to show in the **Parameters (Advanced)**).
Access Level	This setting is important if you want to control if pages are accessible only to registered visitors. See Chapter 9 on user management.
Created Date	Change this value to manipulate the **Created Date** that Joomla! can display with any article. By changing the date, you can bring an existing article to the attention of the visitor because it will reappear in pages with new items.
Start Publishing, Finish Publishing	Sometimes, you'll have prepared content that should only be published for a given period of time; think of a temporary promotion, or a special New Years message. Use **Start Publishing** to enter the date when the new page should appear on the site; set a date in the **Finish Publishing** box to automatically unpublish content after a certain period.

Parameters (Advanced)

Show Title, Intro Text, Section Name, Category Title, Article Rating, Author Name, Created Date and Time, Modified Date and Time, PDF Icon, Print Icon, E-mail Icon

These Parameters control which details should be displayed with the article (either in Blog Layout view or in full article view), as shown in the following screenshot.

In the example below, all extras are set to show. This results in a lot of "article clutter"; it's hard to find the real content in this detail overkill. It's best to only display one or two details – if they add useful information.

Setting Article Rating to Show will display a five point scale below the article title when the full article is shown; visitors can rate the article:

Title Linkable (Section Title Linkable, Category Title Linkable)

When set to **Show**, an article **Title** or **Section or Category** name can be *linkable*; the visitor can click on it to navigate to the article/section/category.

Content Language, Key Reference

These advanced options are only relevant when you have a multilingual site.

Alternative Read more: text

Entering a Read more text will replace the default Read more link with something specific to the article:

On the frontend, it will be shown as follows:

> Just What is Ugly Art?
> The Characteristics of True Ugliness: how do you recognize them?
>
> Recognizing Ugly Art »

Filling out the **Alternative Read more: text** is good for the findability of your content. Search engines attach greater importance to a custom link (Recognizing Ugly Art) than to default text Read more. It's better for usability too, as it allows you to better guide your visitors towards the article content.

Metadata Information

Description, Keywords, Robots, Author

Metadata information is used by search engines. You can add an article description and keywords to help search engines index your content. You'll read more on this in Chapter 12.

Setting preferences for all new articles at once

You'll probably want to set some preferences for all your articles at once: whether you want the author name displayed, whether the title should be a hyperlink, and so on. To enter these site-wide article preferences, navigate to **Content | Article Manager** and click on the **Parameters** button in the toolbar. After you have chosen the appropriate settings, these will apply to all new articles, so it's a good idea to choose these settings before the bulk of your site content is created. Of course, you can override these general settings by setting specific parameter choices when editing individual articles.

Archiving articles

Your website is growing and there's a steady stream of new content. Now what can you do with articles that are outdated? Of course, you can just unpublish them. That way they're still available in the backend, but the site visitor cannot see them anymore.

Another option is to create an archive. Archived articles are still available, but they're no longer part of the "normal" site contents.

Time for action – creating a news archive

Let's create an archive for some old news pages on the SRUP site:

1. Navigate to **Content | Article Manager**. In the **Select Category** filter box, select **General News** to see only the articles in that category.

2. Select two news articles to be archived. In the following example, we've selected **New Ugly Paintings Discovered** and **Bob Ross Exhibition Announced**:

3. Click on the **Archive** button in the toolbar. A message appears to confirm both articles are archived. The article titles have changed to grey and the word **[Archived]** is displayed next to the title.

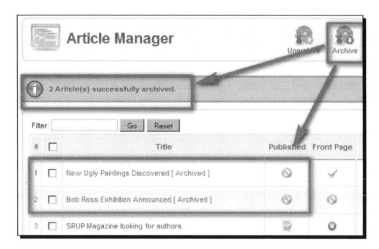

You've created a (tiny) news archive now, but there's no way for the visitor to see the contents. Let's create a link:

> **4.** Navigate to **Menus| Main Menu| New**. Click on **Articles|ArchivedArticle List**. Enter a **Title** for the hyperlink: **News Archive**. Adjust any other settings you like and click on **Save**.

On the frontend, a link to the Archive is shown. The visitor can filter (search) archived articles by keyword or publication date:

What just happened?

You've created an archive for outdated articles. The visitor can see an overview of the archive contents by clicking on the **News Archive** link in the **Main Menu**. Although this archiving system can be useful, there's a catch; archived articles get a different URL. This is a disadvantage because existing links from other sites to your now archived contents will be broken.

You cannot edit archived articles. If you do want to change the content of an archived article, you have to first unarchive it (using the **Unarchive** button in the **Article Manager** toolbar) to make it an ordinary article. After you've made changes, archive it again.

Pop quiz – test your site article expertise

1. The article editor screen in Joomla! allows you to do which of these three things?
    a. Formatting article text.
    b. Inserting images.
    c. Controlling the start and end date of publishing.

2. What's the use of the Joomla! Media Manager?
    a. It allows you to manage all sorts of media (images, movie files, and MP3 files).
    b. It allows you to upload images and insert them into an article.
    c. It allows you to insert images that come with the default Joomla! installation.

3. You open an existing article in the Joomla article editor and see a red dotted line. What does that mean?
    a. Text below the line will not be displayed.
    b. The article text has exceeded the maximum number of characters allowed.
    c. If needed, Joomla! can separately display the intro text and the full article text.

4. How can you break a long article into a series of short ones?
    a. By manually creating several individual articles.
    b. By entering page breaks in an article.
    c. By entering *Read more* links in an article.

5. What's the function of archiving articles?
    a. Archived articles cannot be edited any more.
    b. Archived articles aren't displayed in the frontend.
    c. Archived articles are displayed in a special Archive part of the frontend.

Summary

In this chapter, you've mastered creating article content. This is what we covered:

◆ To create new articles or to edit existing ones, the **Article Manager** is your starting point. From there, click on **New** or select an article and click on **Edit**.

◆ The article editing screen allows you to style your contents and add images. If you want more text editing control, you can set the text editor to show an extra ("Extended") set of buttons.

◆ The **Media Manager** allows you to create new image folders. This way, you can keep the image files on the web server organized.

◆ There are several ways to display article content. It can be one continuous text page, but you can also split the article into an introductory text and the actual article body text.

◆ To break a long article into several interlinked subpages, you add page breaks to the article text. In the backend you've still got one article, in the frontend it will display as a series of pages.

You've now mastered the recipe that enables you to create as much killer content as you like. But all of the beautiful site content that may be accumulating in your sections and categories is useless if your site visitors fail to notice it's there. So, it's time to focus on your site's "shop windows": the home page and other pages that draw your visitors' attention to the content. In the next chapter, you'll learn how to create an inviting home page and alluring overview pages; give visitors an irresistible preview of what your site has to offer.

7
Welcoming Your Visitors: Creating Attractive Home Pages and Overview Pages

In the previous chapters, you've laid the ground work for your site. First, you created content containers (sections and categories), then, you created actual content (articles). You've got a bunch of neatly organized, attractive articles ready to be explored by a worldwide web surfing audience. But how can you entice those casual web surfers to actually read all that valuable content? Why would they bother to drill down the content of your site?

That's where the home page and overview pages come in. The home page lures your visitors in; Joomla!'s overview pages—"second level home pages" that provide a quick overview of section and category contents—direct people to the articles they could be interested in.

In this chapter we will:

- ◆ Customize the home page settings
- ◆ Create a different kind of home page
- ◆ Create and tweak section and category overview pages
- ◆ Create different layouts for different types of overview pages

So, let's start tweaking the SRUP home page!

Up to now, you've set up the home page and and overview pages using the default options. But you might have noticed that Joomla! offers dozens of parameters for these page types. Changing these parameters (settings) can completely alter the way content is presented. In fact, different settings can create very different looking pages.

Let's effectively welcome your visitors and entice them to read all of your valuable content—enter the magic world of home page and overview pages. In the following screenshots, you'll see what page types we're talking about. On the left-hand side is the example home page in the default Joomla! installation, on the right-hand side is an overview page showing contents of the News category:

Why do you need overview pages, anyway?

Typically, Joomla! will lead your site visitor to a section or category content in three steps. Between the **Main Menu** and the actual content, there's a secondary page to show section or category contents:

1. A visitor clicks on a menu link.

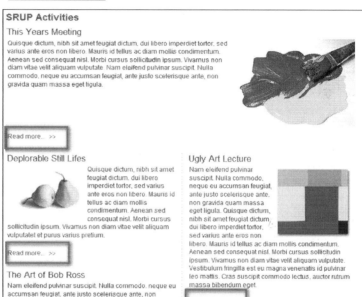

2. They are taken to an overview page with article previews and links.

3. They click to read the full article.

As you can see, what's on the home page and the overview pages (and how it's presented) is vitally important to your site. It's the teaser texts, images, and hyperlinks on these pages that lead your visitor to the actual content.

Of course, people don't always arrive at your site via the home page. Search engine results might take them directly to any page—including overview pages. One more reason to make those pages as enticing as you can!

Overview page, landing page, secondary home page?

Joomla! doesn't have a name for overview pages. Among web builders they're also known as section *start pages*, *category pages*, *department pages*, or *landing pages*. Whatever you like to call it, it's the same thing: a navigational page that provides an overview of site categories. In this book we'll call them section or category overview pages.

Creating the perfect home: Mastering home page layout

The main content area in any Joomla! home page is driven by the Front Page Component—it's the thing that tells Joomla! what to display in the main content area (the mainbody) of the home page. When you've installed Joomla! with the sample data, the home page mainbody will show:

- One introductory article text over the full width of the mainbody
- Four intro texts divided into two columns
- A list of links to other articles

You can see this in action in the screenshot at the beginning of this chapter.

This default setup is suited for many types of content rich sites. But you're certainly not limited to using this one combination of intro texts and links in the home page mainbody. Joomla!'s Front Page Component offers you a vast amount of choices on how to display content in it, and what to display.

Changing the way your home page is arranged

It's your client on the phone, telling you that—happy as they are with their new site—some SRUP staff members find the home page layout too distracting. They don't like the newspaper look that displays the content columns in different widths. Would you be so kind as to tone things down a little? If you could quickly show them an alternative layout, that would be fine. You hang up and dive into the Front Page settings.

Time for action – rearrange the layout of articles on the home page

You decide to rearrange the items on the Front Page. Let's say you want a maximum of two intro texts, both in just one column. Apart from this, you would like to show a few hyperlinks to other articles that could be of interest to visitors browsing the home page.

1. Navigate to **Menus | Main Menu**. In the **Menu Item Manager**, click on **Home** to edit the settings of the home page.

2. In the **Parameters (Basic)** section, the default view settings are shown. There's **1** leading (full width) intro text, **4** intro texts are shown in **2** columns, and there are **4** hyperlinks. If we want a single column on the front page, we'll set the number of intros and columns to zero. Change the values as follows: set **# Leading** to **2**, **# Intro** to **0**, **Columns** to **0**, and **# Links** to **4**.

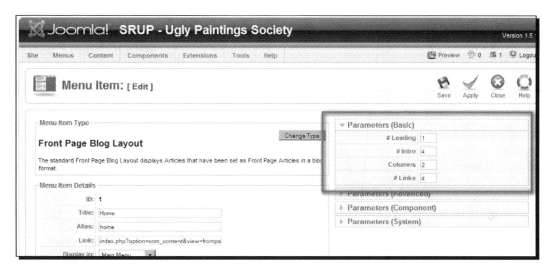

3. Click on **Preview** to see the changes on the frontend. There are now two full-width intro texts. Because up to now only three articles have been assigned to the home page, beneath the two intro texts just one article link is displayed. When you'll assign more articles to the home page, this list will grow to a maximum of four hyperlinks.

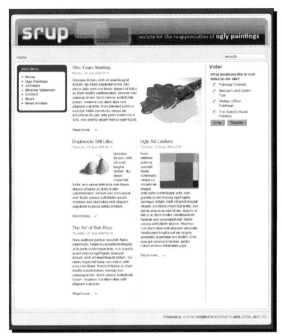

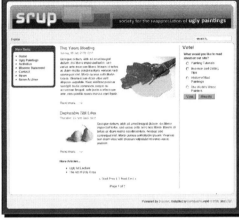

The previous two screenshots show the home page before and after. The updated home page on the right-hand side features the same four articles presented differently in just one column. Instead of four intro texts, the new page shows two intro texts and two hyperlinks.

What just happened?

The Parameters of any menu item allows you to influence the looks of the hyperlink's destination page. In this case, you've tweaked the **Home** Menu Item settings to change the contents of the home page mainbody. The magic numbers of the **Parameters (Basic)** are really powerful as different values can completely change the way content is displayed.

Have a go hero – tweak the home page settings to your liking

Joomla! offers you a long list of other settings you can use to adjust the home page layout. Navigate to **Menus | Main Menu | Home** and have a look at **Parameters (Advanced)**. First, you will probably want to set **Pagination** to **Hide**. That way, you'll hide the pagination links (**< Start Prev Next Last >**) that Joomla! displays when there are more articles available than can be shown on the home page as intro texts. Showing these links on a home page seems suited for web log home pages, where visitors expect to be able to browse through possibly long lists of blog entries. On other types of sites, web users aren't likely to expect multi-page home pages.

Unwanted Pagination Links can be set to **Hide** in the menu link's **Parameters (Advanced)** section.

Have a look at the **Parameters (Component)** to further customize the home page output. These parameters allow you to hide article details, such as **Author Name**, **Created Date and Time**, and **Modified Date and Time**. On a website that's maintained by just one or a few authors, or a website that isn't updated regularly, you might want to hide that information.

In this image, the **Parameters (Component)** are set to show article details, such as the author name and creation date.

Hiding unnecessary article details reduces "article clutter": images and details that may distract the reader. There's more room for actual content in the same space.

On a home page you'll probably also want to hide all of the special function icons (set **Icons**, **PDF Icon**, **Print Icon**, and **E-mail Icon** to **Hide**). It's unlikely that visitors want to print or e-mail parts of your home page content—let alone create a PDF document of part of the home page.

Without pagination and article details, the home page looks similar to the following screenshot. It's a clean looking page, focusing on just two article intro texts without any distracting irrelevant information, links, or buttons. Less is more: the result is a simple but appealing home page without too many intro texts or details.

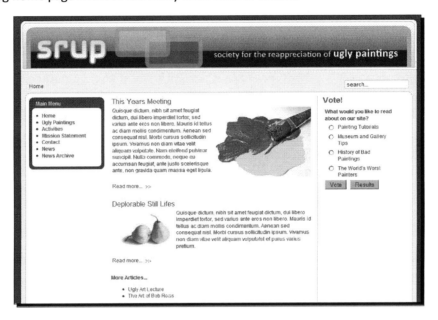

Adding items to the Front Page

In the **More Articles ...** hyperlink list of your home page, just one hyperlink is shown. That's because only three articles are set to display on the Front Page. To add some more, navigate to **Content | Article Manager**. Add any article by clicking on the red cross in the **Front Page** column to the right-hand side of the article title. The cross changes to a green check mark.

In the following example, we've selected a **News** item (**SRUP Magazine Looking for Authors**) to be featured on the **Front Page**:

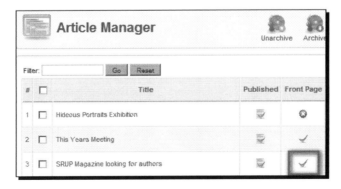

Want to see what this looks like up front? Just click on **Save** and then on **Preview**. The two new Front Page items are shown in the **More articles ...** list on the home page.

Another way to add articles to the Front Page

Adding items to the Front Page takes just a few clicks in the Article Manager **Front Page** column. You can also add an article in the **Article: [Edit]** screen, by selecting **Front Page: Yes**.

Controlling the order of Front Page items manually

Now that you've reorganized your home page layout, you'll probably want to set the order of the Front Page items. By default, the intro texts and links are displayed in the order they have in the Front Page Manager:

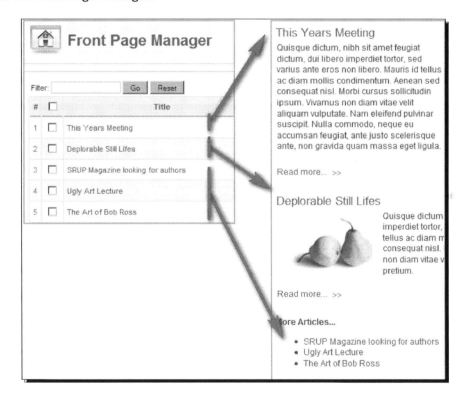

To change the order of the home page items, navigate to **Content | Front Page Manager** and click on the green arrows in the **Order** column to move an item up or down.

What's the use of the Front Page Manager?

In the Front Page Manager, you can't—as you might have expected—add items to the Front Page. As you've seen, you assign articles to the Front Page in the **Article Manager** (or in the article editing screen). You'll probably only use the **Front Page Manager** if you want to manually control the order of front page items, or if you want a quick overview of what's set to be shown on the Front Page. Apart from this, the **Front Page Manager** allows you to publish, delete, or archive Front Page articles—but you can just as easily use the **Article Manager** for that too.

Setting criteria to automatically order Front Page items

Having full manual control over the order of Front Page items can be convenient when you have a fixed set of content items that you want to show up on the home page, for example, when you have a corporate site and want to always show your company profile, an introduction on your products, and a link to a page with your address and contact details.

However, when your site is updated frequently with new content you'll probably want Joomla! to automatically arrange the home page items to certain ordering criteria. The **Parameters (Advanced)** allow you to choose from a wide range of ordering methods.

Time for action – show the most recent items first

The visitors of the SRUP site will probably expect to see the most recently added items on the top of the page. Let's set the **Parameters (Advanced)** to organize things accordingly.

1. Navigate to **Menus | Main Menu | Home**. In the **Menu Item Manager**, click on **Home** to edit the settings of the home page. Click on **Parameters (Advanced)** heading to see which options it offers.

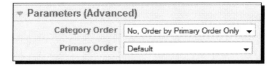

2. In the **Primary Order** drop-down box, choose **Most recent first**.

3. When ordering your articles by date you'll probably want to display the publication date for every article. Navigate to **Parameters (Component)** and make sure **Created Date and Time** is set to **Show**.

4. Click on **Save** and click on **Preview**.

What just happened?

When you check out the home page you'll find that the most recently added articles are shown first now. You control the order of home page items by selecting the appropriate **Primary Order** settings of the Front Page Menu Item (the **Home** link in the **Main Menu**).

Have a go hero – try out the Front Page settings

The Front Page Menu Item Parameters allow you do to much more than just arrange the content. You've got many, many more options. In real web building life, you'll probably set the Front Page parameters once and forget all about them. For now, it's a good idea to get acquainted with the impressive list of settings. Just check them out and discover the outcome on the frontend. Below you'll find a complete reference of all parameters.

Dozens of dazzling parameters—isn't that a bit too much?

You've seen them before (when setting article preferences in Chapter 6), and now they turn up again, those seemingly endless lists of parameters. Maybe you find these lists discouraging. Is it really necessary to check thirty or forty options to create just one menu link? Luckily, that's not how it works. You also get good results when you stick to the default settings. But if you want more grip, if you want to tweak your sites sections, categories, and articles, it is worthwhile to browse the parameter lists and experiment with the different sets of options. You'll see which settings fit your site best; later on, in your day to day web building routine, you'll probably stick to those.

Parameters (Basic)

Under **Parameters - Basic** you'll set the magic numbers. These affect the layout and arrangement of Front Page items.

# Leading	Enter the number of Leading articles you want to display, that is, intro texts displayed across the entire width of the main body.
# Intro	The number of intro texts that you want to show in two or more columns.
Columns	Specify the number of columns; over how many columns should the **# Intro** texts be distributed?
# Links	The number of hyperlinks to other articles (shown below Leading or Intro texts).

Parameters (Advanced)

The advanced parameters give you some more control over the order and presentation.

Category order	Do you want to organize the items on the Front Page by category title? You might want to do this when you have many items on your front page and you want your visitor to understand the category structure behind this. If you want to order by category, set the Category Title (see **Parameters (Component)** explained in the next table) to show; that way, the visitor can see the articles are grouped by category.

These Category order options are available:

- ◆ **No, Order by Primary Order Only**: If you select this option, the items are displayed in the order you set in the Primary Order field (the next parameter in this list).

- ◆ **Title Alphabetical**: Organizes categories alphabetically by title.

- ◆ **Title Reverse-Alphabetical**: Organizes categories reverse-alphabetically by title.

- ◆ **Order**: Organizes categories according to the Order they have in the Category Manager and order the category contents according to the Primary Order (that you can specify below).

Primary Order	You can order the items within the Front Page by date, alphabetically by **Author Name** or **Title**, **Most hits**, and so on. If you choose **Default**, then the items appear in the order they have in the Front Page Manager. This last option gives you full manual control over the order of items on the Front Page. Note: the Primary Order is applied only after the Category Order. Primary Order only has effect if you choose **No, Order by Primary Order Only** in the Category Order box.
Pagination	**Auto**: When there are more Front Page items than fit the first page, Joomla! automatically adds pagination links (<<Start <Previous 1 2 3 Next> End>>). On the Front Page you'll probably want to set Pagination to **Hide**.
Pagination results	If pagination links are shown Joomla! can also display the **Pagination Results**, the total number of pages (as in **Page 1 of 3**).

Parameters (Component)

The **Parameters (Component)** influence how articles are displayed on the Front Page.

Show Unauthorized Links	Do you want to show hyperlinks to articles that are only accessible to registered users, or hide these articles completely?
Show Article Title	Display article titles or not? It's hard to find a reason to select **No**.
Title Linkable	Should the title of the article be a hyperlink to the full article? Select **Yes** here. This is better for usability reasons because your visitor can just click on the title instead of a Read more link. It is also better because search engines love links that clearly define the destination (and the title does a better job in this respect than a Read more link).

News

Bob Ross Exhibition Announced

Mauris id tellus ac diam mollis condimentum. diam vitae velit aliquam vulputate. Vestibulum commodo lectus, auctor rutrum massa biben

Read more... >>

	The article title is clickable—that's good!
Show Intro Text	After the visitor has clicked on a Read more link, do you want them to see a page with just the rest of the article text (select No) or the full article including the intro text (select Yes)?
Section Title, Category Title	Select **Show** if you want to show the section name and / or category name below the title.

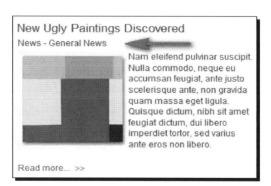

New Ugly Paintings Discovered

News - General News

Nam eleifend pulvinar suscipit. Nulla commodo, neque eu accumsan feugiat, ante justo scelerisque ante, non gravida quam massa eget ligula. Quisque dictum, nibh sit amet feugiat dictum, dui libero imperdiet tortor, sed varius ante eros non libero.

Read more... >>

In the above example, both category and section title are displayed. Showing the Section title on a section overview page doesn't make much sense, as the page title or menu link will already make it clear to the visitor that it is a section overview.

Section Title linkable, Category Title Linkable	If the Section Title or Category Title is shown, should it be a hyperlink to the Section or Category?
Author Name, Created Date and Time, Modified Date and Time	Do you want to show author name, creation date, and/or the date the article was last updated? By default, these options set to **Show**. You may want to choose **Hide** if you've got a small site or a site that isn't regularly updated. In that case you probably don't want to broadcast when your articles were written or who wrote them.
Show Navigation	Do you want to show navigation links between articles?
Read more... Link	Do you want a **Read More** link to appear below an article intro text? You'll probably want to leave this set to **Yes**, but if the title of the article is a hyperlink a **Read More** link can be omitted. Although Joomla! displays the Read More by default, many web builders just make the article title clickable; the following is an example of `http://www.timesonline.co.uk`.

UK BUSINESS NEWS

King cranks up pressure on high street banks

Bank of England Governor says he is considering cutting interest paid on cash that banks have in reserve accounts

RBS pays £10m to attract two top bankers

The packages are two of the most lucrative offered by RBS to attract talent to rebuild business after it almost collapsed

Article Rating/Voting	Should readers be able to rate articles (assign one to five stars to an article)?
Icons	Joomla! can show special function icons. These allow the visitor to create a PDF file from the article, to print it, or to e-mail it. Do you want to display these options as icons or text links?
PDF Icon, Print Icon, Icon E-mail	Show or hide the special function icons? It's often better to altogether hide these extras. Your visitors might want to use the print function, but any modern browser offers a print function with better page formatting options.
Hits	Should the number of hits per article be displayed?
For each feed item show intro text / full text	This option is only needed if you use RSS feeds (see Chapter 12).

Parameters (System)

The **Parameters (System)** are a mixed bunch of settings—the system part is not really clear.

Page Title	Here you can determine which page title appears at the top of the Front Page (that is, the main body). By default, it's **Welcome to the Front Page**. If you google that phrase, you may notice that many thousands of Joomla! Site Administrators have forgotten to change the default title. You can type a custom title here, but remember that a home page doesn't necessarily need a page title (as it often isn't an ordinary page, but an overview of very different types of content).
Show Page Title	If you don't want a **Page Title** on the Front Page, set it to **Hide** here.
Page Class Suffix	This is only important if you want to get more control over the page design: font size, colors, and so on. With the **Page Class Suffix**, you add a suffix to the name of all CSS styles used on this page. To use this, you have to know your way around in CSS. You can read more about CSS in Chapter 11 on using templates.
Menu Image	Should an image be shown in the Main Menu link next to the Home link? Menu images are often used on special function menus; the icons make the menu more attractive and easier to scan. An example of a menu using icons (www.ford.co.uk) is as follows: 
SSL Enabled	Only important if you are using **Secure Sockets Layer** (**SSL**), a protocol for secure web pages.

The alternative way: Creating a single article home page

So far you've used Joomla!'s Front Page Layout for your site's home page. But what if you want something completely different on your site's home page? No problem since Joomla! allows you to set any menu item as the default page.

Time for action – creating a different home page

Let's *not* use the Front Page settings. We'll get the home page to show just a single, full article:

1. Navigate to **Menus | Main Menu**. As you can see, there's a star in the **Default** column next to the **Home** link. This indicates that the visitor will see this page in the mainbody when accessing your site.

2. To change the **Default** page, select the checkbox next to another Menu Item. In this case, select the **Mission Statement** menu item and click on the **Default** button in the toolbar. It's the button with the big yellow star.

3. Click on **Preview**. The results are shown in the following screenshot; an ordinary article has become the **Default** page:

If you want to update the **Main Menu** to reflect these changes, you can hide the old **Home** link (click on the **Unpublish** icon next to the **Home** link) and rename the existing **Mission Statement** link to **Home**.

What just happened?

You've changed the default view of the home page to a clean look, showing just one article. Of course, you can dress up such a "static" home page any way you like. For some sites (a simple "brochure site" presenting a small company or a project) this may be a good solution.

The consequence of this approach is that the Front Page settings (that you find in the **Article Manager** and in the article edit screen) have become redundant. These settings no longer determine what's published on the home page.

Have a go hero – undo!

For our example site, a single article home page doesn't fit the bill. However, you can easily revert to the home page you created earlier. In the **Main Menu**, set the **Home** link to be the **Default** item again and click on the red cross in the **Published** column next to unhide the **Home** link in the menu. Everything is back to normal now.

Creating section and category overview pages

In the previous chapter, you've seen how you organize content with sections and categories. You create sections and categories in the backend; this way, you tell Joomla! how to group things. However, you will also want to present section and category contents on the frontend of the website in one way or another. That's where Joomla!'s section and category pages come in. They provide an intermediate level between the home page and content pages, presenting hyperlinks to section or category contents. They're a bit like 'second level home pages. Joomla! has no name for these pages; we'll call them overview pages or just section or category pages.

You've already seen some basic examples of Joomla!'s overview page when you created menu links of the **Section Blog Layout** type to display sections (see *Displaying sections and categories on your website* in Chapter 5). Now, we'll go beyond the basics and make section and category pages that exactly fit your (client's) needs.

Blog Layout or List Layout?

Of course, being a somewhat advanced Joomler you already know that you create section and category overview pages through specific menu link settings. Creating a link to a section or category takes just the following steps:

1. Navigate to **Menus | Main Menu** and click on **New**.

2. In the **Select Menu Item Type** section, click on **Articles**. To display categories or sections, you have four further options:

   ❑ Category Blog Layout

   ❑ Category List Layout

   ❑ Section Blog Layout

   ❑ Section Layout *(this should be called Section List Layout)*

3. Select the appropriate Layout, select the category or section the menu link should point to, and add a link—that's all there is to it.

There's a small catch to Step 3. How do you choose between a Blog Layout and a List Layout? How do you create the type of overview page that fits the content of a specific section or category? That's what we'll find out now. Let's first have a look at the Blog Layout; it's more common and more powerful than the List Layout.

The first type of overview page: Creating Blog Layouts

The Blog Layout isn't just one layout. Its wide range of settings offers you very different ways of presenting your content. Time to start experimenting!

Time for action – create a facebook using the Blog Layout

Let's use the Blog Layout to create a small facebook, a few pages presenting the SRUP team:

1. For this purpose, create a few more content pages, each for every one of the SRUP founders. Navigate to **Content | Article Manager** and click on **New**. Create three articles in the **Who are SRUP?** category in the **About SRUP** section. In this example, we've used these titles: **Ms. Daiping Suraba, Dr. T. Phaedratski**, and **Dr. A. Fienstein**. Create articles with an intro text, a **Read more ...** link, and a main article text (you've seen this before in Chapter 4).

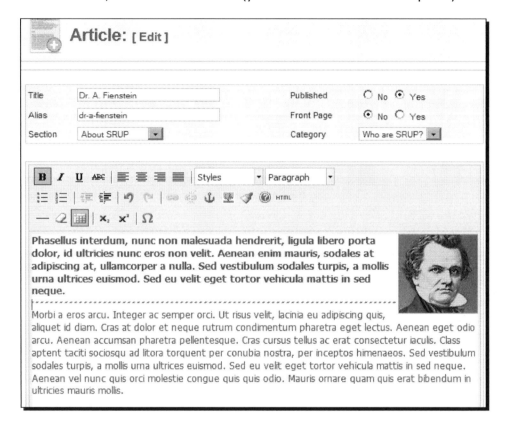

2. Create a new menu link to the category page. Navigate to **Menus | Main Menu** and click on **New**. In the **Select Menu Item Type** list, choose **Article | Category Blog Layout**.

3. In the next screen, give the new link a **Title** (**Who are SRUP?**). In the **Parameters (Basic)** section, select the appropriate category: **About SRUP/Who are SRUP?**.

4. Click on **Apply** and click on **Preview**. So far so good! There's a new link, showing a new category page:

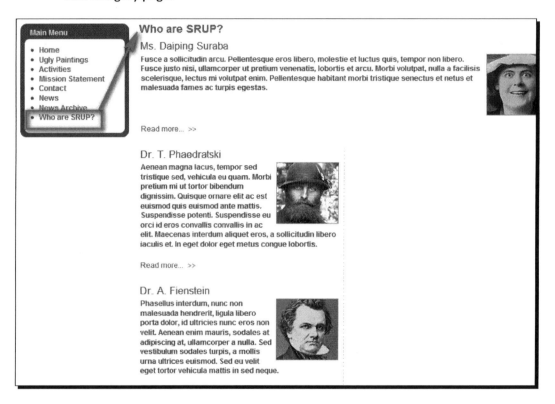

5. As you can see, the default layout is unbalanced. There's a big gap to the right-hand side of the second and third intro text. That's because we have to tell Joomla! how to spread items on the page. In **Parameters (Advanced)**, set **Multi Column Order** to **Across**.

6. Click on **Apply** and then on **Preview**. The outcome is much better:

7. The page looks OK, but there's room for improvement. Why should the first founding member have a wide column and the others a narrow one? Let's divide them evenly over the page. Change the **Parameters (Basic)** of the **Who are SRUP?** menu link as follows:

- ❑ **# Leading: 0**
- ❑ **# Intro: 3**
- ❑ **Columns: 3**
- ❑ **# Links: 0**

8. Click on **Apply** and click on **Preview**. The following is the new outcome:

9. Looks alright, but the three column layout doesn't fit with the overall site design. Let's try one last alternative. Set **# Leading** to **3**, **# Intro** to **0**, **Columns** to **0**, and **# Links** to **0**. Click on **Apply** and click on **Preview**. Voila! A simple and clean one column layout:

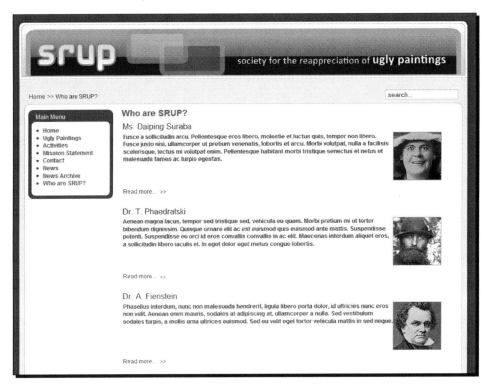

Let's keep it this way. The page looks much more balanced now.

What just happened?

You've seen some different ways in which category pages can show article content. You've added a facebook to the **Who are SRUP?** category by displaying the intro text of these articles in a category overview page; visitors can click on it to read the full article.

Have a go hero – add a category description

Category content doesn't always speak for itself so you might want to give your visitors a short introduction to a category page. Remember the Category Description in Chapter 5? It allows you to show a few descriptive lines at the top of any category page. Why not add one to the **Who are SRUP?** category page?

1. Navigate to **Menus | Main Menu** and open the **Who are SRUP?** menu link for editing. In the **Menu Item Edit** screen, navigate to the **Parameters (Basic)** section and make sure **Description** is set to **Show**.

2. There's no category description to display, so let's add a few lines. Navigate to **Content | Category Manager** and click on the **Who are SRUP?** category title to edit the category properties. In the **Description** field, add some intro text:

3. Click on **Save** and click on **Preview**. A short category description is displayed:

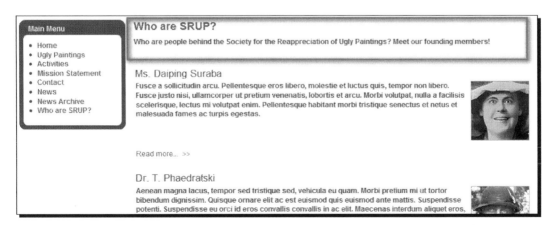

The more menu items you create, the longer and messier the main menu gets. You'll probably want to change the order of menu links—or create submenus to better arrange the long list of menu links. Don't worry, we'll get to building and customizing menus in Chapter 8.

Showing full articles on a category overview page

So far, you've seen how you can show *intro texts* and *links* to articles on a category page. However, you can also use category pages to show a list of *full* articles. In fact, this is probably why this layout is called a Blog Layout. A typical page on a weblog site consists of a number of short articles ordered by subject or by date. Here's an example of a category page showing three full article texts:

To achieve this in Joomla!, you use a category page like the one you created just before. To show full articles instead of intro texts, change the article texts themselves. Navigate to **Content | Article Manager** and select the article you need to edit. In the editor screen, delete the red dotted line indicating the separation between intro text (with a **Read more ...** link) and the rest of the text. This will tell Joomla! not to split the article in two parts, and thus, on any overview page it will show the full thing instead of just its intro text.

Have a go hero – experiment with Blog Layout settings

Just like the Front Page Blog Layout, the Section and Category Blog Layout offers a litany of settings that allow you to adjust the target page. You can set them trough **Menus | Main Menu | [name of link to section or category page]**.

The Component and System Parameters are for the most part the same as the ones you've seen when setting the Front Page Blog Layout preferences. See the section *Have a go hero – Try out the Front Page settings* earlier in this chapter for a full listing.

Just the two first Parameters are specific for Section or Category Blog Layouts. Under **Parameters - Basic** you select the **Section** or **Category** you want to show, and you have the option to add show a section or category **Description** and a **Description Image** at the top of the section or category overview page.

The second type of overview page: Lists

Compared to the Blog Layout, the List Layout provides a simpler view of section or category contents. Instead of a series of intros and links, the visitor is shown only a number of links to categories and/or articles. The following is an example of a Section List page in the default Joomla! installation, a listing of four categories in the FAQs section:

FAQs

- General (3 Articles)
  General questions about the Joomla! CMS
- Current Users (6 Articles)
  Questions that users migrating to Joomla! 1.5 are likely to raise
- New to Joomla! (3 Articles)
  Questions for new users of Joomla!
- Languages (5 Articles)
  Questions related to localisation and languages

Creating Section Lists

If you've already created links pointing to Blog Layouts, creating a link to List Layout will seem very familiar. Navigate to **Menus | Main Menu**, click on **New** and select the appropriate Menu Item Type: **Category List Layout** or **Section (List) Layout**. Provide the necessary details (select the target category or section and type a link title) and you're done.

Time for action – change a Blog Layout to a List Layout

To see the capabilities of the List Layout, let's convert a Blog Layout link you created previously to a List Layout, both targeting the Activities section.

1. Navigate to **Menus | Main Menu**. Click on **Activities** to edit the menu item.

2. In the **Menu Item [Edit]** screen, click on the **Change Type** button:

3. In the **Change Menu Item** screen, select **Internal Link | Section | Section Layout**. A Section List shows no article contents; it just presents a list of categories as hyperlinks.

4. Click on **Save**. Done! Click on **Preview** to view the home page of your site; click on the **Activities** link.

What just happened?

With just a few clicks you have created a section page that displays a list of hyperlinks to categories instead of a series of teaser texts. Clicking on a category title reveals another intermediate page, a list of article titles.

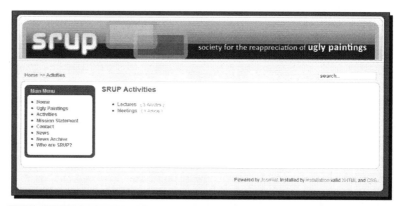

In this example, the **Activities** menu link shows a Section List of two categories.

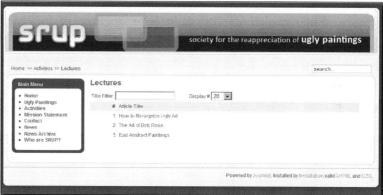

When the visitor clicks on the **Lectures** link, the Lectures category contents are shown as a list of articles. The visitor can even use the Filter field (a search box) to find the desired article.

The List Layout is useful for sections or categories that are crammed with articles. It provides a quick overview, allowing visitors to scan or search for article titles. You might consider using List Layouts on a site with many articles on related subjects, such as elaborate FAQ sections or large numbers of articles in a section with product reviews. Lists enable visitors to find information they search for fast. It's not really suited to attract casual surfers to explore the site's content. For that purpose you can use the Blog Layout.

Have a go hero – undo!

In a site with much content, the List Layout can help your visitors search category and article titles. However, in this case, this layout doesn't really do the trick. It doesn't look very inviting—your site visitors are not likely to click through on an empty page with just a few links to another page with again just a few links. Luckily, you can easily revert your actions. Just navigate back to the Main Menu, click on **Activities** again and change the **Menu Item Type** back to **Section Blog Layout**. In Joomla!, choosing and changing the layout of content overview pages is very easy; it's always possible to reconsider or adapt the layout to the changing contents of your site.

Customizing lists: Exploring Section List Layout parameters

List Layout pages have less parameters than Blog Layouts. To change the settings, navigate to **Main Menu | [name of menu link to the section]**.

Parameters (Basic)

Under **Parameters (Basic)** you can set how you want the items to be arranged on the section page.

Section	Select the section you want to show.
Description, Description Image	Do you want to show a section description and an image at the top of the section overview page? The following example shows an introductory text on the Activities section:

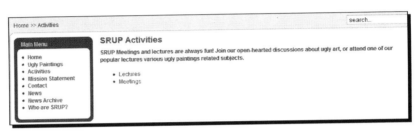

	To add the **Description** (or its image) itself, navigate to **Content | Section** and edit the appropriate section.
Section	Select the section you want to show.
Category List - Section	Select **Show** to display the Categories in the section list.
Empty Categories in Section	Choose **Hide** if you don't want to display empty categories (which are dead-end roads for your visitor).
# Category Items	Select **Show** to display the number of category items (articles).
Category Description	Select **Show** to display a description below each category title. To add a Category Description, navigate to **Content | Category Manager | [category name]**.

The power of Descriptions

In the **Parameters (Basic)**, you can set **Description**, **Description Image**, and **Category Description** to show. This makes a big difference; after all, in its simplest form a List Layout page is pretty bare. By adding descriptions you can make the page a little more interesting and explain what the section and categories are all about. You add descriptions by editing the properties of a section or category itself (through **Content | Section Manager** or **Content | Category Manager**; see Chapter 5 on sections and categories). The following screenshot shows a Section List Layout with a Description of both the section and of the two categories in it. As you can see, a description can also contain pictures.

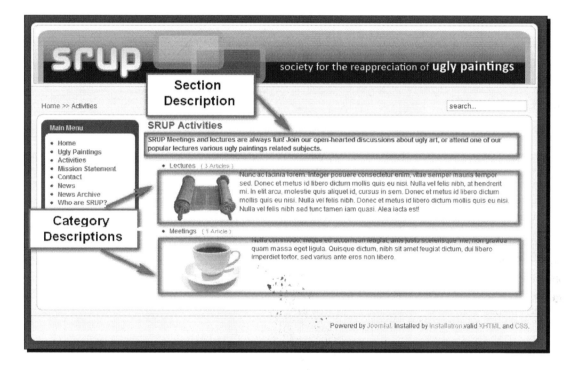

Parameters (Advanced)

The advanced parameters give you some more control over the order of categories on a section list page.

Order	In what order should the categories be displayed? You can order them alphabetically by title, reversed alphabetically, or in the default order that the categories have in the **Category Manager**.
Article Order	The order of the list of articles your visitors see when they click on one of the category names. This means the Article Order doesn't have an effect on the section list page itself (which contains no articles), but on the next page.
Show a Feed Link	Only important if you use news feeds on the site.

Parameters (Component)

These settings apply to the articles your visitor arrives at through this overview page. The options are exactly the same you as the ones you can set in the general preferences for articles (**Article Manager | Parameters**, see *Tweaking the details: Changing article settings* in Chapter 6). Here you can depart from the general settings for the articles and make different choices for this particular section or category.

Parameters (System)

The **Parameters (System)** mainly give you some more control over the display of list pages.

Page Title	The page title that appears above the page content. You can use this to add an appropriate title for your section/category page. If you don't fill this in, Joomla! displays the name of the menu link that points to this page as the page title.
Show Page Title	Set this to Hide if you don't want the section list page to have a Page Title.
Page Class Suffix	This is only important if you want to get more control over the page design (such as font size and colors). Using the Page Class Suffix, you add a suffix to the name of all CSS styles used on this page. You can read more about CSS in Chapter 11 on templates.
Menu Image	Should an image be shown in the **Main Menu** link next to the **Home** link? You can use menu images to make the menu more attractive and easier to read. You can, for example, have a 'house' icon next to the **Home** link.
SSL Enabled	Only important if you are using Secure Sockets Layer (SSL), a protocol for secure Web pages.

Using Category Lists

The Category List Layout is very similar to the Section List Layout. It's a simple list, too, in this case as it features the titles of all the articles in a category. A Filter box (search box) makes it easier to find content should the list of titles be very long.

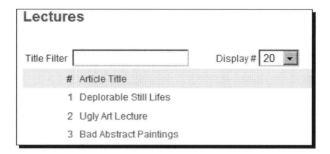

The Category List parameters give you some control over the list presentation.

Parameters (Basic)

The **Parameters (Basic)** allow you to set, in some detail, what you want to be displayed on the category page.

Category	Choose the category you want to show.
# Links	From the drop-down box, select the number of links to articles you want to display in the list.
Table Headings	Select **Hide** to hide the column headers (Article Title, Author, and so on) above the table.
Date Column	Do you want to show or hide the Date Column (with publication dates)?

#	Article Title	Date
1	How to Recognize Ugly Art	Sunday, 05 July 2009
2	The Art of Bob Ross	Thursday, 25 June 2009
3	Bad Abstract Paintings	Wednesday, 24 June 2009

Date format	By default, Joomla! displays the date as in the following example: Wednesday, 19 August 2010. If you want to format the date differently, enter a date format code here. For example, entering the code **%Y-%m-%d** will change the article date format to 2010-09-19. To find out which codes are allowed, check `http://php.net/manual/en/function.strftime.php`.

Filter	In a long list of categories (more than a few dozen) it's useful to set **Filter** to **Show**. The filter gives the visitor the possibility to search the list by entering a keyword in the Filter box.
Filter Field	By default, the Filter box allows visitors to search by title. If you wish, you can specify that the search filter works by author name or number of hits.

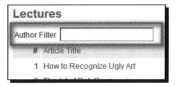

Parameters (Advanced)

The **Parameters (Advanced)** give you some control over the order of list items and the appearance of the list page.

Primary Order	Select the order in which the articles are displayed: by date, alphabetically, and so on. By default, the items are in the same order that they have in the Article Manager.
Pagination	Select **Show** to show Previous and Next navigation links if the section consists of a very long category list that doesn't fit one page.
Display Select	Select **Show** to display a select box allowing the visitor to choose how many items they want to see on the page. This option turned on by default, but it's only useful if the list contains at least a few dozen hyperlinks.

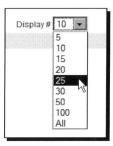

Show a Feed Link	Important only if you use news feeds on the site.

The **Parameters (Component)** and the **Parameters (System)** of the Section List Layout are identical to those of the Category List Layout. To see the Section List options, have a look at the previous section on Category Lists.

Pop quiz – test your knowledge of home pages and overview pages

1. How can you change the arrangement of items on your home page?

    a. By adding new content in the Front Page Manager.

    b. By changing the Main Menu Home link settings.

    c. By selecting 'Display on Front Page' in the Article editor.

2. How do you create an overview page?

    a. By adding a new article in the Article Manager.

    b. By adding a new section or category.

    c. By adding a new menu link to point to a section or category.

3. In what cases would you choose to present content in a Blog Layout?

    a. Blog Layout is used strictly for web logs.

    b. You use Blog Layout to show a row of article titles.

    c. You use Blog Layout to show teaser texts or full articles.

Summary

In this chapter, you've learned all about two types of pages that Joomla! uses to draw the visitor towards the actual content of your site: home pages and overview pages.

◆ When you want to set the layout and arrangement of the Front Page contents, you change the settings of the Main Menu Home link. These allow you to determine how many introductory article texts the home page shows, and how they are laid out.

◆ When you want a completely different home page, you can choose *not* to use the Front Page settings. You can set any Main Menu item to be the default home page contents.

◆ To show your visitor the contents of a section or category, you'll create menu links to section and category overview pages. These provide an intermediate level between the home page and content pages; they're like "second level home pages".

◆ There are two main formats for overview pages, Blog Layout and List Layout.

◆ The Blog Layout is more versatile and is focused on *content*. It provides a taste of the article content. Its purpose is to lure casual surfers.

◆ The List Layout is focused on organization. It shows how sections or categories are structured. It helps visitors quickly scan or search for article titles on sites with lots of related content (such as elaborate FAQ sections, or large numbers of articles in a section with product reviews). This layout enables visitors to find information quickly in long lists of items.

In the previous chapter, you've created content; in this chapter, you've focused on presenting that content (through the home page and overview pages). In the next chapter, you'll master another critical aspect of web design: creating great navigation. You'll learn how to design menus that guide your visitors and help them to easily find what they're looking for.

8

Helping Your Visitors Find What They Want: Managing Menus

Menus and content in Joomla! are closely intertwined. In the previous chapters, you have seen that menu links don't just point to existing pages, as you might expect if you have experience building websites the old fashioned way. When adding a menu link, you don't just tell Joomla! what page the menu link should point to, but you rather instruct it to make that page. When adding content to your site in previous chapters, you've seen how this works. By creating menu links, you created different types of pages.

However, to your visitor, Joomla! menus are no different from other website menus. To your visitor, menus should provide an easy means of navigation. In this chapter, we'll concentrate on menus as a means to navigate. We'll focus on how you can make and tweak menus to design clear and intuitive navigation, and also on how you can help the visitors find what they want without difficulty.

Up to now, you've added menu links using mainly the default settings. Let's find out how we can enhance menus and improve the navigability of the site.

This is what you'll learn:

- ◆ Adding a new menu
- ◆ Creating submenus
- ◆ Adjusting menu module settings
- ◆ Creating hyperlinks in article texts

How many menus can you have?

On any Joomla! website you can create as many menus as you want. The default sample site that you installed in Chapter 2 is a good example as it contains no fewer than six menus. On the home page four of those are shown: the horizontal **Top Menu**, the **Main Menu**, the **Resources Menu**, and the **Key Concepts Menu**. In the backend, all of the menus are listed in the Menu Manager (**Menus | Menu Manager**).

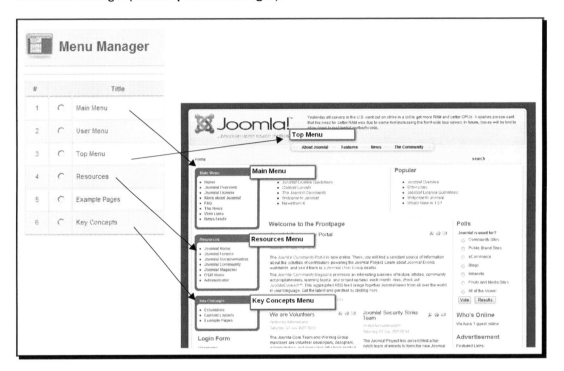

At least one menu, the **Main Menu**, is needed for Joomla! to function properly. The other ones, such as the **Top Menu** (the top horizontal menu) and the **User Menu** (a menu that's only visible after users have logged in), are only there to showcase Joomla!'s menu possibilities. In real life you'll probably just confuse your visitors with that amount of navigation options popping up on different pages and places.

However, it's great to be able to create as many menus as you like. This allows you to set up different menus for different functions and different users. You can have a main menu (at the top of the page) containing primary links, and another menu (somewhere down the page) containing secondary links. You might also want to have a special menu with action links (such as Login, and Register) and another menu that's only shown to visitors who have logged in.

Menus are modules (and why that's important)

You've already seen some examples of *modules* in action, such as the Poll module. Remember, modules are Joomla!'s magic building blocks that can contain all kinds of functionality. Menus are modules too. In fact, every new menu you add is a new instance of the *mod_mainmenu* module. This makes menus very flexible. Not only can you have as many menus (menu modules) on your site as you like, but you can also tell Joomla! exactly where (on what part of the screen, in which *module position*) and when (on which specific pages, for which specific users) you want these menus to show up.

Sounds confusing? Don't worry, we'll practice adding and customizing menus in this chapter—and once you get the hang of it, you'll really appreciate Joomla!'s amazing menu flexibility.

Creating user-friendly navigation: Cleaning up the Main Menu

When building a site, you'll start by adding links to the Main Menu. It's the mandatory menu that is always part of the Joomla! installation, even if you don't install sample data. But as your site evolves, it can become a long and cluttered list of hyperlinks. Even the menu of our SRUP example site already contains eight links. When you find the Main Menu gets long and messy, what options do you have to improve site navigation?

Option 1: Change the order of menu items

By default, a new menu item is added to the end of the existing menu. If you were to add a new link called **New Menu Item**, it would show up at the bottom:

In our example site we've haven't paid much attention to menu item order. However, the order in which you add items isn't necessarily the order in which you want them to be displayed to your visitor.

Time for action – change menu item order

On the SRUP example site main menu there are eight menu items (as you've just seen in the previous screenshot). Let's move things around to present the links in a more logical order. The items that we want to get most attention should be in the top half of the menu; links to less important or static content should be placed down below.

1. Navigate to **Menus | Main Menu**.

2. In the **Order** column, enter numbers to reflect the desired order of menu items.

3. Click on the little disc icon on the top row of the **Order** column to apply the new order.

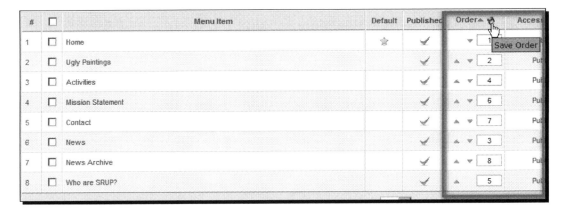

What just happened?

The menu items now show up in the order that you've chosen. **News** and **Who are SRUP?** have been moved up from their humble position. On the frontend you can see that the order of items has changed:

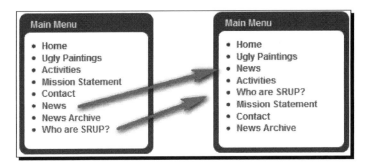

A quick way to change the position of multiple menu items is to enter the desired order by numbers, as you've just seen. If you only want to move one or two menu items up or down you can also click on the green up and down arrows in the **Order** column.

Option 2: Add a separate new menu

Rearranging menu items is a first step—but there are definitely more powerful ways to improve a menu. You can also clean up a menu by removing links that don't really fit in, and create a separate menu for these links that you can show somewhere else on the page. This way, you can either emphasize those links in the visual hierarchy of the web page—or you can choose to make them less prominent.

Let's have a look at the SRUP Main Menu items. Imagine your client has asked you to reorganize the navigation to enable visitors to quickly find the information on ugly paintings that this site is about. As the current **Main Menu** is rather long, it's difficult for the visitor to distinguish between links on actual *ugly painting contents* and links on the *organization behind the site*. A good solution would be to create a separate menu on SRUP-related contents.

Time for action – step 1: Create a new, empty menu

In the **Main Menu** of the example site, three items are suited to be shown in another menu. These links are of interest to visitors who want to know more are about the SRUP organization. Let's create a new menu "About SRUP" so that we can move the menu links **Who are SRUP?**, **Mission Statement,** and **Contact** there.

1. Navigate to **Menus | Menu Manager**. Click on **New**.

2. In the **Menu : [New]** screen add a **Unique name**. This is the name that Joomla! uses to identify the menu; it won't be visible on the frontend. Enter a name without spaces or special characters. In the following example, we have entered **aboutsrup**:

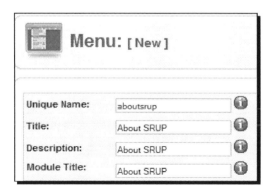

3. Enter the **Title**; this is the name that may be displayed with the menu. Enter a **Description** and a **Module Title** too. The Module Title will show up in the **Module Manager**.

4. Click on **Save**. You'll be taken to the **Menu Manager**. At the bottom of the list you can see a new entry. The menu **About SRUP** has been created:

What just happened?

In the **Menu Manager** you've created new menu. It's visible in the Joomla! backend—but of course it's still empty.

Time for action – step 2: Move hyperlinks to the new menu

One way to fill a new menu is by creating brand new links (**Menus | About SRUP | New**). In this case, however, we'll *move* three existing links from the Main Menu to our new menu:

1. In the **Menu Manager**, locate the **Main Menu**. Click on the icon in the **Menu Item(s)** column next to it to edit it.

2. Select the menu items you want to move to the new menu. In this example, we've selected **Who are SRUP?**, **Mission Statement**, and **Contact**.

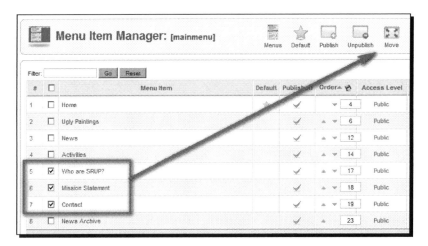

3. Click on the **Move** button in the toolbar.

4. In the next screen, select the destination menu. In the **Move to Menu:** list, select **aboutsrup** and click on the **Move** button to confirm.

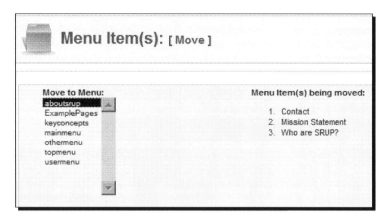

5. The **Menu Item Manager** screen now displays three new items in the **About SRUP** menu:

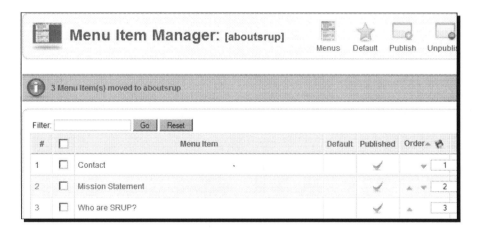

6. Let's put critical content links in the highest position. In the **Menu Item Manager**, click on the arrows in the **Order** column to rearrange the items in this order:

- ❏ Who are SRUP?
- ❏ Mission Statement
- ❏ Contact

What just happened?

Everything is set up fine now; the new **About SRUP** menu contains the desired hyperlinks in the desired order. There's just one thing left to do now—make it visible on your website.

Time for action – step 3: Tell Joomla! where to display the menu

To actually get the menu to show on the site, you edit the settings of the appropriate menu module. The module is the "functionality block" that contains your menu. Let's tell Joomla! where you want it to show:

1. Navigate to **Extensions | Module Manager** and locate the new module, **About SRUP**. Click on the **Module Name** to edit the module:

2. In the **Module: [Edit]** screen, select **Enabled: Yes**. This sets the menu to show. Leave **Position:** set to **left** for now. This will make the new menu appear in the same column as the **Main Menu**.

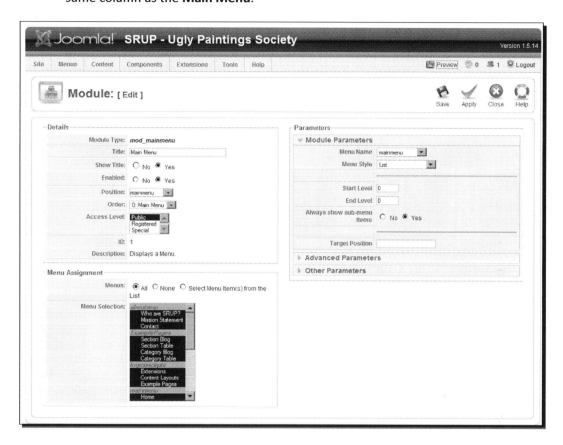

3. Click on **Apply** and click on **Preview**. There you are! A separate menu appears. The new **About SRUP** menu is displayed at the top position in the left-hand side column:

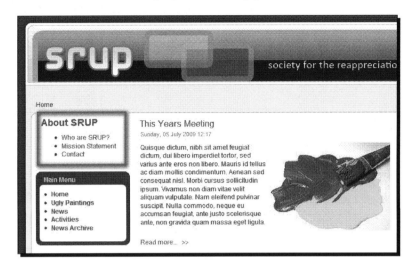

You're almost there! We've got our new menu showing up in the left column, but we obviously want it to appear *below* the **Main Menu** to establish a better visual hierarchy. This takes just one extra step. If you've clicked out of the module editing screen, navigate back to **Extensions | Module Manager** and select the **About SRUP** module to edit the menu again.

4. In the **Details** section, there are two settings that control where the menu will turn up on the frontend. Again, we'll leave **Position** set to **left** (to keep the menu in the left-hand side column). In the **Order** drop-down box, the current value is **0: About SRUP**. The number indicates that the menu is now the top item in the **left** position. To change this value, select **2: Main Menu**. This will position the new menu below the **Main Menu**.

5. Click on **Apply** and then on **Preview** to check that the secondary menu is now published in the right place:

What just happened?

In this example, we've chosen to take three links out of the main menu and show them in a separate menu. We've succeeded in cleaning up the previously overcrowded **Main Menu**; it now shows just five main links. All links that point to content about the SRUP organization have been moved to a separate menu.

More on menu module settings

Up to now, you've use the menu module settings screen (the **Module : [Edit]** screen) only to adjust the position of the menu on the web page. However, there are dozens of other menu module settings that you can tweak to your liking. See the *Exploring menu module settings* section later in this chapter for a full overview.

Tweaking the menu styling

You'll have noticed the second menu (the **About SRUP** menu) has a different style from the **Main Menu**. If you want both menus to share the same styling, navigate to **Extensions | Module Manager | About SRUP**. Navigate to the **Advanced Parameters** and look up the **Module Class Suffix** box. By default, it's empty. Enter **_menu** as **Module Class Suffix**. Click on **Apply** and then on **Preview**. The two menus now share the same styling. In the default Joomla! template, modules with the suffix **_menu** will display the specific formatting that's reserved for menus:

The rhuk_milkyway template is set up this way. Its stylesheet contains specific menu styles, ending in the suffix _menu (such as module_menu instead of just module). By adding the _menu Module Class Suffix to this module we make use of these specific styles—and our menu will be formatted accordingly.

Don't worry if you don't like the default formatting of the Joomla! Main Menu and submenu. Many templates allow for attractively styled menus. If you have some CSS coding skills you can edit the menu styles yourself. You'll see examples of styling with CSS in Chapter 11 using templates.

Time for action – tweak the menu position and orientation

Placing a second menu in the left-hand side column makes it very prominent. You might notice that site visitors find this second menu distracting. And after all, the static links to information about SRUP aren't really that important. Why not move the menu somewhere down the page? We'll publish the SRUP links as a horizontal menu at the very bottom.

By default, at the bottom of the screen there's a copyright notice. We'll start by removing this to make room for the new menu.

Removing the copyright notice involves deleting a few lines of code from the template HTML. If you want to move the menu to any other screen position you can skip the first three steps:

1. Navigate to **Extensions | Template** Manager. Select the **rhuk_milkyway** template and click on **Edit HTML**.

2. In the HTML editor screen, find and select the following code:

```
<p id="power_by"> <?php echo JText::_('Powered by') ?>
<a href="http://www.joomla.org">Joomla!</a>.<?php echo
JText::_('Valid') ?> <a href="http://validator.w3.org/check/
referer">XHTML</a> <?php echo JText::_('and') ?> <a href="http://
jigsaw.w3.org/css-validator/check/referer">CSS</a>.</p>
```

3. Press the *Delete* key to remove the selected code and click on **Save**. You can preview the frontend to check if the copyright notice has effectively disappeared.

To have the About SRUP menu occupy the free position, we'll edit the menu module properties:

4. Navigate to **Extensions | Module Manager** and click on the **About SRUP** menu module.

5. In the **Position** drop-down box, select s**yndicate**. This is the bottom most position in this template.

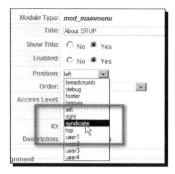

6. In the **Parameters** section, click on **Module Parameters** and set the **Menu Style** to **Legacy – Horizontal**. This will make Joomla! display the links horizontally side by side in a table row.

7. Click on **Other Parameters**. In the **Spacer** text box, enter a character to display in between the horizontal links. In this example, we'll enter two dashes. The effect is that the menu links will be displayed as follows:

   Who are SRUP? -- Mission Statement -- Contact

8. Click on **Apply** and click on **Preview**. The menu has been moved to the bottom of the page:

What just happened?

We've just removed the copyright notice that by default appears at the bottom of the template. This creates room for a separate "About SRUP" menu. To get this menu to display at the bottom position we've changed its module position and the menu style (the links orientation) from the default values. The result is that the menu is now displayed as row of links at the bottom of the page. This makes them much less prominent. Only visitors looking for these links will really notice them.

This kind of presentation is a good choice for links that don't fit the main navigation menus. In this example, we've moved links on the organization behind the site to the bottom menu. In real life, it's common to publish static links there (such as About This Site, Disclaimer, and Sitemap).

Menu Manager or Module Manager?

To customize a menu, you'll sometimes use the Menu Manager, and sometimes use the Module Manager. What's the difference? The Menu Manager is used for everything that has to do with the *contents* of the menu. Anything to do with the *display* of the menu module you control through the module settings.

Option 3: Creating submenu items

There's still room for improvement in our **Main Menu**. Although there are now only five links left, the way they're organized might still confuse visitors. Having a **News** link and a separate **News Archive** link, both on the same menu level, is odd. Visitors will expect a *News* link in a main site menu, but *News Archive* shouldn't really be a top-level link. Joomla! allows you to add a secondary level to a menu so let's change *News Archive* into a secondary link that will only display after the News link has been clicked.

Time for action – create a secondary menu item

Let's remove the **News Archive** link from the primary level in the **Main Menu** and show it as a sublevel link:

1. To edit the **Main Menu** contents, navigate to **Menus | Main Menu**.

2. Click on the title of the item you want to edit, **News Archive**.

3. In the **Menu Item Details** section, the parent item is set to top. Change the parent item to **News**:

4. Click on **Save**. In the list of menu items in the **Menu Item Manager**, the new sublevel menu item is shown indented:

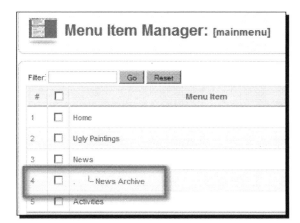

5. Click on **Preview** to see the output on the frontend. The **Main Menu** now shows four primary links. When the visitor clicks on **News**, a secondary link **News Archive** is displayed:

What just happened?

By assigning a parent item to a menu link you can create a submenu item. Of course, submenus aren't the only way to make secondary content visible. In Chapter 7, you've seen that main links can point to overview pages with links to content from sections or categories. Those "secondary home pages" can make secondary menu links superfluous.

However, sometimes it's better to add sublevels in the menu itself. If you have items outside of the section or category structure (such as uncategorized pages), submenus can clarify the coherence of the site. You can have main ("parent") links and secondary ("child") links.

Creating split submenus

When you want to use submenus on your site, you can also choose an altogether different presentation from what you've just seen. You're not limited to having submenu items shown *within* the main menu, as it's also possible to place main navigation links horizontally along the top of the page and display second level links in a *separate* menu (for example, in a vertical menu in the left-hand side column). This creates a clear visual distinction between the main menu items and their submenu items. At the same time the visitor can see that those two menus are related. The parent item can be displayed as "active" (using a different style or color) when the related submenu is displayed.

An example is shown in the following screenshot. The primary link, **Activities,** is shown in a (horizontal) main menu bar. When this link is clicked a separate submenu shows secondary links (submenu links) to two category overview pages (**Meetings** and **Lectures**):

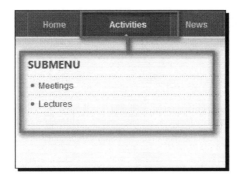

How do you build this kind of menu system in Joomla!? In short, you create a copy of the main menu, set the original main menu to show only the top-level links, and set the copy to show only the second-level links. Joomla! will automatically display the appropriate submenu when the parent item is chosen in the top menu.

We won't add a split menu system to our example site as it doesn't have the amount of content that would justify an elaborate multi-level navigation. However, feel free to experiment on your own website, as this is a very powerful technique. The following are the required steps in more detail:

1. Suppose you have created a Main Menu with two or more links to sublevel items. Navigate to **Extensions | Module Manager**. Select the **Main Menu** module and click on **Copy**.

2. The same list now contains an item called **Copy of Main Menu**. Open that copy and enter another title (for example, **Submenu**). Select **Position: left**.

3. In the **Module Parameters**, set the **Start Level** to **1** and the **End Level** to **1**. This will make the menu display only second-level menu items.

4. Now edit the **Main Menu** module to show only the top-level items. Set **Start Level** to **0** and **End Level** to **0**.

The menu is done! The submenus now only display when the corresponding main-level link is clicked.

Have a go hero – arrange menus any way you like

Joomla!'s split menu capabilities allow you to design exactly the type of navigation that's appropriate for your site. You can place a row of main menu links at the top of the page and position secondary (submenu) links in the left-hand side or right-hand side column. Try to figure out what arrangement of main and secondary links fits your site best and how you can realize this in Joomla!. Here are a few suggestions (some common arrangements of site navigation) to get you going:

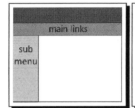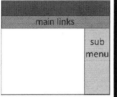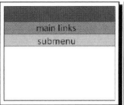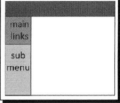

By default, Joomla's main menu links are displayed as a vertical row in the left-hand side column. How can you achieve a horizontal row of main menu links, as shown in the first three images above? Have a look again at the *Time for action - Tweak the menu position and orientation* earlier in this chapter. It shows the easiest way to change the menu orientation in Joomla!, selecting the appropriate Menu Style in the menu module editing screen. However, there are templates that are specifically designed to support horizontal menus. These contain the appropriate module positions and module styling for a main horizontal menu (and do a much better job at this than the default Joomla template). We'll see an example of this in Chapter 11 on templates.

Exploring menu module settings

When creating or editing a menu module, the module details and parameters allow you to control exactly where the menu is shown and how it displays. In many cases, the default settings will do—but if you really want control over your menus, it's a good idea to explore the wide range of additional possibilities these settings provide. In the **Module Manager**, click on the menu name (such as **Main Menu** or **About SRUP**). The **Module: [Edit]** screen appears.

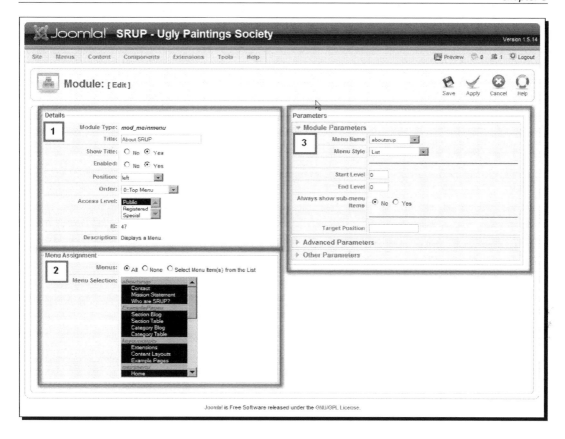

The three main sections of the **Module: [Edit]** screen are **Details**, **Menu Assignment**, and **Parameters**.

Details

The **Details** section controls basic properties, such as the menu title and the menu position.

Properties	Description
Title	Enter the **Title** of the module, that can be displayed on the frontend.
Show Title	In many cases, you can set the **Title** to hide. After all, why should a main menu be called **Main Menu**? Web visitors recognize a menu when they see one. Only special function menus (Login) should show a title. In the example site, I've left it to show so that you can easily identify the Main Menu on the page, but in real life you should go ahead and unpublish it!

Properties	Description
Enabled	Select **Yes** to show the menu module on the site, select **No** to hide it.
Position	Select the pre-defined position where you want the module to be displayed. The options you have here depend on the template you're using. Template designers can add as many positions as they like, giving you maximum flexibility in assigning positions to menus and other modules.
Order	There can be more than one module within a **Position**; by changing the **Order** setting, you can control the order of the modules in the **Position** you've selected. The drop-down box shows all modules in the current **Position** (for an example, see *Changing the order of menu items* earlier in this chapter).
Access Level	When you apply different access levels to different parts of your site, here you can determine who has access to this menu. When set to **Public**, every visitor can see the menu. Choose **Registered** to only give registered users access and **Special** to give only users with author status or higher to have access.

Menu Assignment

The **Menu Assignment** section allows you to control on which pages (through which menu links) the menu module will be accessible.

Properties	Description
Menus, **Menu Selection**	By default, a module will be shown on all pages. Choose **Select Menu Item(s) from the List** to make a selection in the **Menu Selection** box. This selection controls on which pages (that are linked to through the listed Menu Items) the module is displayed.

Module Parameters

You'll only have to edit the **Module Parameters** in some special situations.

Parameter	Description
Menu Name	The name you've entered when creating this menu in the **Menu Manager**. The default name is **mainmenu**.
Menu Style	The style determines which HTML code Joomla! generates to create a menu link list. The **List** option generates the most generally applicable code. **Legacy - Vertical** provides a vertical table; **Legacy - Horizontal** provides links in a horizontal table. **Legacy - Flat List** is an outdated method. The image below shows an example of a menu in the default Joomla! example site using the Legacy – Horizontal setting.
Start Level, End Level	**Start Level** and **End Level** allow you to split a menu showing primary links at the top of the page and secondary links in a split menu in some other position. See *Creating split submenus* earlier in this chapter for an example.
Always show sub-menu Items	Should submenu items be displayed even when the parent is not active (not selected)? Select **No** to have sub-menu items display only when the parent menu item is clicked.
Target Position	This is only relevant in some templates to specify the location of drop-down or pop-up menus.

Advanced Parameters

The **Advanced Parameters**, too, you'll probably only adjust in some special situations.

Parameters	Description
Show Whitespace	This setting doesn't have any effect on the way the page is displayed; it only affects the appearance of the source code. Should spaces be shown?
Caching	If you have set a caching value in the Global Configuration you can override it here for this module.
Menu Tag ID, Menu Class Suffix, Module Class Suffix	You can set the **Menu Tag ID**, **Menu Class Suffix**, and **Module Class Suffix** to tweak the layout of the menu. These options are only relevant if you want fine control over the layout of your menu through the CSS stylesheet.
Maximum Menu Depth	What's the maximum number of child menu levels you want the menu to show?

Other Parameters

The **Other Parameters** controls the display of menu images and some other menu display settings.

Parameter	Description
Show Menu Images, Menu Image Alignment, Menu Image Link, Indent Image	These settings are important if you want to show images next to individual menu items, such as an icon next to each main category link. The settings here control whether images will be displayed and if these images should function as hyperlinks.
	Before you can get any images to display next to menu items, you should add these images for each separate menu item through the menu item's parameters. In the menu item's **Parameters (System)** section, use the **Menu Image** option.
Expand Menu	Submenu items are shown after the visitor has clicked on the corresponding main level link. Do you want to always display the submenu items? Select **Expand Menu: Yes**.
Activate Parent, Full Active Highlighting	By setting **Activate Parent** and **Full Active Highlighting** to **Yes,** the menu will give the visitors a better indication of where they are in the site. If the menu has sublevel links, **Activate Parent** ensures that the parent level is indicated as "active" when a sublevel link is chosen.
	Full Active Highlighting allows the visitor to see where he is, on each page he visits—directions to the page he sees in the (active, otherwise styled) menu item **Contact**
Spacer, End Spacer	When using a horizontal menu, you can enter the character that should be shown between links. For example:
	About Us | Contact | Site Policy
	The end spacer is shown after the last horizontal menu item.

Have a go hero – try out available menu settings

In this chapter, you've seen how easy it is to create new menus, move links around, and place the menu anywhere on the page through the menu module settings. You might want to experiment a little; choose one of the menus on your site and try out some different module settings. Try, for instance, selecting other Menu Assignment settings; you'll see the menu will only display on the pages that you select.

Creating menu links

Up to now, we've focused on creating menus and tweaking menu display and settings. Of course, menus are about hyperlinks, so let's have a closer look at the way these are created and modified. As creating menu links is an essential activity in Joomla!, you're already familiar with the basic steps it takes to create these: navigate to **Menus**, click on the name of the menu, and click on **New**.

Every time you make a new link you're presented with an impressive list of Menu Item Types:

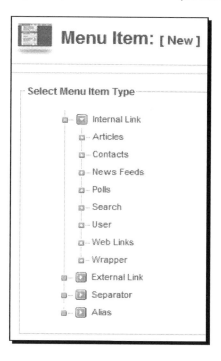

 This list can be different in your particular Joomla! installation. After you've installed a component that contains its own new page types, these can show up in the Menu Item Type list too.

When building the example site you've added links using some different Menu Item Types. You've created links pointing to articles (**Internal Link | Articles**): some pointing directly to content pages and others pointing to article overview pages (section and category pages). You've also added a link through **Internal Link | Contacts** to add a special function page: a contact form.

But you'll have noticed there are many more hyperlink types, as the above image shows. Clicking on the items shown here will reveal even more subitems. These menu item types are not about different types of menu navigation, they are about creating different types of content. They represent different preset ways of displaying all kinds of content.

The following table provides a short overview of what these Menu Item Types mean and how you can use them. We won't go into the details (as these Menu Item Types are targeted on creating content), but it's a good idea to browse the menu options mentioned next to get a quick impression of what they're about. We'll cover relevant Menu Item Types in more detail in other chapters about adding content (the references to these chapters are shown in the table):

What types of Menu Links can you create?	
Name	**What type of link is it?**
Internal Link	A link within the current website.
◆ **Articles**	A link to an article, a section or category overview page, or an article archive page (see Chapter 6 and 7)
◆ **Contacts**	A link to a page with data from one or more contacts (see Chapter 4).
◆ **News Feeds**	Link to a page with RSS feeds, new blocks of other sites.
◆ **Polls**	Link to a page with a poll, a survey (see Chapter 4).
◆ **Search**	Link to a page with the site search engine.
◆ **User**	Links to pages for specific users, such a registration and login page (see Chapter 9).
◆ **Web Links**	Link to a page with a collection of links to other sites.
◆ **Wrapper**	Link to a page within this site that shows an external web page (within a frame).
External Link	Link to an external site.
Separator	Not a link, but a line used to visually separate different parts of the menu.
Alias	A copy of a link to an existing menu item.

Have a go hero – try out some Menu Item Types

The extensive list of Menu Item Types looks inviting; why don't you have a go at the different types of menu items? Add a new menu link to the main menu and choose a menu item type you haven't used yet. Check out the **Search**, **External Link**, or the **Separator** menu item types; they're pretty straightforward. Some others, such as the **User** link, are quite complex and won't immediately make sense—but don't worry, they won't mess up your site permanently and you can easily delete unwanted menu items in them again. In the course of this book, you'll learn to use many of these menu item types.

Why do you have to create menu links manually, anyway?

You might wonder why you have to add menu links yourself—isn't that a boring job? Well maybe, but creating menu links gives you a huge amount of control. Not only do you control the type of page the link points to, but also which links are displayed, in what order they appear, on what pages they show up, in which menu they appear, and so on. Moreover, you can choose a menu structure that doesn't have be identical to the site structure. If you want to link from the home page menu straight to a registration page, you can do that (even if that page isn't part of your main site structure). This way, you can limit the number of clicks and lead your visitors through your site easily.

And don't worry, you'll only make menu items pointing to the main pages and content groups—not to each and every page. Menus usually point to overview pages, some selected articles, and special function pages (such as a login form, contact form, search page). Joomla! *will* automatically create links to any amount of articles below the main levels, using overview pages, as you've seen in Chapter 6.

Creating plain text links

Sometimes you'll want to show hyperlinks that are not part of a menu, but are embedded in an article text. How do you create these? It's doable, but it does take quite a few steps.

Time for action – creating text links

The SRUP website is in desperate need of an internal hyperlink from one page to another, a link from the **Mission Statement** page to the **Ugly Paintings** overview page. Let's create this link:

1. Before you can create a hyperlink, you have to get the URL of the target page. Navigate to the **Menus | Main Menu** and open the target page to edit it.

2. In the **Link:** field, select all of the text (press *Ctrl + A*) and copy it (press *Ctrl + C*).

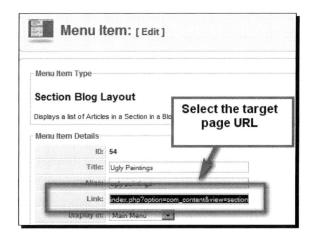

3. Now create a link to the URL you just copied. Navigate to **Content | Article Manager** and open the article that needs to contain the link in the editor. In this example, we've selected the **Mission Statement** article.

4. Select the word or words that should be a hyperlink and click on the hyperlink icon in the editor:

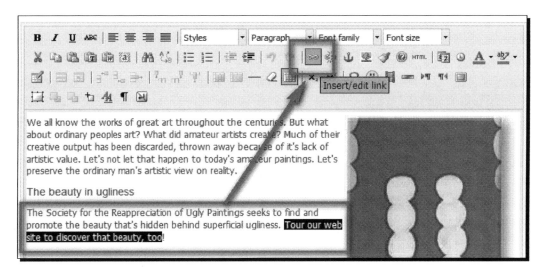

5. A pop-up screen appears. In the **Link URL** box, paste the target page URL and add a **Title** for the hyperlink. The **Title** will show up when the visitor hovers the mouse pointer on the link. In this example, we've entered **Discover Ugly Paintings** as link **Title**.

6. Click on **Update**. The pop-up screen closes. In the editor screen, click on **Save** and click on **Preview** to see the results on the frontend.

Check out the article on the frontend to see if the text is now a hyperlink:

What just happened?

You've created a text hyperlink from an article to another page in the same site. You can only create a link to a page that has a menu link pointing to it. To be able to create a text hyperlink, you first have to explore the menu link of the target page and get the URL information you need.

In the previous screenshots, you can see the editor buttons and pop-up screens available when Joomla!'s default text editor, Tiny MCE, is set to **Functionality: Extended**. Although the normal functionality setting will do in most cases, you might want to consider activating these advanced options. See Tip: *Extending the text editor* in Chapter 6.

If you often need to add text links to articles, it's much easier to use another editor, the **Joomla! Content Editor (JCE)**. Its approach is much more intuitive and it allows you to just click and select the target page (without first having to look up the target page URL). To know more about the JCE editor, see Chapter 10.

Pop quiz – test your menu knowledge

1. How many menus can you add to your website?

    a. Six Menus (the Main Menu and five other menus).

    b. As much as you want.

    c. You can only have one Main Menu.

2. How can you add submenu items to a menu?

    a. By creating "parent links" and "child links".

    b. By assigning a different Parent Item to a menu link than the default (Home).

    c. By creating a new menu.

3. When you create a new menu link, why does Joomla! show such a big list of Menu Item Types?

    a. To enhance navigation.

    b. To enable you to create new menus.

    c. To enable you to create different types of target pages.

Summary

In this chapter, we learned a lot about creating user-friendly navigation through Joomla! menus. This is what we covered:

- By default, new menu links are added to the bottom of the menu link list. You can move menu links up and down in the Menu Item Manager.

- You can set up a second menu that functions completely independent from the main menu. That way, you can move links that don't fit the main menu to a separate, less prominent position. You can create as much separate menus on your website as you like.

- Menus can be more than one level deep. By assigning a parent item to a menu link, you create a submenu item.

- You can also create interrelated menus, such as a main menu showing parent links and a secondary menu on a different page position that automatically shows child links.

- Submenus aren't the only way to make secondary content visible. Main links can point to overview pages with (automatically generated) links to content from those sections or categories.

- To create hyperlinks in an article text, you first have to retrieve the URL of the target page and copy it when creating a hyperlink in the article text editor.

You've now finished making a basic, functional, and easy to navigate website. In the next chapters, we'll take things further—after all, dynamic database-driven CMS magic doesn't stop at creating *basic* sites. In the next chapter, you'll learn how to add extra functionality, such as the ability for your visitors to contribute content or to register as site members.

9

Opening Up the Site: Enabling Users to Contribute and Interact

In the last few chapters you have set up a site for your client. It's a very up-to-date Joomla!-powered site, but there's still something old fashioned about it. After all, you're still the only person who has access to it and who is allowed to add and manage content. You haven't yet benefited from Joomla!'s built-in tools to create a team of specially designated power users who can log in to the site to add or edit content. In Joomla!, you're allowed to add as many content contributors as necessary and you can give them permission to create or edit articles, or to do even more.

But opening up your site to the world doesn't end there; Joomla! offers some powerful methods to engage your Web visitors and turn them into active users. You can enable visitors to register and give them exclusive access to premium content. Also, you can allow them to rate articles, giving others a good indication of must-read content.

In this chapter, you'll learn:

- ◆ Creating and managing user accounts: enabling Web team members to log in and maintain the site contents
- ◆ Configuring self-registration for site visitors and creating content for registered users only
- ◆ Allowing users to rate articles

Creating user accounts for team members

After you've installed Joomla!, there's only one user: the Super Administrator. When you take a look at the User Manager (**Site |User Manager**), you can check the user details of the Super Administrator: the default **Name** (by default this is **Administrator**), the **Username** (**admin**), whether this user is currently **Logged In**, whether his account is **Enabled**, the user's **E-mail** address, the time of the user's **Last Visit**, and the user's **ID** (an identifying user number that's only used by the system):

What different types of user accounts can you create?

In the **User Manager** you can create new users and assign them to a specific **Group**, granting them various levels of access to the site. There are five groups available, each with their own set of permissions:

1. Registered users

These are regular site visitors, except for the fact that they have registered and activated their account. After they have logged in with their account details, they can view content that may be hidden from ordinary site visitors ("guests") because the **Access Level** has been set to **Registered**. The site administrator can select this access level for all kinds of content, from modules and menu items to individual articles (through **Parameters (Article)**):

Registered users may have special access rights, but they can't contribute content. They're part of the user community, not of the Web team. We'll discuss user registration later in this chapter (see the section *Allowing visitors to register*).

2. Frontend content contributors

Up to now, you've only experienced Joomla!'s backend editing capabilities. However, it is also possible to log in to the frontend, to edit or add articles to the site. We'll see how that works in a moment. The idea behind having frontend editing possibilities is to lower the threshold for non-technical content contributors. They don't have to bother to learn the backend interface and can edit, and add, articles directly in an interface that they already know—the public frontend of the site.

The following are the three types of frontend content contributors, each having their own permission levels:

- **Authors** can submit new content for approval by a Publisher or someone higher in rank, but they can't edit existing articles.

- **Editors** can submit new articles and edit existing articles. A Publisher or higher must approve their submissions.

- **Publishers** can submit, edit, and publish articles in the frontend.

Authors and editors can't publish content. Only after approval by a Publisher (or someone higher in rank) will the content they submit be visible. Although this has its advantages—someone will be double-checking all content before it's published—having to review all of the new articles can create an extra workload for those with publishing permissions, and it could possibly turn into a bottleneck impeding a steady flow of new content. That might be a reason to instead assign Publisher permissions to your Web team members. Publishers have the same permissions as authors and editors, but (as you might have guessed) they are the ones who can also publish content.

> Generally, assigning a user to the Publisher group will be a good choice when you want Web team members to be able to individually add and publish content, without you having to grant them access to the (more complex) backend of the site. Publishers can easily create new content without having to learn their way around in the backend—or being able to create havoc by changing things they shouldn't.

3. Backend content contributors and administrators

Finally, there are three types of backend users. They have all the permissions of the frontend group, but they are also allowed to login to the backend to add and manage content and to perform administrative tasks:

- **Managers** can do all that Publishers can, but they are also allowed backend access to add or delete articles, and they can also create and manage sections and categories. They have limited access to administration functions.

◆ **Administrators** can do all that Managers can and have access to more administration functions. They can manage users, add or remove extensions, and change the site template.

◆ Super Administrators have no restrictions. They can do everything possible in the backend. When Joomla! is installed, there's always one super administrator account created. That's usually the person who builds and customizes the website. In the current example website, you're the super administrator.

Time for action – giving a user frontend authoring permissions

Suppose your client wants to create a Web team—a couple of people who should become responsible for content maintenance—let's create user accounts for these content contributors.

1. Navigate to **Site | User Manager**, Joomla!'s backend manager where you can view, edit, and create site users.

2. There's just one user, you. By default, Joomla! calls this first user **Administrator** (although this user belongs to the **Super Administrator** group). To add another user, click on the **New** button in the toolbar.

3. In the **User: [New]** screen, add **User Details** as desired. In this example, we've entered **Jim Van Gogh** in the **Name** field. In the **Username** field we've entered **jvgogh**. Enter a valid E-**mail** address and a password for the new user.

4. In the **Group** box, select **Author**. This will allow the new user to submit and edit content (after logging in to the frontend of the site).

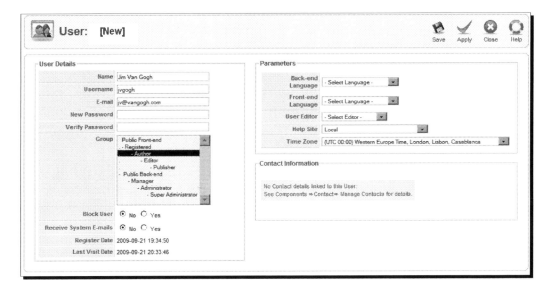

5. Click on **Save**. The **User Manager** screen now shows the new **User**:

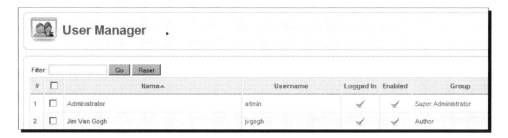

What just happened?

In the site user list in the **User Manager**, you're no longer on your own. As Mr. Van Gogh has been assigned to the **Author** user group, he is now permitted to log in to the frontend of the site and add content. However, to enable the new user to do anything we'll have to create a way for him to log in to the frontend. After all, the method of logging in that you yourself have been using (through a separate backend URL like `http://www.yoursite. com/administrator`) is only accessible to users with back end access—and Mr. Van Gogh doesn't have those permissions.

Enabling team members to log in to the frontend

Once you've assigned users to the Authors, Editors, or Publishers group, you'll have to create an entrance to the site frontend. Otherwise, they proudly own a shiny key to a secret part of the site—but there's no door to open!

Time for action – create a Login Form

Let's enable the Login Module. It's part of the Joomla! default installation, but it has to be enabled to become visible.

1. Navigate to **Extensions | Module Manager**. In the **Select Type** drop-down box, select **mod_login**. This will filter the long list of installed modules; only the **Login Form** module will be shown.

2. Click on the name **Login Form** to edit the module settings. Select **Enabled: Yes** to publish the module. The **Position** is set to **left** to display the Login Module on the left-hand side column, below the **Main Menu**.

3. Make sure **Menu Assignment** is set to **Home** only; this way, the Login Module will only show up on the home page. We can safely assume that users will probably want to log in to the site directly from the home page, so there's no need to clutter valuable screen real estate with a login form on other pages.

4. In this example, we'll leave the **Parameters** as they are. You could enter some **Pre-text** or **Post-text** here: a short text that is shown before or just below the Login Module.

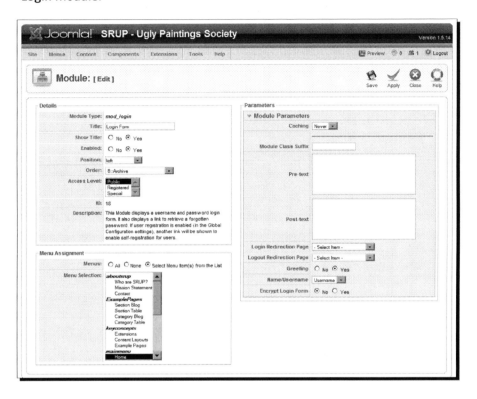

5. Click on **Save** and click on **Preview** to check the output on the frontend. In the left-hand side column, the **Login Form** is now shown below the **Main Menu**:

What just happened?

You've now enabled users to access your site through a **Login Form**. Maybe you've noticed that as soon as you add this form, it also displays a **Create an account** link. By default, Joomla! is configured to allow user self-registration. If you don't want users to be able to register, change a **Global Configuration** setting. Navigate to **Site | Global Configuration** and select the **System** tab. In the **User Settings** section, make sure **Allow User Registration** is set to **No** (the default value is **Yes**). Now the **Create an account link** will disappear. You'll read much more on user self-registration later in this chapter (see the section *Allowing visitors to register*).

Threw out the Login Form? Create a new one!

In the previous example, we're just publishing a Login Form that was already there because it is part of the Joomla! default installation sample data. If you haven't installed sample data, or have accidentally thrown away the Login Form, you can easily create a new one. After all, the sample Login Form is just an instance of the Login Form module that's built into Joomla!. To create a new Login Form, navigate to **Extensions | Module Manager** and click on **New** in the toolbar. Now select **Login**, click on **Next**, enter a **Title** (such as **Login**), and set **Menu Assignment** to **Home**. Make sure to set **Enabled:** to **Yes**. Click on **Save**. The Login Form will now appear in the left-hand side column, just like we've seen in the previous screenshot.

Time for action – logging in as a frontend content contributor

You now have one user who's the member of the Author group, you have a Login Form set up to enable this user to enter the site—so why don't we try how our Author can log in and submit content?

1. Navigate to the frontend of the site and use the **Login Form** to log in as the new user (in this example **jvgogh**):

2. Below the **Main Menu**, a **User Menu** appears. This is part of the Joomla! default installation and it's set to be only visible when a user has logged in—that's why it turns up all of a sudden. The **User Menu** provides links to functionality only available to registered users. For example, it allows the **Author** to view and edit his or her user details. However, we're primarily interested in the possibility of entering new content, so let's click on the **Submit an Article** link. Now here's a surprise; the Joomla! frontend turns into a live web page editor!

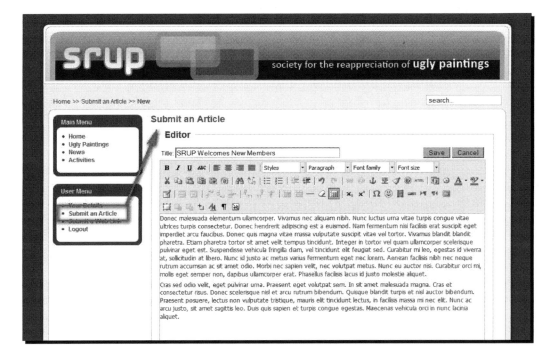

3. For testing purposes, enter some article text, add a title, and select the appropriate **Section** and **Category** (you'll find a **Section** and **Category** drop-down box if you scroll down on the **Submit an Article** page). In this example, we've created a dummy article called **SRUP Welcomes New Members** in the **News** section and **General News** category.

4. Click on **Save** to submit the article. You'll see a notice: **Thank you for your submission. It will be reviewed before being posted on the site**.

What just happened?

You've just logged in to your own site as if you were part of the Author user group. As an Author, you're able to contribute content on the frontend of the site.

Have a go hero – create a frontend User Menu

In the above example, you've seen a **User Menu** suddenly appear when a registered user has logged in. This **User Menu** is pre-installed when you choose to install Joomla! with sample data. Now what if you haven't installed sample data? You'll obviously want your logged in Authors to be able to submit content. To do this, add a **Submit an Article** link to any of the existing menus or create your own dedicated menu for frontend users (just like the **User Menu** that's included in the Joomla! sample site).

The procedure is pretty straightforward; these are roughly the steps involved. In the **Menu Manager**, create a new menu and call it what you like (for example, **User Menu**). You've now have an empty menu—click on the **Menu Items** icon to add some new menu links. If you want to enable Authors (or higher) to submit an article, in the **Menu Item Type** list add a link of the **Article Submission Layout** type. Save your changes to display and make sure to set your new menu module to display (set it to be *enabled* in the **Module Manager**). If you're a bit rusty on menu creating skills, please have a look again at Chapter 8 on navigation.

Allowing users to manage their accounts

The default login form already enables users to log in, create a new account, and retrieve their password or user name. However, instead of using the login form you can also create separate menu links to a login page, a self-registration page, or to a page enabling users to manage their account details (for example, to change their password). You'll find these particular link types in the **User** section of the **Menu Item Type** list. We'll try a few of these User links out later in this chapter, in the *Allowing visitors to register* section.

Reviewing and publishing team content submissions

Up to now, you've seen how you can create user accounts for team members on your site and how you can enable them to login. You've also switched to another role to see your site through the eyes of a logged in team member: an Author, someone who's able to submit (but not publish) content. Now let's see how you can get content submitted by Authors to show on the site.

Time for action – reviewing submitted content

Sorry, I'll have to ask you now to switch back once again to your original role—being the site administrator. After all, once an Author has submitted an article you (or another user with publishing permissions) should review and approve the new content to get it to display on the site. Let's see how this works:

1. Log in to the backend of your site as Administrator. Navigate to **Tools | Read Messages** (or click on the little envelope icon next to the **Preview** button in the backend Control Panel). You'll see this message:

A new Article has been submitted by [jvgogh] titled [SRUP Welcomes New Members] from Section [News] and Category [General News].

> ### Receiving submission reminders
> The Private Messaging icon isn't really conspicuous—you're bound to overlook messages alarming you about new submissions. Do you want to get an e-mail notification every time new content is submitted? Navigate to **Tools | Read Messages** and click on the **Settings** button in the toolbar. Select **Mail me on new Message: Yes.**

2. To review and publish the new article, navigate to **Content | Article Manager** and locate the new article. You'll notice a red cross in the **Published** column indicating the article is still unpublished. You can click on the title of the article to view and edit it as desired.

3. When you're satisfied with the article, click on **Save**. In the **Published** column of the **Article Manager**, click on the cross. It will turn into a green check mark.

4. Click on **Preview**. In the **News** section, the new article is shown:

What just happened?

Logging in as the site administrator again, you're able to check articles that have been submitted by authors. You can review the article, possibly edit it, and publish it if you're happy with it.

Have a go hero – explore different User Group permissions

So far you've seen what Authors are allowed to do in Joomla!. Why not explore other User Groups permissions? It's a good idea to log in as a user with different permissions to get a grasp of the possibilities. Changing user permissions only takes a few clicks. Here are a few pointers to get you going.

Find out what editors and publishers can do

Navigate to **Site | User Manager** and click on the name of the user (in our example, Jim Van Gogh) who you've added earlier and who you assigned to the Author group. Now, in the **Group** box, select **Editor** to give the user new frontend editing permissions. Click on **Save** and login to the frontend with the username and password of Mr. Van Gogh. You'll notice a small difference. Next to every article, a little pen and paper icon is now displayed:

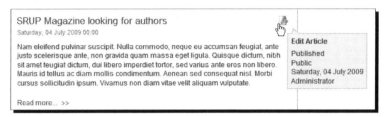

This old school icon opens up a range of new possibilities. When clicking on it, the web page turns into an editor screen just like the **Submit an Article** screen (see *Time for action – logging in as a frontend content contributor* earlier in this chapter). This shows what Editors can do (and Authors cannot). Editors can create articles, but they can't publish them themselves. However, they can change the text of existing articles by editing them in the frontend of the site—and immediately publish the changed article. This basically means they can't add content on their own, but they are allowed to make changes to existing content on their own (without approval of a Publisher or higher).

To find out what Publishers can do, change the Group that Mr. Van Gogh belongs to again. You won't notice any differences after logging in to the frontend. However, after you've edited or created an article, saving the article will immediately publish it. The article won't be submitted for review first.

Find out what backend users can do

A final step in "upgrading" user accounts is assigning one of the three backend accounts: Manager, Administrator, or Super Administrator. For example, try changing the existing Publisher account and assign the user to the Manager group. You can now log in with this user's **Username** and **Password** to the backend of the site
(via `http://www.yoursite.com/administrator`):

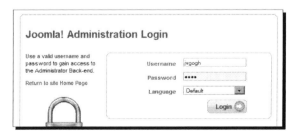

After logging in you'll be taken to the backend Control Panel where you can add and edit content the same way you're used to in your role as site administrator. As the new user has been assigned the Manager role, he has permissions to do most things with content that site administrators can (that is, creating new sections, categories, and articles).

Allowing visitors to register

In the previous section, you've set up new user accounts manually in the backend using the User Manager. Giving a team of content contributor's access to the site is a great way to share responsibilities and to collaborate in maintaining the site and keeping its contents up to date.

Another way to open up your site is to enable user self-registration. That way, a user community can develop and any amount of users can register themselves without the site administrator having to do or approve anything (of course, the administrator is still in charge and has the ability to block or remove users).

Registered users usually don't have permissions to contribute content; they do have exclusive access to parts of the site where the access level is set to—you guessed it—Registered. Let's first find out how to create "members only" content and enable visitors to join through self-registration.

How do you enable users to create an account?

It may have skipped your attention, but as soon as you've set up a Login Form (see *Time for action - create a Login Form* earlier in this chapter), you've enabled user self-registration at the same time. By default, the Login Module not only allows existing users to log in, it also contains a link inviting visitors to create a new account:

Displaying a link to a Login Form

In the above example, we've added a Login Form that displays in the left-hand side column of the home page. You may find this too big or too conspicuous. If you'd rather show just an small "Login" link pointing to a separate login page (a login form in the main content area), that's possible too.

To add a Login link to the Main Menu, navigate to **Menus | Main Menu**, click on **New,** and in the **Select Menu Item Type** section select **User | Login | Default Login Layout**. Add a title for the link (for example, **Login**) and click on **Save**. Set the **Login Form** module to hide (navigate to **Extensions | Module Manager** and set **Enabled** to **No**). Now the Login Form will only be displayed after the visitor has clicked on the **Login** link:

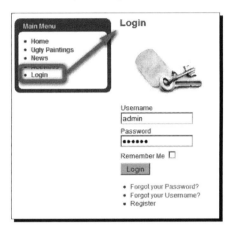

Time for action – register yourself and log in

Let's see what site visitors have to do to create an account. We'll create a dummy user account ourselves.

1. On the frontend, click the **Create an account** link below the Login Form in the left-hand side column (if you've created a menu link to a separate login page, as described above, then click on this menu link and click on **Register**). This will take you to the **Registration** page. Enter your details and make sure to use a valid **E-mail** address.

2. After clicking on **Register**, you are taken to the home page. On the home page, Joomla! displays a system message: **Your account has been created and an activation link has been sent to the e-mail address you entered. Note that you must activate the account by clicking on the activation link when you get the e-mail before you can login.**

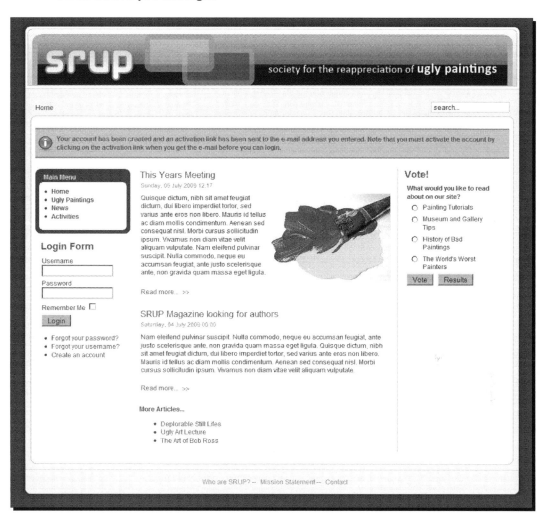

3. Joomla! will now send an automatically generated e-mail that contains a link you must click on to activate your new user account. You'll be taken to the home page and a confirmation message will be displayed: **Your Account has been successfully activated. You can now login using the username and password you chose during the registration**.

What just happened?

You're now officially a member of your own site! Try it out by using the **Login Form** on the home page. Enter your **Username** and **Password** and click on the **Login** button.

However, logging in as a registered user doesn't make much sense now since there's no special content that only registered users can access yet. We'll take care of that in a minute.

You can also enable users to register *without* having to enter a valid e-mail address. To do this, navigate to **Site | Global Configuration** and in **System | User Settings**, set **New User Account Activation** to **No**. However, be aware this can lower the threshold for spammers to create fake member accounts on your site.

Hiding content for non-registered users

Creating exclusive "member content" doesn't take much more than setting the access level of an item to Registered. This item will be hidden for regular users, but it will show up for those who have logged in. Most of Joomla!'s building blocks can be set to a specific Access Level. Whether this block is just one specific page or a module or all of the contents of a specific category, you can set it to be visible to registered users only. This basically means that you can make your site look very different to different types of users. Public users may only see a basic website; registered users have the same content plus a whole bunch of extra articles, menus, menu links, or modules.

Time for action – hiding content for non-registered users

Let's explore how how hiding content works. By default, every menu item is visible: the **Access Level** is set to **Public**. We'll change that setting for the **Ugly Paintings** link that's currently the second link in the menu:

Let's make this **Ugly Paintings** only visible for registered users that have logged in.

1. In the **Main Menu**, select the **Ugly Paintings** link to edit it.

2. In the menu links **Parameters**, set the **Access Level** to **Registered**, and click on **Save**.

What just happened?

That's it! By changing a single menu item parameter you've effectively hidden the menu item for non-registered users. The output is shown in the screenshot below:

The Ugly Paintings will only be displayed after a registered user has logged in.

Have a go hero – change access level settings

Have a look at the way you can change access levels for different items on your site. Explore the parameters or details of any article, menu item, or module. You'll find out that you'll always have the same set of **Access Level** choices you can set. Here's an example of the **Menu Item Details** you just changed:

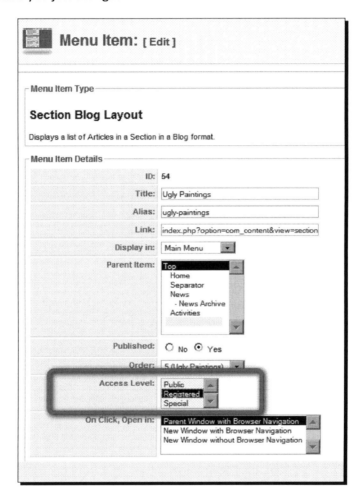

If you would like to make a whole menu display only for registered users, you'd set the **Access Level** of that particular menu module:

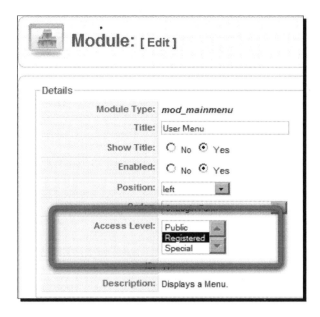

> **What's the special access level about?**
>
> You'll have noticed that there are three access levels: **Public**, **Special**, and **Registered**. Whatever is set to **Special** level is only accessible to administrators. You can use this level to show content that's meant for logged in administrators only.

Getting your visitors to 'register to read more'

It's great to be able to completely hide contents for non-registered users, but this approach does have one drawback. It doesn't encourage users to register as they simply can't see what they are missing out on. Sometimes, it's better to show non-registered users only part of an article and invite them to join (register) to read more.

On the example site, we'll do just that. We won't completely hide content for registered users, as this would leave a very sparse website for first time visitors, that wouldn't really persuade them to explore the hidden stuff.

Time for action – partially hiding content from non-registered users

Suppose your client wants to offer their site members some exclusive content; anyone registering to the SRUP site can enjoy special discounts on art supplies and other goodies. Let's create this content and make sure it's only partly shown—unless users register:

1. To create a new section, navigate to **Content | Section Manager** and click on **New**. Call this new section **Member Area**.

2. To create a new category, navigate to **Content | Category Manager** and click on **New**. Call the new category **Member Discounts**. Set the **Section** to **Member Area**.

3. To create a new article, navigate to **Content | Article Manager** and click on **New**. Assign the new article to the **Member Area** section and the **Member Discounts** category.

4. Make sure to divide the article in an intro text and a main body text by placing the cursor directly after the intro text and then clicking on the **Read more...** button. A red dotted line indicates where the intro text ends and the Read more link will appear.

5. In the **Parameters (Article)**, set the **Access Level** to **Registered**:

6. If you like, you can create another article in the same category. In this example, we've named the article **Special Discounts for Members**. Make sure to set the **Access Level** to **Registered**.

7. Create a link pointing to the new section. Navigate to **Menus | Main Menu** and click on **New**. In the **New Menu Item Type** section, select **Articles | Section Blog Layout**. Enter a **Title (Member Area)** and in the **Parameters (Basic)**, select the **Member Area** section as the link target. In the **Parameters (Component)**, set **Show Unauthorized Links** to **Yes**:

This last step takes care of the Register to Read More magic. Instead of completely hiding non-public articles, Joomla! will now partially display them.

What just happened?

You've created some web pages that can be fully viewed by registered users only. When you preview the site, you'll see a Main Menu link pointing to the **Member Area**. Clicking on this link shows the teaser texts of the articles in the **Member Area** section are displayed with a **Register to read more...** link. This way, unregistered users get a taste of the registered content:

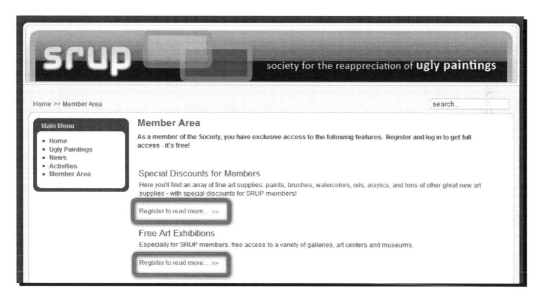

When site visitors click on the **Register to read more...** link they are automatically taken to a separate login page:

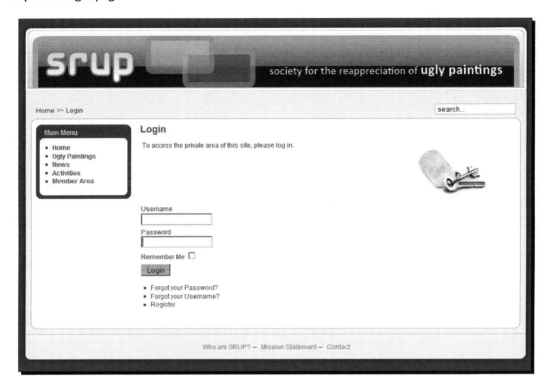

Visitors that haven't yet created an account can click on **Register** to do so now. If the visitors already have an account, they can login here. You can check this out for yourself by logging in now with the dummy user account you created earlier.

Enabling users to rate articles or write comments

Allowing your visitors to register is a first step to create user involvement. If you want more community interaction, you might consider enabling your visitors to rate articles. This option is built-in; when editing an article, navigate to **Parameters (Advanced)** and set **Article Rating** to **Show**. Now, users can rate an article on a five point scale from **Poor** to **Best**.

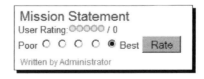

If you want to enable visitors to rate articles, you may want to set this for all articles at once. Navigate to the **Article Manager**, choose **Parameters** and set **Article Rating/Voting** to **Yes**. This will enable article rating for all articles you write from now on, unless you disallow rating for specific articles.

Another great way to get visitors involved is to allow them to post comments to your articles. This gives them an opportunity to give feedback on the subjects you cover and to participate in discussions with other visitors. Moreover, it can show you which issues your site visitors care about. In Joomla! 1.5, a commenting system isn't pre-installed. However, there are many commenting extensions available, such as the free !JoomlaComment, YvComment, and Disqus components. You can find more information on using extensions in Chapter 10; specific information on commenting systems is available through the Joomla! extensions website: `http://extensions.joomla.org/extensions/contacts-and-feedback/articles-comments`.

Pop quiz – test your knowledge of Joomla! user management

1. What's the difference between registered users and ordinary site visitors?

    a. Registered users can add content to the site.

    b. Registered users are able to view "registered" content.

    c. Registered users are team members.

2. What's the use of displaying a login form on your website?

    a. To allow users to log in or to register.

    b. To allow anyone to log in to the backend.

    c. To allow users to activate their account.

3. What's the advantage of using "Register to read more" links?

    a. Site visitors will feel encouraged to add content.

    b. Site visitors will feel encouraged to register to read partly hidden content.

    c. Site visitors won't be able to know what content is hidden.

Summary

In this chapter, you learned a lot about different ways of user interaction in Joomla!. The following is what we have covered:

◆ In the User Manager you can create new users and assign them to a specific Group, granting them various levels of access to the site. There are five groups available, each with their own set of permissions.

◆ Some users have access to only the frontend of the site; others have more permissions and can login to both the frontend and the backend of the site.

◆ To allow users to login to the site, you'll have to create an entrance: a login form where they can enter their username and password.

◆ Some frontend users are only allowed to submit or edit content; they can't publish it. Another user with publishing permissions has to review their submissions and makes them visible on the site.

◆ By enabling user self-registration a user community can develop. Registered users have exclusive access to "members only" content.

◆ To invite visitors to register you can show them only part of an article. This way, you can encourage them to explore all the hidden stuff.

◆ If you want your visitors to interact you can allow them to rate articles or to add comments, using a dedicated commenting component.

Up to now, you've steadily built a fine website. It's looking good, organized clearly, easy to expand, and easy to navigate. Moreover, you've now added some advanced features to the site using Joomla!'s built-in user management capabilities. What more can you want? Much more! Now it's time to look further and explore the vast range of powerful extras by extending Joomla!. In the next chapter, you'll enhance your site and make it even better and much more fun to use.

10

Getting the Most out of Your Site: Extending Joomla!

When you've got your basic Joomla!-powered site up and running, and you've got all of your content and functionality covered, chances are you'll want more. Maybe your client has some specific requirements, or maybe you just want to increase the wow factor of your site and add some eye candy or cool effects. Doing more things with Joomla! and make your site stand out from the rest of them—that's where extensions come in.

The real power of Joomla! lies in its extensibility. If you need any functionality that's not built into the basic Joomla! installation (or "core"), you'll very likely find it in the huge treasure house that's called the Joomla! extension database. Extensions are little pieces of software that you can download and install to become part of the backend, extending Joomla!'s capabilities.

In this chapter, you'll:

- ◆ Use Joomla!'s core extensions
- ◆ Download and install extensions
- ◆ Put extensions to work to enhance the frontend of your site or your backend workspace

Don't let the term *extension* confuse you; some extensions are part of the Joomla! core. They are integrated into the basic Joomla! package. Many of these provide essential functionality so you can't even uninstall them. Joomla!'s search function, it's menu system, or it's Contacts functionality are examples of these pre-installed extensions. This means you already have some extensions experience. As soon as you start using Joomla!, you deploy extensions.

In this chapter, we'll focus on the possibilities of some core extensions that we haven't covered yet and also on using third-party extensions. We'll install some must-have extensions and find out how they work.

Extensions in all shapes and sizes

Before digging into the wonderful world of extensions, it's good to know they come in different shapes and sizes. Basically, there are three types of extensions:

♦ The big ones called **Components**. You manage them through a special **Components** menu in the backend. They are the most comprehensive extensions, sometimes providing lots of administration options and settings. Component output is usually displayed in the main content area. An example is the Contacts components (to manage a system of contacts, contact details, and contact forms).

♦ The medium ones called **Modules**. Modules are "blocks" that contain special functionality. You've already seen examples at work, such as the menu module. You manage modules in **Extensions | Module Manager**. Modules usually turn up around the main content area: in the left-hand side and right-hand side column, or in the header and footer. These module positions ('left', 'right', and so on) are predefined by the template designer. In the following screenshot, you can see the default template is packed with module positions:

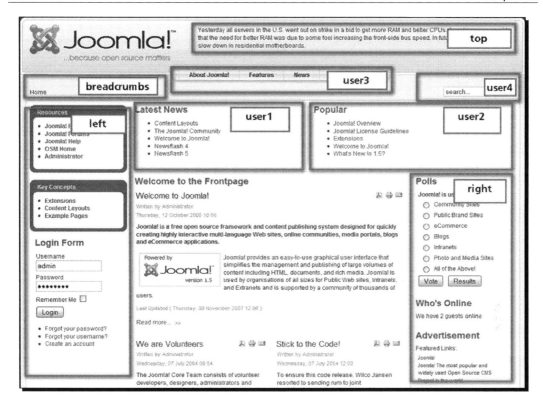

- ◆ Tiny extensions called **Plugins**. These are usually minor enhancements, such as an extra button in the text editor that makes it easy to insert hyperlinks.

Don't worry, you don't have to memorize this extensions typology. Although technically and practically there are important differences between these three extension types, the bottom line is that they all extend Joomla!'s capabilities by adding extra functionality in the backend of your site. You just choose the tool that does the job—sometimes this means you'll use a component, sometimes a module, and sometimes a plugin (and sometimes even a combination).

In the **Extensions** menu you'll also find **Template Manager** and **Language Manager**. We won't cover them here as they have very specific purposes:

Templates determine the site's layout, colors, and typography. See Chapter 11 on using templates.

Language files allow you to set the default language for the frontend and the backend of the site. On the frontend, this will translate all preset texts (such as *Read more* and *Written by*) to a language of your choice. See Chapter 2 on installing Joomla!.

Where do you get them from?

Apart from the few dozen extensions that are part of the default Joomla! installation, you can find thousands of additional extensions developed by third parties on the Web. Most of these are listed on `http://extensions.joomla.org`, the **Joomla! Extensions Directory** (or **JED**, as it is fondly called by the Joomla! community):

Here you'll see that extensions offer a wealth of new possibilities, whether it's better content presentation (through menus, link lists, and galleries), user interaction (using forums and comments), or backend tools (interface enhancements).

Browse the JED categories (navigation systems, forums, and so on) every now and again and keep an eye on the *New and Noteworthy* section. Make sure to check out the *Editor's Picks* and the *Most Popular* extensions to find some true gems. It's a good idea to read other users comments. They will often give you a good indication of whether an extension is mature enough and whether the support by the developer is up to standards.

The JED lists very many extensions, but there are much more extension portal sites and developer sites. Just google for "Joomla! extensions" or "Joomla! extensions must-haves" and make sure you've got enough coffee prepared to embark on a long and adventurous online treasure hunt.

What do they cost?

Many Joomla! extensions are free or available for a reasonable fee. Sometimes, developers require registration before you can download the extension.

Enhancing your site using core extensions

Let's explore some extensions that are part of the Joomla! core package. We'll put a few modules to work.

Time for action – adding a Newsflash to the home page

When your site grows, it's important to make sure the home page properly reflects all of the content categories to prevent your valuable new content from staying unnoticed. Using the Front Page Manager (see Chapter 4) you can set a selection of articles to show in central area of the home page. But there are more ways to attract attention to specific articles. In this case, we'll use the Newsflash module to show a random article intro text from a selected category each time the page is loaded. Every time the visitor returns another item will be displayed in the Newsflash module position.

1. Navigate to **Extensions | Module Manager**. It may be hard to locate the Newsflash module in this multi-page listing, but there's a quick way to find it. In the **Type** drop-down box, select **mod_newsflash**. Now just this module is shown:

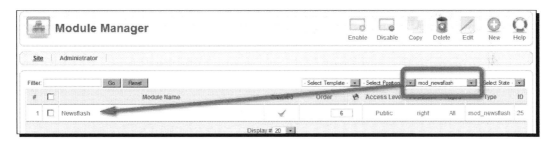

2. Click on the **Module Name (Newsflash)** to edit the module properties. In the **Title** box, replace the default title **Newsflash** with an appropriate title. In this example, we'll enter **Recent Lectures** as the module title.

3. Select **Enabled: Yes** to get the module to display.

4. Select **Position: right** to display the module in the right-hand side column.

5. In the **Menu Assignment** section, select **Select Menu Item(s) from the List** and set the module to show on the **Home** page only.

6. In the **Module Parameters** section, select the **Category** from which Joomla! should show one or more article intro texts.

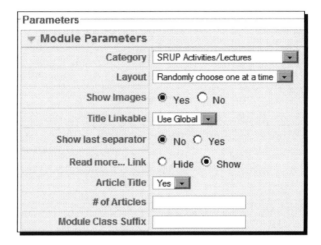

7. In the **Layout** drop-down box, choose **Randomly choose one at a time**. This will make the module display one random article from the selected category each time the visitor revisits this page (if you were to choose **Horizontal** or **Vertical** here you could display a number of article intro texts listed either horizontally or vertically).

8. Set **Show Images** to **Yes**; this way the images in the article's intro text will be displayed. Images will only fit if they aren't wider than the available module position, as bigger images aren't resized automatically. In this case, images are displayed if they aren't wider than the right-hand side column (which is about 230 pixels).

9. Set **Title Linkable** to **Yes** to turn the title of the article into a hyperlink.

10. Select **Read more... Link: Show** to show a **Read more...** link after the intro text.

11. Select **Article Title: Yes** to show the article title (and not just the intro text).

12. Click on **Save** and click on **Preview**.

The Newsflash module is shown above the Poll in the right-hand side column:

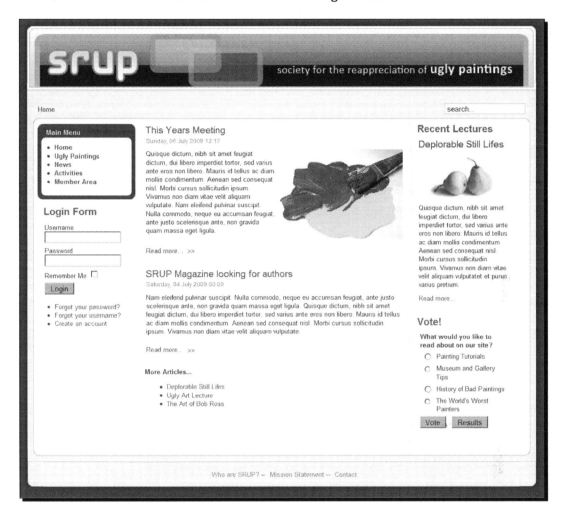

What just happened?

The Newsflash module can help you attract attention to a specific set of articles; every time the page is revisited (reloaded in the visitor's browser), a new random article intro text from the selected category is shown. Don't let the name *Newsflash* fool you as the module is obviously not just for news items. You can use it to show items from any category. The fun part is that you can surprise the visitor with different content at every revisit, without having to actually refresh your site.

Have a go hero – change the Newsflash settings

As with almost any module, the settings and parameters greatly determine the output of the Newsflash. In the following screenshot, you can see what the output can look like if you change the position and layout settings:

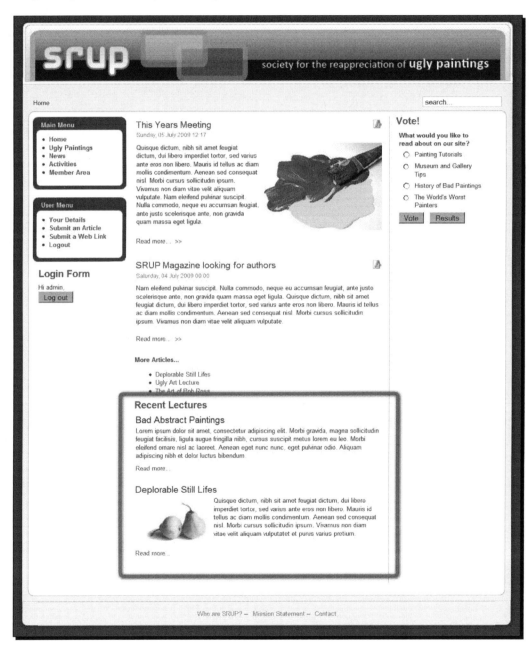

Here, the **Position** is set to **Footer** and the **Layout** is set to **Vertical**. In **# of Articles** we've entered **2** to display two article intro texts from the **Lectures** category in one column. This way, the Newsflash module allows you to display article intro texts *from a selected category*, something you can't achieve with the Front Page settings only. The Front Page Blog Layout shows articles that are set to "Show on Front Page", regardless of the category they belong to.

Using the same module twice (or more)

Suppose you want to use the Newsflash a few times on the same page. Is that possible? Yes, you can have multiple instances of any module on a given page. You've already seen an example of this if you have installed Joomla! with sample data, as the sample site shows various menus together on one page (such as **Main Menu**, **Top Menu**, and **User Menu**). These are all copies of a single module type: **mod_mainmenu**.

Being able to use many instances of the same module means you can also have one Newsflash module showing a few teasers from Category A, and another one just below that showcasing Category B. To do this, just navigate to **Extensions | Module Manager**, select the Newsflash module, and click on **Copy** in the toolbar. In the **Module Manager** a copy will show up named **Copy of [module name]**. Edit this copy to set it to show just what you want to. You'll probably want to give it another **Title** and set the source to another **Category**.

Another option—instead of copying an existing module—is to create a new instance of the desired module from scratch; navigate to **Extensions | Module Manager**, click on **New,** and select the type of module you want (we'll cover an example in the following section).

Creating a custom HTML block

Imagine you want to add a block of information on your site, for example a short announcement in a sidebar. You can't use an article for this, as this will be displayed in the main content area. But there's a nifty little module available in the Joomla! core that will help you out. It's called the Custom HTML module.

Time for action – add a short content block

On all the pages of Ugly Paintings, the SRUP people would like to announce a forthcoming series of articles. Let's use the **Custom HTML** module to achieve this.

1. This module isn't in use yet, so we can't adjust an existing copy of it. Let's create a new instance of it. Navigate to **Extensions | Module Manager** and click on **New** in the toolbar.

2. In the **Module: [New]** screen, select **Custom HTML** and click on **Next**.

3. In the **Module: [Edit]** screen, enter the details. First set the **Title** to something appropriate (in this example, we've entered **Hacking Ugly Paintings**). Set **Show Title** to **No**.

4. Make sure **Position** is set to **left**; the module will display below the **Main Menu** (which is also assigned to this module position).

5. In the **Menu Assignment** section, choose **Select Menu Item(s) from the List** and in **Menu Selection:** select the **Ugly Paintings** link. This will make the module show up on all of the pages that this menu link leads to.

6. In the **Custom Output** screen, enter the text and images you'd like to show in this block. You can format the text using text editor buttons. In this example, we've centered the text, made it bold, and added an image.

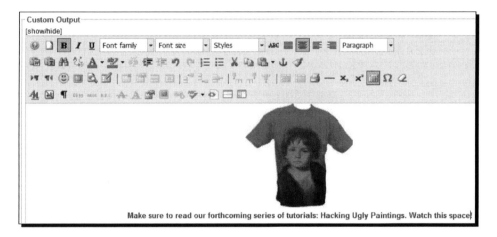

7. Click on **Save** and click on **Preview**. In the frontend **Main Menu**, click on the **Ugly Paintings** link to see the results:

What just happened?

Using the **Custom HTML** module, we've added a special little content block. It will only show up on specific pages. Usually, modules contain dynamic content, such as links or a login form. The **Custom HTML** module is different; it allows you to determine the module content from scratch. You can use it to display a fixed text on some pages, such as a welcome note, a note on the section that the reader finds on those pages, or some "static" hyperlinks.

 If you're a scripting wizard you can also add dynamic HTML code (JavaScript). However, by default the Joomla! editor TinyMCE will clean up dynamic code from the text when saving. If you do want to be able to enter (and save!) any code here, navigate to **Extensions | Plugin Manager**, select **Editor - TinyMCE 2.0,** select **Code cleanup on save: Never,** and click on **Save**.

What other extensions are part of the Joomla! core?

Navigate to **Extensions | Module Manager** to see which modules are part of the default installation.

Module Name	Type	What can you do with it?
Archive	mod_archive	When you archive items in Joomla! you can use this module to display a list of links to archived articles (sorted by date). We've explored archiving articles in Chapter 6.
Breadcrumbs	mod_breadcrumbs	This displays a set of hyperlinks that helps visitors understand where they are (that is, **Home | Category | Article**)
Custom HTML	mod_custom	This is a simple, but very flexible module to display content anywhere on the page. See the previous section for an example of its usage.
Feed Display	mod_feed	This displays a list of hyperlinks to news updates (newsfeeds) from another website.
Latest News	mod_latestnews	This module shows a list of hyperlinks to show the last articles added to certain sections or categories. The name is confusing because it is really about "latest content", not just news.
Login	mod_login	This module shows a form that users can use to log in or create a new account. You've seen this in action in Chapter 9.
Main Menu	mod_mainmenu	The mod_mainmenu module is Joomla!'s default menu module. All menus in Joomla! are in fact instances of the basic menu module mod_mainmenu. In other words, in spite of the name this is not just a "Main Menu" module, it's Joomla!'s menu functionality—period.
News Flash	mod_newsflash	You've read about this module earlier in this chapter. It's not just for news, but it allows you to display the intro texts of a set of articles in any category.
Popular	mod_mostread	Add this module to display a list of hyperlinks to the articles that have been accessed most often.
Random Image	mod_random_image	Shows a random image from an image folder any time the page is reloaded; a simple way to surprise the visitor with a page that looks different on every visit, even when there's no new content added.

Module Name	Type	What can you do with it?
Related Items	mod_related_items	Shows a list of hyperlinks to pages with a subject matter related to that of the current page. The relationship is based on the meta tag keywords of the articles. If the current page and two other articles contain the keyword *tutorial*, then two items will appear in the link list.
Search	mod_search	Shows the site search field.
Sections	mod_sections	Shows a list of hyperlinks to all sections in the site.
Statistics	mod_stats	Shows a set of website statistics, such as the number of content items and visitors hits.
Syndicate	mod_syndicate	This shows a RSS Feed link; users can click on this to subscribe to updates for the current page and read them in a special application (a news reader).
Who's Online	mod_whosonline	Shows how many users are logged in.
Wrapper	mod_wrapper	Allows you to show an external page (a page from another site) within your site.

Every module in the **Module Manager** has a **Module Name** and a **Type**. The name is the (customizable) **Title** of the module that you show at the frontend of the site. The module **Type** is the (fixed) name Joomla! uses internally. As you saw above, you can repeatedly use the same module type (for example, mod_mainmenu), but you distinguish module copies with their name (for example, Top Menu, or User Menu).

Navigate to the **Components** menu to see which components are part of the Joomla! core. A short overview:

Component Name	What can you do with it?
Banner	Manage banner ads on your website. You can create new banners and manage banner clients.
Contacts	Add and manage contact information and link contacts to registered users. See Chapter 4 for an example.
News Feeds	Add newsfeeds from other sites to your Joomla! site.
Poll	Create multiple choice surveys. See Chapter 4 for an example.
Search	Access search statistics to see how many searches were done for certain keywords or keyword combinations.
Web Links	Add and categorize links to other websites (to display on your site through the Web Link Menu Link type).

Enhancing your site using third-party extensions

When you run into the limitations of the basic Joomla! installation and the core extensions, it's time to check out some more sophisticated, dedicated extensions. Any functionality you can think of is likely to already exist in the form of a component, module, or plugin (or a combination). It takes just a few steps to add an extension to your website. First you download the extension (as a ZIP file), then you install it through Joomla!'s Extension Manager, and finally you adjust its settings to get it to work the way you want to.

Trying out an alternative News flash

Earlier in this chapter, you've explored a core module, Newsflash. This is a great module for attracting attention to a few selected articles, but it has some limitations. For example, content can be inadvertently shown *twice* on your home page. In the following example, an article intro is displayed because it's set to show on the Front Page, but its title is also shown because the article is part of the Newsflash category:

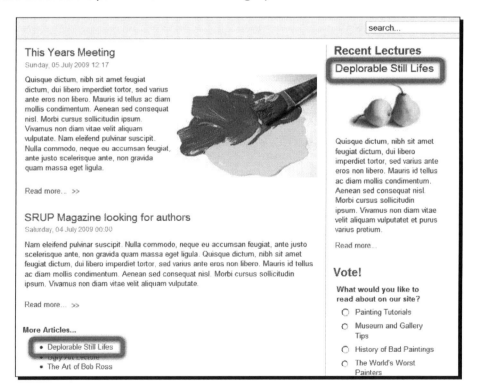

To prevent this, you have to manually check for double home page entries. However, there are dedicated content presentation modules available that can do this automatically (and do much more). We'll check out an example.

Time for action – downloading and installing an extension

Let's install an alternative news module, News Show Pro:

1. Navigate to `http://tools.gavick.com` and select the **News Show Pro** link.

2. Click on **Download** to download the file `mod_news_pro_gk1_J15!.zip` file containing the extension files. You'll be asked to login or register. Click on **Register** to register as a user and log in to the site. You'll be taken to the download page where you can download the ZIP file.

3. In the backend of your site, navigate to **Extensions | Install/Uninstall**. You'll be taken to the **Install** screen of the **Extension Manager**:

4. Now install the extension by clicking on **Browse** to select the extension ZIP file on your computer. Click on **Upload File & Install**. Once the installation is complete, you'll see a message (**Install Module Success**).

Time for action – putting the extension to work

Now, let's get News Show Pro display an article teaser text in the right-hand side column on the front page. If you've followed along and installed the NewsFlash module earlier, it's time to hide that module again, as we'll replace it. To do so, navigate to **Extensions | Module Manager**. Locate the **NewsFlash** module and click on the green check mark in the **Enabled** column to hide it on the frontend.

1. In the **Module Manager**, locate the **News Show Pro** module and click on the **Module Name (News Pro GK1)** to see the huge list of available options.

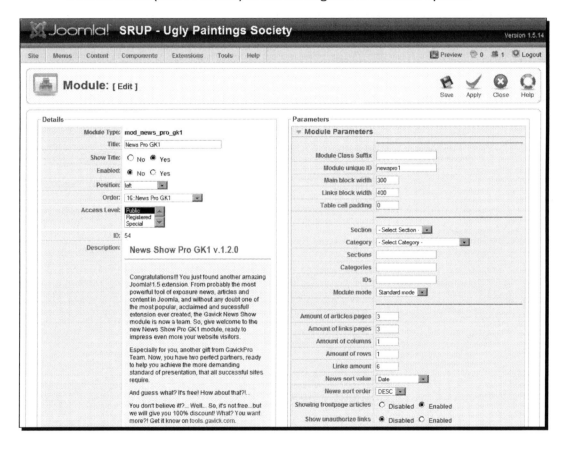

This is a bit different from the default Newsflash module! If you scroll down, you'll see News Show Pro has more than 70 different **Module Parameters**. But don't despair, you'll only have to tweak a few settings to get this beast to work.

2. In the **Title** field, enter **Recent Lectures**.

3. Set **Enabled:** to **Yes** and select **Position: right**.

4. In the **Menu Assignment** section, set the module to display on the **Home** page only.

5. In the **Module Parameters**, set **Main block width** to **200**. This defines the maximum width of the displayed module contents.

6. In the **Category** field, select **SRUP Activities/Lectures**.

7. In the **Amount of columns** and **Amount of rows** boxes, enter **1**. This will display one news item at a time.

8. Set **Showing frontpage articles** to **Disabled**. This will hide category contents that's already set to show in the Front Page mainbody.

9. Set **News image height** and **News image width** both to 50px. This will automatically reduce any images (in the article intro texts) to small thumbnails when displayed as part of the News Show Pro module.

10. Set **Autoanimation** to **Enabled**. This will create an automatic sliding display.

11. Click on **Save** and click on **Preview**.

What just happened?

The right-hand side column still shows a teaser text, but the differences are in the details:

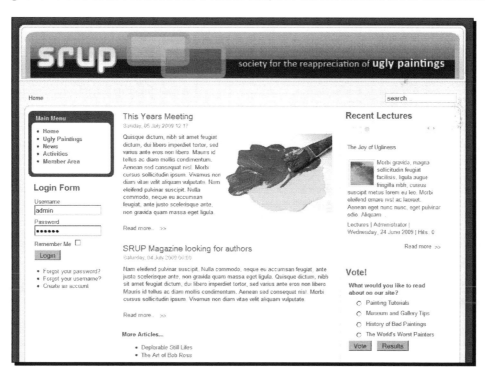

1. There are no double front page entries any more. Whatever appears on the front page, is automatically filtered out of the News Show module.

2. Every second or so a new teaser text will automatically slide in to reveal other category contents:

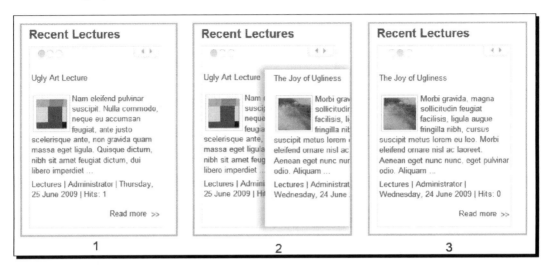

Moreover, there are some controls allowing the visitor to manually browse the available teasers from this category. Of course, automatic panel animation might be a bit too much for your sophisticated site – but it's cool to have this option.

3. The images in the article intro texts have been converted to small thumbnails to make better use of the limited screen real estate of the front page column.

 If you just see *one* teaser text and no other content sliding in, chances are the category you've chosen doesn't contain enough articles. Create some new (dummy) articles to see the effect.

News Show Pro is a good example of the difference between Joomla!'s built-in extensions and the extensions that are available through third-party developers. Generally, the core extensions are lightweight, simple, and do their job just fine. However, dedicated third-party extensions are bound to have more options and features. Moreover, you usually can choose between several excellent extensions to perform the same kind of functionality. Another great extension for displaying article teasers, for example, is Mini Frontpage (http://www.templateplazza.com/minifrontpage-module).

Have a go hero – experiment with News Show settings

Try out the many different options that the News Show module offers. You can change the layout and set all sorts of combinations of teasers, links, and sliding panels. When downloading the extension, you'll notice there's a separate PDF manual available for download that contains instructions and examples to help you on your way. The following is an example from the developer's demo site:

Showing images in a gallery

On our art website we'd like to display our art pictures really big, allowing the visitor to enjoy as much of the ugly details as possible. This means we definitely need an image gallery using a lightbox. You'll no doubt have seen this trick used on the Web; images are displayed small (as thumbnails) on the web page itself, to be maximized only after the visitor has clicked them. Then, the image opens in a lightbox, greybox, slimbox, or whatever different developers like to call this method. It not only looks cool, but it's functional too, as it allows you to show a lot of pictures on the page, leaving it to the visitor to pick which pictures he or she wants to have a better look at:

Time for action – create an image gallery

To show all images in a folder as a gallery, we'll use the plugin Simple Image Gallery available from JoomlaWorks.

1. Download the Simple Image Gallery extension ZIP file from
`http://www.joomlaworks.gr`.

2. Navigate to **Extensions | Install/Uninstall**. Select the ZIP file you downloaded and click on **Upload File & Install**. You'll see a message when the installation is finished (**Install Plugin Success**).

3. As this is a plugin, we'll use the Plugin Manager to enable this extension. Navigate to **Extensions | Plugin Manager** and locate the **Simple Image Gallery** plugin. Click on the cross in the **Enabled** column. The cross turns into a check mark, indicating the plugin is now active:

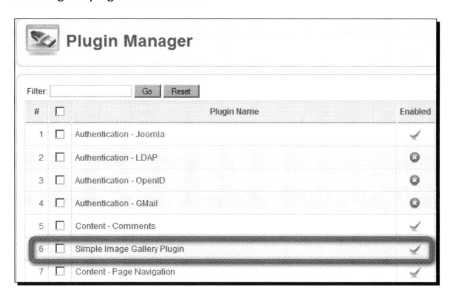

4. Click on the Plugin Name (**Simple Image Gallery Plugin**) to set **Image thumbnail width** and **Image thumbnail height** both to **100px**. This will reduce the thumbnail size to a maximum 100 pixels, allowing for a good deal of small thumbnails on the page:

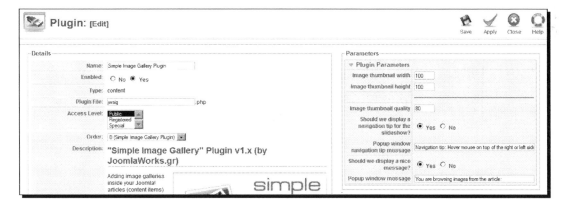

5. To actually create a gallery, we need a folder containing all of the pictures we want to show. Let's upload them to a folder /images/stories /paintings.

6. To do this, navigate to **Site | Media Manager**. Navigate to the **stories** folder and create a new folder **paintings**. Open this folder and upload your images to it.

7. You're all set. Now you only have to create a new article (or edit an existing one) that will contain the gallery pictures. Navigate to **Content | Article Manager** and click on **New**. In the following example, I've created an article titled **Ugly Paintings Gallery** and assigned it to the **Ugly Paintings** section and the **Facts** category.

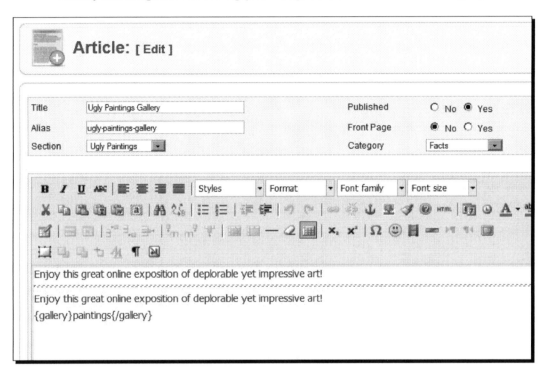

8. In the article enter this code: **{gallery}paintings{/gallery}**. This will instruct the plugin to display all image files from the `images/stories/paintings` folder.

9. Click on **Save**. You're done. On the frontend, click on the **Ugly Paintings** link in the **Main Menu** to navigate to the new article. It will display as follows:

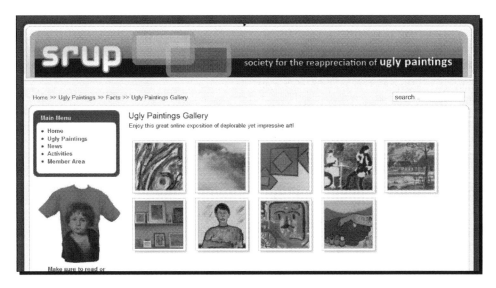

What just happened?

You've set up a gallery that will impress your visitors. Clicking on any of the thumbnails opens a lightbox with the full-size image, allowing the user to browse through through the available set of images:

The plugin automatically searches `images/stories` to find the specified images folder. If the target folder would be `images/stories/food/bagels`, then you would enter `{gallery}food/bagels{/gallery}`.

Do you want more from your photo gallery?

The Simple Image Gallery plugin is—as you might expect—quite simple. If you're looking for a more sophisticated gallery tool that allows you to manage a large number of images and show them to your visitors in a structured way, you might want to consider using a gallery component. An example is Phoca (`www.phoca.cz/phocagallery`). Phoca can present large image collections using categories and subcategories. Visitors can browse the photos using lightbox pop-up screens:

Using extensions to enhance your work space

Extensions don't just extend the functionality of the frontend of your site. There are also extensions available that enhance and extend the backend. For example, you can replace the backend article editor by a more powerful one.

Time for action – replace Joomla!'s default text editor

The default text editor is allright for entering text, but some of the advanced capabilities (such as adding images or inserting hyperlinks) aren't really easy and intuitive. Let's install the Joomla! Content Editor, a popular and freely available replacement for Joomla!'s default editor (which is called TinyMCE). For many Joomla! users, JCE is the first thing they add after installing Joomla!:

1. Go to `http://www.joomlacontenteditor.net` and download the "single installation package" (containing the two extensions JCE: the **Editor Plugin** and a **Component)**. The installation package is a ZIP file.

2. Navigate to **Extensions | Install / Uninstall**. Click on **Browse** to locate the ZIP file you just downloaded and click on **Upload File & Install**. Once both are installed you'll see the message: **Install Component Success**.

3. Tell Joomla! that you want JCE to be the default editor. Navigate to **Site | Global Configuration**. On the **Site** tab panel set **Default WYSIWYG Editor** to **Editor - JCE**.

What just happened?

You've just installed the JCE editor. What's the big deal? At first glance, the differences between JCE and the default editor might be inconspicuous—but they will make a big difference in day-to-day article editing! Here are some examples of the benefits:

◆ You can now quickly create text links (hyperlinks to other articles). In Chapter 8 (section *Creating plain text links*) you've seen that you can't do this from the default editor screen. In JCE, you just select some text and click on the hyperlink icon (**Insert / Edit Hyperlink**). JCE now lets you select the target article (or another link destination) from a drop-down list:

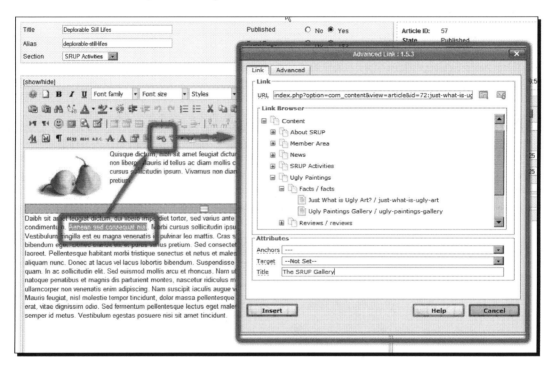

In the **Attributes** section, add a link **Title** (the little pop-up text the visitor sees when hovering the mouse pointer over actual link) and click on **Insert**. That's it.

- ◆ Another improvement you and your colleague content editors will appreciate is the easy way to images with JCE. To add an image to an article, you no longer use the **Image** button below the editor screen. Instead, click on the **Insert / Edit Image** icon to open JCE's own **Image Manager**:

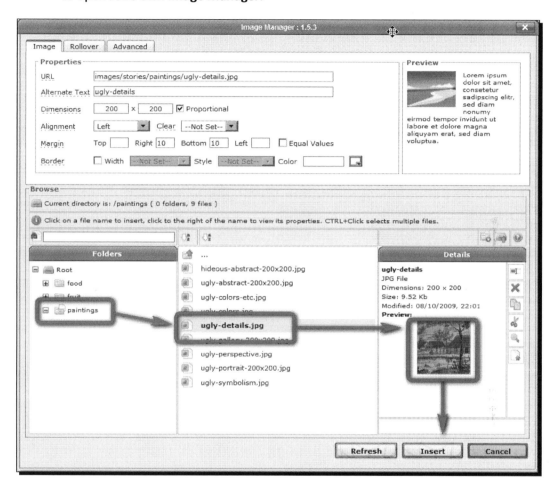

To add an image, click on the desired folder, select the image file, check the preview, and click on **Insert**.

◆ If you need to control the image alignment, that's possible too. For example, set the image **Alignment** to **Left** and the **Margin** at the **Right** and the **Bottom** to **10** pixels to have the text flow nicely around the image:

◆ The Image Manager also makes it possible to directly upload more than one image simultaneously from your hard drive to the web server. You can move, remove, or rename images and preview them full-size.

In short, JCE makes it possible to do more things with text and pictures, and it makes editing much easier.

You can adjust JCE's settings via **Components | JCE Administration | Control Panel**. Among others, JCE has a comprehensive system of Groups that allow you to determine what different users (for example, editors or webmasters) may see and do in JCE. This functionality will come in handy if you want to limit what different types of users can do, for example if you don't want to allow editors to add images to an article.

So much more to explore

With thousands of extensions available, the best way to find the perfect addition to your site is by exploring the Joomla! Extensions Database. To whet your appetite, here's a little taste of the different types of functionality they offer:

AllVideos: Show YouTube (or other) videos inside articles

Plugin Googlemaps: Display Google Maps within articles, modules, or components

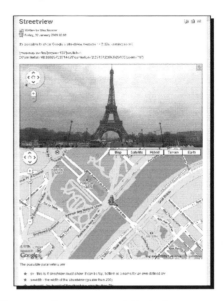

Virtuemart: Integrate an e-commerce shop within a Joomla! site

Kunena: A component that allows you to deploy a community forum on your site

You can find all the above extensions by searching www.extensions.joomla.org for the extension name.

Finding unmissable extensions

Every Joomla! user probably has his own particular favorite extensions—but there sure are some great ones around that almost everybody using Joomla! seems to deploy. A good way to find great extensions is to do a web search for "best Joomla extensions" or "must-have Joomla extensions". You'll get some great tips on cool extensions, both for enhancing the frontend and backend functionality of your site.

Pop quiz – test your knowledge of Joomla! extensions

1. What's the difference between components and other extensions?

    a. Components are more powerful and more complex.

    b. Components are only available to selected users.

    c. Components are shown in different module positions.

2. What's the use of the Newsflash module?

    a. To allow visitors to subscribe to newsfeeds.

    b. To show just one news item in a module position.

    c. To show one or more article intro texts in a module position.

3. What's the use of installing modules?

    a. Modules can make it easier entering new content.

    b. Modules can contain any kind of advanced functionality.

    c. Modules can contain lists of hyperlinks.

Summary

In this chapter, we've covered the magic of Joomla! extensions:

- If you need any functionality that's not built into the basic Joomla! core you'll very likely find it in the Joomla! Extension Directory (JED). The JED lists very many extensions, but there are many more extension portal sites and developer sites.

- There are three types of extensions: components (the big ones), modules (the medium ones), and plugins (the small ones). Components have their separate menu item in the backend of your site; the other extensions are found through the Extensions menu.

- The Joomla! core already contains several components, modules, and plugins. You'll find an overview browsing the Components and Extensions menu of the Joomla! backend.

- ◆ To add a third-party extension to your website, you download it from the Web and install it. When it's installed, you can adjust the extension in the backend and activate it (*enable* it, in Joomla! terms).

- ◆ Some extensions enhance the frontend of your site; they provide cool ways to present content. Others focus on extending the backend capabilities.

Now that you've explored how extensions work and added a few to your site, it's about time to focus on one special extension type: templates! In earlier chapters, you've already made some changes to the default template. However, Joomla!'s template capabilities are much more powerful. In the next chapter, you'll learn how to find and install templates and apply a brand new design to your site.

11

Creating an Attractive Design: Working with Templates

You probably don't want to make websites that all look like "typical" Joomla! sites. That's where templates come to the rescue. Because Joomla! allows you to install another template in a few minutes, giving your site a fresh look and feel is really a breeze. There are thousands of templates available on the Web making it possible to apply any style imaginable to your site. Moreover, you can easily personalize templates to meet your needs. And if you're a web building wizard yourself, you can create your own template from scratch.

Now we'll explore the power of templates further. In this chapter, you'll learn about:

- ◆ Finding and installing a template
- ◆ Customizing a template
- ◆ Downloading and installing templates
- ◆ Customizing templates: tweaking CSS and HTML

This is what templates do

A Joomla! template is a set of files that contain the HTML and CSS code defining what your website will look like. HTML is the code used to build web pages and CSS is the code used to style them. You could say that HTML is the bricks and mortar of your site, whereas CSS provides the wallpaper and paint. Let's see how this works.

Without any CSS applied, your web browser would display a typical Joomla! site as follows:

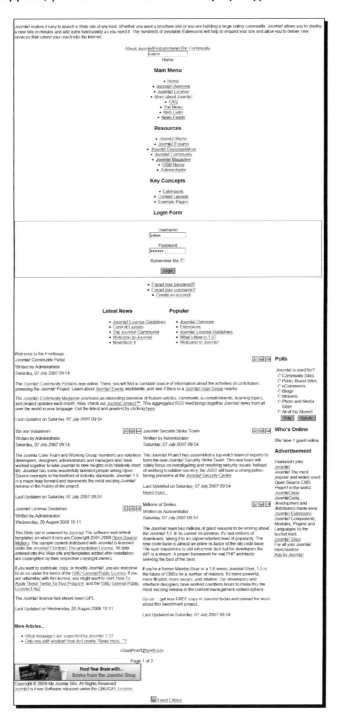

With CSS styles applied, the same content is displayed—but now the overall page layout and design is added:

Actually, a template contains more than pure HTML and CSS. To the basic HTML, it adds some instructions (written in the PHP language) that tell Joomla! what content it should place at which position within the HTML page structure. This way, the template instructs Joomla! exactly where it should put the central content, menus, and other modules.

So that's what a template does. Joomla! as such generates only the basic HTML; the template adds to this instructions on how to layout that page, what content to place at which positions, and what all this content should look like. This powerful mixture of PHP, HTML, and CSS determines just about any part of the design, from the number of columns on the page to the position of elements, the colors, the graphics, or the choice of fonts.

This is why templates are so much fun

Artsy, basic, flashy, grungy, corporate, or clean—whatever your taste in templates may be, you're very likely to find a template that meets your needs. The following is a tiny selection of the free Joomla! templates on offer on the Web—showcasing just a few of the stunning designs possible:

Make sure that the template you download is suited for the current version of Joomla!. There are still many Joomla! 1.0 templates around that won't work in Joomla! 1.5. The previous examples are templates developed for Joomla! 1.5. The details of these examples can be found at: `www.rockettheme.com` (Quasar template), `http://bamboopixel.com` (Pluralism template), `www.pure-joomla.com` (PJEnchanted template), and `www.veero.net` (Paros Villas template).

Where can you find templates?

If you search the Web for "Joomla! template", you'll get a dazzling number of results. It can take hours to find the one template that's just right for your goals. Instead, you might want to start your template search in dedicated Joomla! template gallery sites.

- Good starting places are template sites such as `www.joomla24.com`, `www.osskins.com`, and `www.cmslounge.com`. These sites offer hundreds of templates. Browse the collections and check out live previews of the templates you like.

- Check the collections of professional Joomla! template developers, such as `www.rockettheme.com`, `www.joomlashack.com`, `www.gavick.com`, `www.yootheme.com`, and `www.joomlabamboo.com`.

- ◆ Another great resource is `www.bestofjoomla.com`; it makes finding the right template easier by allowing you to filter your search according to all sorts of criteria (License, Menu Type, Compatibility, Developer, and so on).

Many templates are offered by commercial developers; a number of template clubs allow members to regularly download new templates for a subscription fee. However, you'll also be able to find many quality templates completely free.

Enough tempting template information for now—let's get into action! First, you'll activate one of the Joomla! default templates, after that, you'll download a new one from the Web.

Changing the default template

If you've followed along up to now you've built an example website using Joomla!'s default template. Let's assume your client has some more specific requirements: they have introduced a new visual identity and want their website to reflect this. They've updated their logo and have chosen new corporate colors. It seems it's time for a general overhaul of the site's look and feel, let's establish a new layout and design for the SRUP site.

Time for action – activating a different template

Time for a little experiment! Let's try a different template on for size. Joomla! comes with a few different templates. They're pre-installed; you only have to set them to be the new default template. In this example, we'll choose the JA Purity template:

1. Navigate to **Extensions | Template Manager**.

2. Select the radio button next to **JA Purity**. Click on the **Default** button in the toolbar to set **JA Purity** to be the default template. Click on **Preview** to see the results:

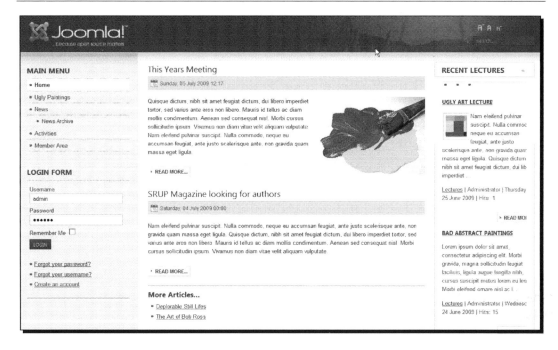

What just happened?

Same content, different design; by setting JA Purity to be the new default template you've given the site a completely new look. The ability to change templates in a few clicks is one of the things that really makes Joomla! stand out. Without needing any coding skills you can completely transform the site's appearance.

Have a go hero – adjust the template settings

The JA Purity template has a many settings (or Parameters, as Joomla! calls them). They allow you to tweak the template's looks and behavior. Navigate to **Extensions | Template Manager** and click on **JA Purity** to open the **Template: [Edit]** screen.

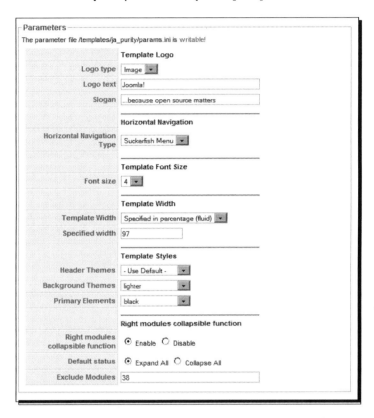

The JA Purity template parameters allow you to change (among others) the menu style, the basic font size, and the template width. In the **Parameters** section you can also enter a different **Logo text** and **Slogan** to display on the site header:

Not every template contains this same set of parameters. Template builders can decide to add parameters—or to leave them out. If you're using another template you'll probably have other (and often less) parameters. This doesn't limit your options though. You can still edit the template properties by looking under the hood and change the CSS or HTML code. We'll look into this later in this chapter.

Downloading and installing a new template

Of course, the templates that ship with Joomla! are just a few examples of the possible designs. Do you need a different layout or do you want a more attractive design? There are tons of templates available on the Web.

Physically, a Joomla! template is a bunch of files. When you download a template, these files are packed together in a compressed format (usually a ZIP file). Joomla! provides you with a powerful one-click-method to upload and unpack the ZIP file, installing all of the required template files on the web server, ready for use.

Time for action – step 1: Downloading and activating a new template

For your site redesign, you've hit upon a great looking template on the Web. Let's download and install it:

1. Navigate to `www.bestofjoomla.com` and enter the Joomla! Templates section. In the Search box, enter **Lightframe**.

2. On the results page, the **Lightframe** template (**tem_lightframe**) is shown. Click on the **Download** button to download the template ZIP file to your computer.

3. Unpack the ZIP file you've downloaded; the template file `tem_lightframe.zip` is itself encased in a larger ZIP file along with some documentation files.

4. Navigate to **Extensions | Install/Uninstall**. Browse to the `tem_lightframe.zip` file. Select it and click on **Upload File & Install**. If all goes well, you'll see a message: **Install Template Success**.

5. To set the new template as the default one for the site, navigate to **Extensions | Template**, select the desired template, and click on the **Default** button (a yellow star) in the toolbar.

Basically, this is all it takes to start using a new template. Click on **Preview** to have a look at the frontend of the website:

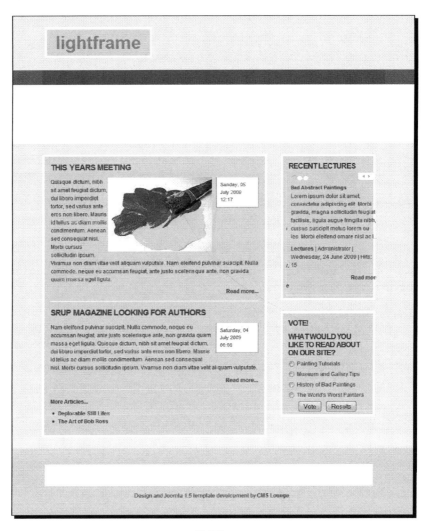

What just happened?

Installing a template works much the same way as installing an extension. Clicking on the **Upload File & Install** button, in fact, automates the process of unpacking the files contained in the template ZIP file and storing them in a subfolder of the `templates` folder, located at the root of a Joomla! site.

You've successfully installed and activated a new template. However, the transformation isn't complete. There are still a few empty spaces in the template: you'll notice that the **Main Menu** doesn't show. Let's fix that.

Time for action – step 2: Getting the Main Menu module to display

The new template doesn't use the exact same module positions as Joomla!'s default templates. In this case, the menu module is still assigned to the **left** position. As the LightFrame template doesn't have a left-hand side column, this position isn't available—which means Joomla! doesn't get any instruction to do anything with the menu module. Let's assign the menu module to the appropriate position. In this particular template, this position is called **mainmenu**:

1. Navigate to **Extensions | Module Manager**. Click on the **Main Menu** module. Change its position to **mainmenu**.

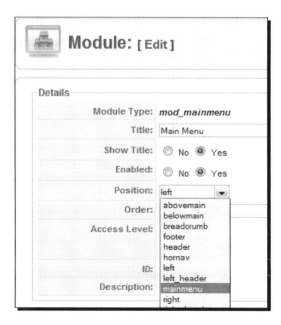

2. The menu will now display in the correct position, but it won't function properly. That's because the template uses a horizontal drop-down menu, requiring some specific menu module settings. Adjust these as follows:

   a. Navigate to **Extensions | Module Manager | Main Menu** and set the **Module Style** parameter to **List**.

   b. Set **Always Show Sub Menu Item** to **Yes.**

   c. In the **Advanced Parameters**, remove any **Module Class Suffix** (the default template uses the **_menu** class suffix; this new template doesn't).

3. Click on **Save** and click on **Preview**. The drop-down menu now displays fine:

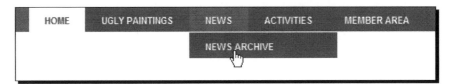

What just happened?

By installing and activating the LightFrame template, you've changed the overall design of the site. The template features a horizontal drop-down menu (controlled by CSS code). To get it to display and function properly, you've tweaked the menu module settings to match the new template properties.

Remember, the menu module Parameters allow you to tweak the presentation of the menu. By setting the parameters you can determine the menu position or its horizontal or vertical orientation. For an overview of the options, see the section *Exploring menu module settings* in Chapter 8 on navigation.

Have a go hero – fill those module positions!

Module positions differ from template to template. This means after you've installed a new template you'll most likely have to check if all existing modules are still visible and if they're assigned to the desired positions. You've just done this for the Main Menu, but there are some more empty spaces in the template indicating module positions without content. To get things right you'll first have to find out the names of the module positions that are available. After that, you can fill these with the desired modules.

Find out which positions are available

How do you know which positions the template designer has made available in a specific template? Many templates come with some sort of documentation; in that case, you're likely to find an overview of module positions there. If not, there's an alternative way: navigate to **Extensions | Template Manager**, select the template, and click on **Edit**. If you now click on the **Preview** button (the button with the magnifying glass, not the **Preview** link just above it), you'll see a special template preview with all positions and their position names displayed in pink letters: header, right, footer, and so on.

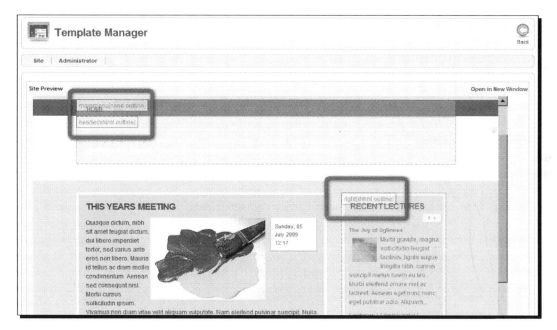

Assign content to empty positions

The overview of menu positions shows a few empty boxes:

1. At the top, below the menu, you'll notice a position called **header**. It's still blank. You can place any module here, such as a newsflash, a banner, or maybe a short message (using the **Custom HTML** module, that you've seen in the section *Creating a custom HTML block* from Chapter 10). In the following screenshot, we've added a short welcome message using a **Custom HTML** module that's assigned to the **header** position:

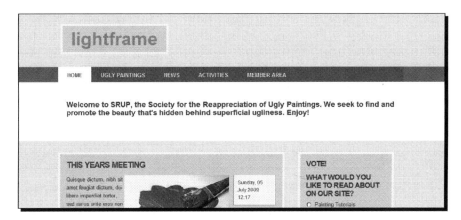

2. If you scroll down, you can see there's another position that's still blank: **User3**. There's no content (no module) assigned to it. That's good because we've still got an orphan module left from our original SRUP site design: the horizontal **About SRUP** menu module. To show this in the **User3** position, navigate to **Extensions | Module Manager | About SRUP** and select **Position: user3**. The menu will now display in the box below the main content:

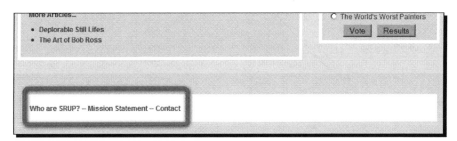

3. If you want the Search box (that was visible in the original template) to appear again, assign it to any of the available template positions. For example, to show it in the right-hand side column, navigate to **Extensions | Module Manager | Search** and select **Position: right**.

Customizing a template: Tweaking CSS styles

Many Joomla! users are perfectly happy using templates out of the box. However, often a template needs just a few tweaks to make it fit your needs.

In the beginning of this chapter you learned that Cascading Style Sheets (CSS) take care of your website's look and feel. If you want to change way the site looks, you'll edit the styles in its CSS file (or CSS files, as the template designer may have chosen to split the necessary code in different stylesheet files).

If you're not familiar with CSS and what it does, have a look at the basic explanation in the following section. After that, we'll see how tweaking CSS code works. Later in this chapter you'll find some useful resources explaining CSS in more detail (see *Expanding your CSS knowledge*).

Understanding the very basics of CSS

Before we try this out on our example site and customize the template we've just installed, let's have a look at the basics of CSS coding. In Joomla!, HTML and CSS codes are contained in separate documents. This way, several web pages (HTML documents) can be linked to the same CSS stylesheet. That's a huge advantage in terms of customizability. By updating a few lines in just one stylesheet you change the looks of several pages (without having to touch the underlying HTML).

Joomla! provides a simple text editor to open up the CSS file (or files) the template uses and to modify the code. This is great for making some quick changes to the template. Don't worry if you're new to this because basic CSS code isn't difficult to understand. Typically, the rules in a CSS stylesheet look like this:

```
h1 {
color: red;
font-weight: bold;
}
```

This rule applies to the h1 element (a top level heading) in the HTML document. It tells your browser to style this heading by setting the text color to red and the font-weight to bold. CSS rules always are enclosed in curly braces. The lines that are part of a CSS rule ("declarations" such as color:red;) are always separated by semicolons.

If you want to change the background color of all `h1` headings to blue, you adjust the `h1` style rule in the CSS file and replace the original value (that is, `red`):

```
h1 {
color: blue;
font-weight: bold;
}
```

Here's another example of a CSS style rule:

```
.contentheading {
color: red;
font-weight: bold;
}
```

This style has its own class name, `.contentheading`. In this example, the properties `red` and `bold` will be applied to any element in the HTML page with the `.contentheading` class. Assigning this class name to a heading or paragraph will make the browser render the text red and bold.

That's it—this concludes your five-minute crash course in CSS. If you want to dive deeper into CSS, you'll learn more about some great Web resources on this subject later on. For now, let's go and experiment!

Tweaking template CSS, part one: Changing site colors

There are two changes you'll usually want to make when adapting a template: changing the main colors of the site and replacing the default logo. Let's apply both changes to the template you've just installed.

Time for action – adjusting the template colors

The template you just installed looks clean and fresh, but the logo and colors of the LightFrame template don't match with the new corporate identity of your client. Let's adjust the template colors and get it to look just right:

1. Navigate to **Extensions | Template Manager**. Select **Lightframe** and click on **Edit**.

2. In the next screen, click on **Edit CSS**, select the template `template_css.css` file, and click on **Edit** again. You're taken to the editor of the **Template Manager**:

3. To change the background color of the page find the BODY style definition. Change it as follows. The highlighted code below is changed to a different value; enter whitesmoke as the color name:

```
BODY (
margin: 0;
padding: 0;
text-align: center;
background:whitesmoke;
)
```

4. To change the background color of the main content area to white, find the style definition that starts with .content, #content-inside. Change the background value to white:

```
.content, #content-inside {
padding:14px;
border:5px solid white;
background:white;
}
```

5. To change the background color of the right-hand side column to white, find the style definition that starts with `#right .moduletable`. Change the background color value to `white`:

```
#right .moduletable,
#right .moduletable_text,
#right .moduletable_menu {
border:5px solid white;
background:white;
margin-bottom:2em;
padding:6px;
}
```

6. To change the background color of the big white box below the menu and the footer to grey, find the style definition that starts with `#footerbg`. Change the background value to `grey`:

```
#footerbg {
Background:grey;
padding:2em;
padding-top:1.5em;
}
```

7. To change the background color of the big white box below the menu and the footer to grey, find the style definition that starts with `#whitebar`. Change the background value to `grey`:

```
#whitebar {
background:grey;
height:130px;
height:100px;
margin-bottom:2em;
}
```

8. To see the results, click on **Apply** and then click on **Preview**.

What just happened?

Because all main colors have changed, the site will look very different from the default output of the **Lightframe** template. Tweaking the colors is a quick way to customize the looks of your site:

In CSS you have several options to specify colors; a quick and easy way is using common English names that are available for a limited set of a few hundred colors. For an overview, see `http://www.w3schools.com/HTML/ html_colornames.asp`. Once you get into building websites you'll probably want to use hexadecimal color values (such as `#FFFFFF` for white), that offers *millions* of color values. Hexadecimal (or hex) color values start with a hash symbol and consist of a combination of six letters or numbers. See `http://www.w3schools.com/Html/html_colors.asp`.

Tweaking template CSS, part two: Adding a graphic logo file

The logo in the header of this template consists of formatted text. It retrieves this text from the **Site Name** that you have specified in the Joomla! Global Configuration when setting up the site. Let's replace this with a graphic logo file. In Chapter 4 you have already applied this trick to another template. Basically, it involves uploading an image file and adding the CSS code to point to that file.

Creating an image file

First, prepare an image file in your favorite graphic editor software. Don't worry if you don't have Photoshop or another fancy graphics program; there are some great online solutions available. You may want to try Pixlr, a free editor that you use directly in your web browser. Just go to `www.pixlr.com/editor` and click on **Create a new image**. Create a file with a width of 600 pixels and a height of 120 pixels. Add a background color (we've chosen `#ffa700` as the color value). You can use the Airstrip font (if you installed it on your computer in Chapter 4 it will be available in Pixlr's font list) and add some slogan text:

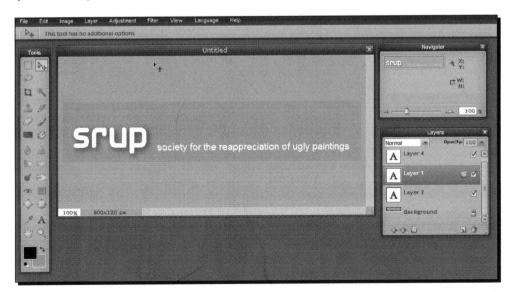

The image file should look similar to the example in the following screenshot:

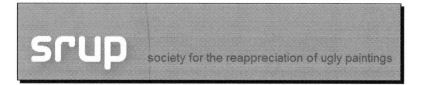

Time for action – replace the header text with an image

1. Let's upload the logo image file and make the template point to this image. In your FTP program, browse to the folder `templates/tem_lightframe` and create a new subfolder called `images`. Upload a logo file with the name `sruplogo.png` to this `images` folder.

2. In the Joomla! backend, change the stylesheet to refer to the new image file. Navigate to **Extensions | Template Manager** and click on **tem_lightframe**. Select the CSS file **template_css.css** and click on **Edit**.

3. In the CSS editor, find the `#logo` style rule. It looks like this:

```
#logo {
width:240px;
height:120px;
float:left;
position:relative;
}
```

4. Change the `width` of `#logo` from `240px` to `760px`; this will make the logo background box cover the full width of the main content area.

5. Add a background using a combination of the logo image and a background color. The style definition should look as follows:

```
#logo {
background: url(../images/sruplogo.png);
background-repeat:no-repeat;
background-color:orange;
width: 760px;
height:120px;
float:left;
position:relative;
}
```

6. Click on **Apply** and click on **Preview** to see the results so far. Okay, this is not really what we had in mind! The text logo displays on top of the new logo image:

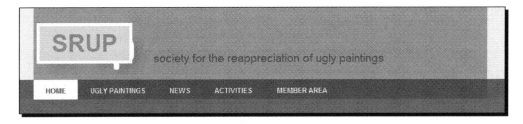

7. To make the text logo disappear, we'll change one last bit of CSS. In the CSS editor, find the style that starts with this code:

```
#logo a:link,
#logo a:visited {
```

Change it by adding the `display: none` declaration. This means the element will not be displayed at all in the browser:

```
#logo a:link,
#logo a:visited {
display:none;
background:#DDECEF;
color:#87AAAe;
text-decoration:none;
font-size:40px;
position:absolute;
padding:20px;
font-weight:bold;
top:25px;
left:5px;
border:5px solid white;
}
```

8. Click on **Save** and click on **Preview**.

society for the reappreciation of ugly paintings

HOME   UGLY PAINTINGS   NEWS   ACTIVITIES   MEMBER AREA

Welcome to SRUP, the Society for the Reappreciation of Ugly Paintings. We seek to find and promote the beauty that's hidden behind superficial ugliness. Enjoy!

THIS YEARS MEETING

Quisque dictum, nibh sit amet feugiat dictum, dui libero imperdiet tortor, sed varius ante eros non libero. Mauris id tellus ac diam mollis condimentum. Aenean sed consequat nisl. Morbi cursus sollicitudin ipsum.

Sunday, 05 July 2009 12:17

Vivamus non diam vitae velit aliquam vulputate. Nam eleifend pulvinar suscipit. Nulla commodo, neque eu accumsan feugiat, ante justo scelerisque ante, non gravida quam massa eget ligula.

Read more...

SRUP MAGAZINE LOOKING FOR AUTHORS

Nam eleifend pulvinar suscipit. Nulla commodo, neque eu accumsan feugiat, ante justo scelerisque ante, non gravida quam massa eget ligula. Quisque dictum, nibh sit amet feugiat dictum, dui libero imperdiet tortor, sed varius ante eros non libero. Mauris id tellus ac diam mollis condimentum. Aenean sed consequat nisl. Morbi cursus sollicitudin ipsum. Vivamus non diam vitae velit aliquam vulputate.

Saturday, 04 July 2009 00:00

Read more...

More Articles...

- Deplorable Still Lifes
- The Art of Bob Ross

RECENT LECTURES

◄ ►

Bad Abstract Paintings
Lorem ipsum dolor sit amet, consectetur adipiscing elit. Morbi gravida, magna sollicitudin feugiat facilisis, ligula augue fringilla nibh, cursus suscipit metus lorem eu leo. Morbi eleifend ornare nisl ac l...

Lectures | Administrator | Wednesday, 24 June 2009 | Hits: 15

Read more

VOTE!

WHAT WOULD YOU LIKE TO READ ABOUT ON OUR SITE?

○ Painting Tutorials
○ Museum and Gallery Tips
○ History of Bad Paintings
○ The World's Worst Painters

Vote   Results

Who are SRUP? – Mission Statement – Contact

What just happened?

Mission accomplished! You've successfully changed the looks of the SRUP site. You've changed the color scheme and made the CSS file point to a new logo image file. To prevent the site name to display on top of the new logo, you've made the original logo text invisible.

When you learn more about CSS you'll find that there are many techniques to achieve certain design goals. The solution we've chosen here to replace a header text by an image is certainly not the only possibility. Do a Web search for "CSS image replacement" to find out more about this technique and some alternative methods.

Have a go hero – tweak the layout to your taste

Feeling confident? Why don't you have a look around in the CSS editor to find out what other changes you can make to enhance the design. Explore the stylesheet to get familiar with the layout elements in the template and the styles assigned to them. Maybe you want to change the width of the main content area (`#content`) and the right-hand side column (`#right`). If you find the big grey block below the header takes up to much space, you can change the height of `#whitebar` to a smaller value to make it a less conspicuous graphical element within the overall page design. Here's an example of the `#whitebar` set to `30px` (30 pixels):

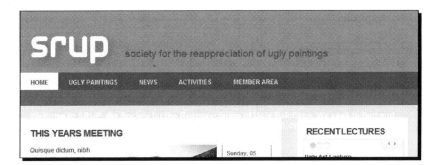

Diving deeper into Joomla! CSS tweaking

In the previous examples, you've changed some CSS styles in the Joomla! editor—but you might be wondering how you find out which particular CSS styles you have to edit in order to get the desired effect. Joomla! uses dozens of different styles and templates, and extensions developers can throw in any number of additional styles. How do you find out, for example, that the main content block is styled through the `#content` style?

In Joomla!, your best chance is to go to the Template Editor and try to figure out what's the appropriate style by analyzing at the CSS stylesheet. But there's a much easier way. It does require you to use the Firefox browser along with a web development plugin called Firebug. Both are open-source software and cost you nothing. If you want to edit the Joomla! template CSS more than once, you should really consider using this nifty set of tools. I'll show you the benefits right now; you can read along without actually using Firefox and Firebug to see if you like this approach and if you find it worthwhile to start using them.

Time for action – editing CSS on the fly using Firebug

Let's say you want to make the text-size of article headings bigger. Now how do you find out the name of the style that you have to edit? We'll check this out the Firebug way:

1. Open the frontend of your Joomla!-powered website in the Firefox browser. Activate Firebug by clicking on the Firebug icon (in the bottom right corner of the browser window). In the bottom half of the browser window, the Firebug screen is displayed, showing both the HTML source and the CSS of the current web page.

2. In the normal browser screen, click on the heading **THIS YEARS MEETING** to see the current HTML and CSS displayed in the Firebug window below. The CSS secret is revealed; this heading is styled by `h2.contentheading`.

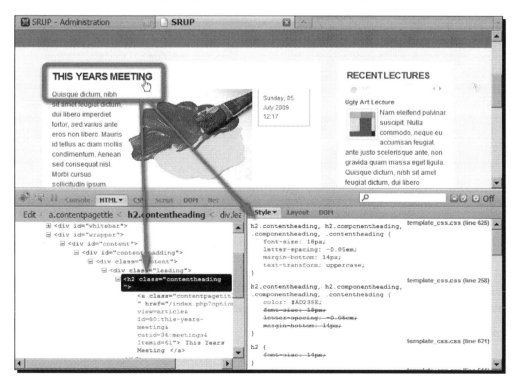

3. In the Firebug Style window, edit `h2.contentheading` by changing `font-size: 18px;` to `font-size: 40px;`. The effects of your edits are immediately shown in the browser window:

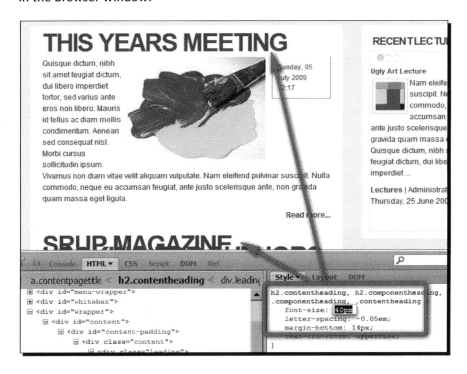

The huge font size is probably not what you're after. Just enter different values until you're pleased with the output you see.

What just happened?

The Firefox extension Firebug enables you to analyze and edit the CSS of any site in your browser. This way, you can edit the CSS and immediately see the effects. Firebug doesn't store your edits; it doesn't have access to your Joomla! template. If you're happy with any changes you've made, you can copy the new code and change the current Joomla! template accordingly in the Joomla! CSS editor.

Expanding your CSS toolkit

If you're convinced Firefox and Firebug are indispensable CSS tools, browse to www.mozilla.org to download and install the Firefox browser. You'll find the Firebug plugin at www.getfirebug.org, along with more elaborate instructions on getting the most out of it.

Firebug is arguably one of the most powerful and popular web development browser add-ons, but there are many more plugins available designed to help you understanding and tweaking CSS code. Examples are CSS viewer for Firefox and Internet Explorer Developer Toolbar for Microsoft Internet Explorer. You may want to do a Web search to pick your favorite set tools.

Expanding your CSS knowledge

Do you want to get deeper into the fine art of creating and editing stylesheets? You'll find plenty of helpful resources on the Web. Just search for "CSS tutorial" or take a look at:

1. The basic tutorial article CSS from the Ground Up: www.wpdfd.com/issues/70/ css_from_the_ground_up.

2. The CSS Tutorial: http://www.csstutorial.net/introductionCSS.php.

3. W3Schools' CSS tutorials, examples and demo's: http://www.w3schools.com/ css/css_intro.asp.

Editing the template HTML

If you want to make some more fundamental changes to a template, Joomla! allows you to edit the HTML. There's an HTML editor available in the Joomla! backend, just like the CSS editor screen. If you want, you can thoroughly change the template code. You can add, change, delete, or move any existing page element—columns, header, and footer, whatever you like. Of course, you should only do this if you know your way around in HTML; don't risk messing up the site layout.

Even if you're not aiming to immerse yourself in the nitty gritty of HTML, being able to change the template HTML directly in Joomla! is still useful. It allows you to change or remove unwanted items that are sometimes "hard coded" (that is, a fixed part of the HTML code) into the template, such as a footer text or copyright notice.

Time for action – removing the fixed footer text

At the bottom of the page there's a hyperlink to the template designers website:

Design and Joomla 1.5 template development by **CMS Lounge**.joomla 1.5 templates

Let's delete it:

1. Navigate to **Extensions | Template Manager**. Select **tem_lightframe** and click on **Edit**.

2. In the next screen, click on the **Edit HTML** button. You're taken to the **HTML editor** screen.

3. In the editor, find this text and delete it:

   ```
   <p> Design and Joomla! 1.5 template development by CMS Lounge
   <a href="http://www.cmslounge.com/"> </ a>. </ p>
   ```

4. Click on **Save** and click on **Preview**; the footer text has disappeared.

What just happened?

Using Joomla!'s HTML editor screen, you can change the template HTML. In this case you've removed the copyright notice. Some template developers kindly ask you to display a link to their site in exchange for their free template. In that case, you shouldn't remove this text.

Backing up and restoring a customized template

Editing a template directly in Joomla! is a great way to tweak the layout as you go. You're able to apply changes in the backend and immediately preview the effects of every adjustment you've made. However, there is a drawback: all changes in the template files are only stored on the web server. If for some reason you were to re-install the template, these changes would be lost.

To prevent this from happening, backup the template as soon as you've finished customizing it. This is how:

1. Start up your FTP program and browse to the folder that contains the template you want to backup. In case of the **tem_lightframe** template, this would be something like `/httpdocs/templates/tem_lightframe`. The rhuk_milkyway template is in the `/httpdocs/templates/rhuk_milkyway` folder (in both cases `httpdocs` is the root folder of the Joomla! installation on the web server; in your situation the root folder might have another name, such as www or `htdocs`). The set of template files and folders will look as follows:

2. Download the template folder (including subfolders and their contents) to your computer.

This folder contains all template files. If you want to re-install the template later, just upload this folder to the same location on the web server again: the `templates` folder in the root directory of the Joomla! installation.

A different approach: customizing a template offline

In this chapter, you've customized a template by editing the template files in the Joomla! template editor screen. Another option would be to download the template files first, open them for editing in the web editing program of your flavor, and uploading them again after you've finished customization. This can be a good idea if you know your way around in (and like working with) web editing tools such as Notepad++ or Adobe Dreamweaver. The *Template building resources* mentioned in the next section should help you on your way if you like to explore this method.

Creating your own template

Using an existing template (and customizing it) will help you getting great results while saving lots of time, compared to creating your own template from scratch. However, if you want full control or need a unique layout you can make a Joomla! template all by yourself. It isn't really complicated, but it does require a good deal of HTML and CSS coding skills. If you know how to build a website without Joomla!, using HTML and CSS, then you won't experience any problems converting your design into a Joomla! template. Most of your time and effort will go into creating a page design from scratch rather than into the adjustments needed to adapt that design for Joomla!

As it is mainly a question of HTML and CSS coding, we won't cover template creation in full detail here. To get you started, here are a few pointers. These are the five main steps it takes to create your own template:

1. **Sketching:** Design an overall layout for your website (yes, you may use old school offline media, such as pencil and paper). Where do you want the main content, the navigation, and the other page elements? Think blocks, just like Joomla! does. Divide the page into blocks containing menus, articles, and images. The result is a schematic representation of the page.

2. **Designing:** Create a layout in a graphic editor, such as Photoshop or the GIMP. The result is a mockup of the site design. You'll only use bits and pieces of that image in the final template, such as the logo image or some image parts containing shadow effects.

3. **Coding:** Turn your design into real web page code using HMTL and CSS. You can use a web development tool such as Dreamweaver that allows you to immediately see the results of your coding.

4. **Customizing the code for Joomla!:** Adapt the CSS and HTML code to create Joomla! template files. In the main template file you'll insert codes telling Joomla! where it should place its dynamic content (such as modules).

5. **Putting your template together:** Any template consists of a set of required files, such as a file containing information about the template (author name, copyright, and so on). Finally, you'll include all of these files in a compressed file (a ZIP file). Now your template is ready to be uploaded and installed it via **Extensions | Install & Uninstall**.

Template building resources

There are many tutorials on the Web that can help you on your way when you want to create Joomla! templates. A Web search for "Joomla! template tutorial" will surely help you on your way:

1. An easy beginners tutorial: `http://net.tutsplus.com/tutorials/other/creating-your-first-joomla-template`.

2. An excellent step by step article series is `www.compassdesigns.net/tutorials/208-Joomla!-15-template-tutorial.html`.

3. Links to tools for creating Joomla! templates using Adobe Dreamweaver: `www.justdreamweaver.com/dreamweaver-joomla-tools.html`.

4. If you are looking for inspiration, make sure to browse the Joomla! community showcase (`http://community.joomla.org/showcase`).

Pop quiz – test your knowledge of Joomla! templates

1. What does a Joomla! template actually do?

    a. It changes the colors and the header graphic.

    b. It determines the overall layout and design.

    c. It allows you to set all sorts of Parameters.

2. After installing a new template, you notice some empty boxes in your site layout. What does this mean?

    a. Something went wrong and you should re-install the template.

    b. You have to assign modules to the available (empty) positions.

    c. You have to add content to some (empty) modules.

3. What's the use of adding Firebug to you Joomla! toolkit?

    a. You can preview CSS edits and automatically save changes to your template.

    b. You can edit CSS in the backend of your Joomla! site.

    c. You can analyze and edit CSS styles of any website, and you can preview the effects of any changes you make.

Summary

In this chapter, you've learned much about the power of Joomla! templates:

◆ A Joomla! template is a set of files containing the HTML and CSS code that defines what your web page looks like. Joomla! comes with a few different templates. They're pre-installed; you only have to set them to be the new default template.

◆ Some templates have built-in Parameters that allow you to tweak the look and behavior in the Template Manager.

◆ If you want another layout, there are tons of templates you can download from the Web, and a good many of them are available for free.

◆ After you've installed a new template, check if all existing modules are still visible and if they're assigned to the desired positions. If not, you can find out the names of the available module positions through the Template Manager's Preview function and assign the appropriate modules to these positions.

◆ Customizing an existing template is a great way to personalize the look and feel of the website. Joomla!'s Template Manager allows you to change the CSS styles the template uses—for example, when you want to change the color scheme or replace the default logo image.

◆ The Firefox extension Firebug enables you to analyze and edit the CSS of any site in your browser. This allows you to do something you can't do in Joomla! itself: edit CSS code and immediately see the effects.

◆ If you want to make some more fundamental changes to a template, you can also edit the template HTML code in the Template Manager.

As far as content, functionality, and looks are concerned, your site is about finished; but there are still a few important things to take care of. In the next chapter, you'll learn what measures you can take to attract visitors and get search engines to pick up your site.

12
Attracting Search Engine Traffic: Tips and Techniques

*You've created a great site—now it's time to get the world to discover that it's there! Up to now, your attention has gone towards the site's content, navigation, and its extra features and its design. In this chapter, let's see what you can do to attract more visitors (or site traffic, as it's usually called). You'll deploy some essential techniques and basic settings in Joomla! that can influence your search engine rankings. This is called **Search Engine Optimization** (or **SEO**) and it's a really hot topic among website builders.*

The first and foremost SEO rule is to make sure you offer great content. If you don't have a site that's regularly updated with quality content, people won't bother to visit (and certainly won't bother to come back). Only if your site offers relevant content is it worth optimizing that content for best search engine results. In this chapter, you'll find out how you can tweak your site to make its content really easy to find—both for human beings and for search engines.

In this chapter, you'll learn about:

- ◆ Optimizing articles
- ◆ Adding metadata to your content
- ◆ Using search engine friendly (SEF) URLs
- ◆ Creating internal hyperlinks
- ◆ Making it easy to find your content using RSS and site maps

SEO is a subject surrounded with many secrets and myths—and with gurus claiming they have the definite answer to all questions. As search engines obviously won't reveal the secret algorithms they use to calculate their search results rankings, these definite answers do not exist. There's no SEO technique or mix of SEO techniques that will bring you overnight success. However, there are some common sense techniques you can apply in your Joomla!-powered site to optimize your visibility for search engines and to get them to pick up your content.

Why do you need to accommodate for search engines?

Search engines are probably the main tool people will use to get to your site. To add your site to their database, search engines use software to scan the World Wide Web looking for relevant content. Of course, search engines can't *see* your site. They'll analyze the source code text of the site (shown on the left-hand side in the following screenshot) and try to understand what your site is about, and what data in it could be important to search engine users:

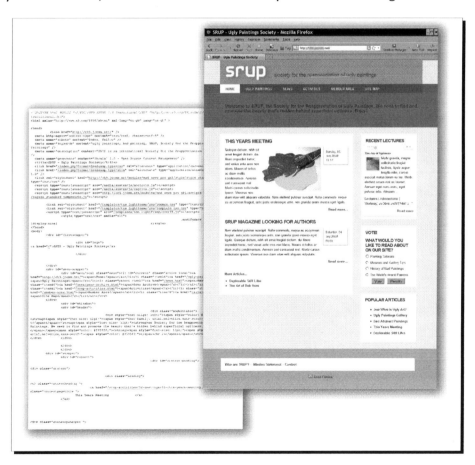

That's why it's so important to accommodate for search engines and to make your site contents search engine friendly—that is, easy to find and understand. All SEO techniques really boil down to increasing the visibility of your content to the search engines. How can you make it as easy as possible for search engine robots to interpret your web pages' source code and to find, understand, and index your content? We'll explore a few different techniques, starting with the stuff it's all about: articles.

Optimize your articles

When writing or editing articles in Joomla!'s article editor, what can you do to optimize your content for search engine visibility? Let's start with some simple good practices that you, or your fellow content creators, can deploy when writing and formatting articles.

1. The article title: Make it meaningful

The first thing to think about carefully is the article **Title**, the very first piece of data you enter in the article editor:

Article titles are important data. In Joomla!, the title entered in the article **Title** field will be displayed on two key positions. It's of course shown above the article itself:

And the title is also displayed in the browser title bar:

This means an article title is important to search engines. It's a good idea to use strong, meaningful, descriptive, and specific titles. Don't use a similar title for different articles. Make sure you know what people are looking for on your site; if possible, use relevant keywords in your article titles. If you're aiming at amateur painters, it's good to have clear titles carrying keywords that appeal to your readers such as *Ten tips to create better paintings, How to Paint like the Pros,* or *Painting techniques tutorial*.

Being as specific as you can means it's better to have a title such as *Ugly Paintings Society Annual Meeting* than just some general title such as *This Year's Meeting*. In the example site, we've used a few randomly picked titles. You'll notice there's room for improvement there. A title such as *The Art of Bob Ross* doesn't make it clear that the article is about a *lecture* on this subject. Something more specific would be: *Art Lecture on Bob Ross Paintings*.

Although it's good to be specific, you should also aim to keep things short. Bear in mind the page title will usually be shown as the first line in the site description on the search engine's results page (and might be truncated). Google, for example, will only display the first 66 characters.

2. The article structure: Use clear formatting

Search engines expect your HTML documents are formatted according to a few simple rules, clearly defining the structure of the page. This means you shouldn't have headings that are just plain text styled as bold type, for example—your visitors might recognize those lines as headings, but search engines won't. Search engines scan HTML documents for headings that follow a hierarchal structure. The main page heading should be formatted with a `Heading 1` (or `H1`) style, the secondary level headings should have a `Heading 2` (`H2`) style, and so on. Make sure every heading marks the beginning of a new section.

In Joomla!'s article editor, you apply **Heading 1** through **Heading 6** using the article editor **Format** drop-down box:

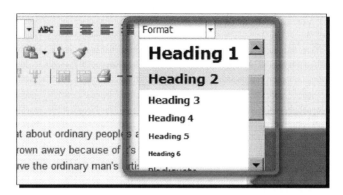

Search engines give headings more weight than regular article text, which means you can emphasize keywords by using them in your page headings. Instead of generic headings ("Lesson Two" or "Improve your art skills") use specific heading texts ("How to Paint Great Landscapes").

As it's the main heading of the page, the title of your article should be styled using the H1 tag. However, Joomla! doesn't allow this as the text in the article **Title** field will automatically get a CSS style called `contentheading`. If you want to comply with the search, there are templates available that override Joomla!'s default styles to comply with search engine friendly page structuring standards. They use so-called template overrides. For more resources on this do a Web search for "Joomla! search engine friendly template".

3. The article body text: Use relevant keywords

It's a good idea to use relevant keywords in your article body text. When writing or editing your text, ask yourself what words your visitors would use when searching for the content you offer? Try to anticipate on the different search terms, synonyms, and abbreviations that different types of visitors would use.

If you're stuck for keyword inspiration, you should definitely consider using one of the many online tools available. The *Google Adwords Keyword Tool* is an excellent example; you'll find it at `https://adwords.google.com/select/KeywordToolExternal`. The screenshot below shows how it works. Just enter any keyword and you'll be presented with a range of related or additional keywords:

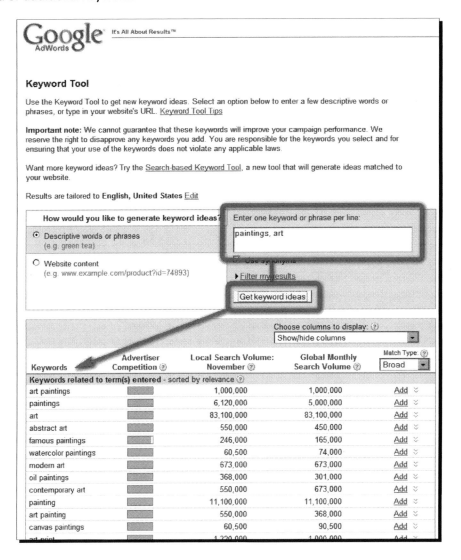

In Joomla!, you can enter relevant keywords in the article body copy. Make sure you use keywords and synonyms throughout the article, but don't stuff your article with keywords just to get search engines to pick up your article—their robots won't be amused.

You'll work with the same set of keywords in the article *metadata* too. We'll get to these in the section *Add meaningful metadata*.

4. The images: Explain what they're about

Search engines scan and analyze text, but they can't interpret images. To search engine spiders, an image is just a meaningless data file. This means you can help search engines by using distinct filenames for any image you use. Moreover, when inserting an image in the Joomla! article editor, add a specific **Alternate Text**. Here's what the **Alternate Text** box looks like on the Joomla! Content Editor Image Editor screen (see also Chapter 10 to read more about this editor):

This **Alternate Text** (or "alt" text) is the short description that shows when the image itself isn't displayed for some reason. You might also want to add a similar description to the **Title** field (under the **Advanced** tab). This title text pops up when the visitor's mouse pointer hovers over the image:

Update articles regularly

Try to regularly add quality content to your site. Adding a few pages every week will make both your visitors and search engines happy. Search engine spiders visit your site regularly; aim to have some new content added when they come around. This doesn't mean that the bigger the site is, the better your search results will be; it's good practice to delete or archive outdated content.

More on SEO-aware writing

Of course, creating great content isn't a Joomla!-specific art. If you want to read more on SEO-aware writing, there are many resources on the Web.

To get a clear overview of the basics, download Google's Search Engine Optimization Starter Guide from www.google.com.

Sites such as Copyblogger.com (try searching this site for "SEO Copywriting") offer a number of tips on writing effective copy for the Web.

Add meaningful metadata

Up to now, we've focused on actual content. You've seen how you can optimize articles to present their content in a clear and well-structured way. However, web pages also contain information that's not shown to site visitors, but is aimed specially at search engine robots: metadata.

Metadata is information about the contents of the HTML document hidden in the documents source code. Browsers (and search engines) will read it; humans won't know it's there (unless they specifically look for it by selecting the **View Source** option in their web browser).

By default, your Joomla!-powered site will only contain some dummy metadata, consisting of a short description and a few Joomla!-related content keywords. Let's change these to something more appropriate.

Time for action – personalize the site metadata

You'll find the controls for optimizing your site for search engine traffic in the backend Configuration Panel. First, let's add some global keywords that characterize the site's content:

1. Navigate to **Site | Global Configuration**. On the **Site** tab, there's a section called **Metadata Settings**.

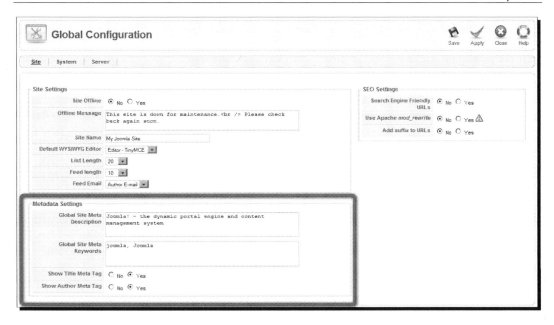

2. Change the **Global Site Metadata Description** default text to a short summary of the content of your website. In our example, we'll enter **SRUP is the international Society For the Reappreciation of Ugly Paintings**.

3. In the **Global Site Meta Keyword** text box enter a few keywords that match the content of your website. Make sure to use the words and synonyms the visitor might use to search for your site's contents. You'll probably use a few words that are also part of the site description. In our example, we'll enter these keywords: **ugly paintings, bad painting, bad art, SRUP, Society For the Reappreciation of Ugly Paintings**. The **Metadata Settings** should now look similar to the following screenshot:

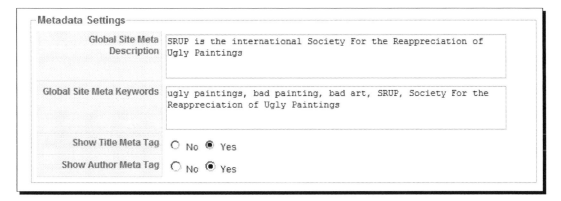

4. Leave **Show Title Meta Tag** and **Show Author Meta Tag** set to **Yes**. This way, Joomla! will not only add global (site-wide) meta keywords to the pages, but it will also include the metadata keywords from the individual pages. You can add this Article Metadata for each individual article in the article editor; we'll see how this works later in this chapter.

5. Click on **Save** and click on **Preview**.

What just happened?

By entering metadata for your site you've added some global keywords and descriptive text to your site. This information will be included in every page of your Joomla!-powered site. Metadata will remain invisible to your visitors, but search engine spiders use this information when crawling your site. Although it seems search engines don't give much weight to meta keywords any more when indexing sites the site description is still very important (and will show up when your site appears on a search results page).

However, don't expect overnight success. You won't instantly see the effect of your metadata changes in search results, but in due time search engines should pick it up and use it to analyze your site's contents. They'll display the site description metadata in the search results. If you need to convince yourself, just google for the default description text in the Joomla! demo site (**Joomla! - the dynamic portal engine and content management system**). You'll get a huge list of results, all links to Joomla!-powered websites that haven't yet personalized their global site description:

Joomla 1.5.xx Recly Demo Site - [Vertaal deze pagina]
Joomla! - the dynamic portal engine and content management system. ... Joomla! - the
dynamic portal engine and content management system ... JWeather. ...
www.recly.com/demo/joomla2/.../jweather - In cache - Vergelijkbaar - 💬 🔼 ⊠

Sites near ajax high school. Joomla - the dynamic portal engine ... - [Vertaal de
Joomla - the dynamic portal engine and content management system SEMESTER II
Classes for second semester resume Thursday January 29 at 8:55am. ...
geourl.org/near?p=www.freewebtown.com/... - In cache - Vergelijkbaar - 💬 🔼 ⊠

Joomla! - the dynamic portal engine and content management system ...
Joomla! - the dynamic portal engine and content management system.
www.humsurfer.com/joomla-the-dynamic-portal-engine-and-content-management-system
- In cache - Vergelijkbaar - 💬 🔼 ⊠

Have a go hero – find metadata to fit your site

All that Ugly Painting business is okay for the example site, but what kind of metadata description and keywords would fit your particular site best? First, do a little research and use the Google keyword tool mentioned before (or a similar tool) to get a few keyword ideas. Another great way to get going is to have a look at how others do it—what kind of keywords and descriptions do similar sites use? Of course you won't copy that text (as that will be of little use in making your site a unique source of information), but it may inspire you.

Here's how you can explore metadata; point your browser to a site you'd like to explore and select the option to look under the hood of the current website—it's probably called something like **View Page Source**. A new browser window or tab will open showing the HTML source code of the current page. You'll find the meta tags in the `<head>` section of the document. The `description` tag looks like this:

```
<meta name="description" content= "A few lines explaining what the
site is about">.
```

The `keywords` tag looks like this:

```
<meta name="keywords" content= "first keyword, second keyword, and
so on">
```

Exploring a few examples of websites offering the same type of content will get you going—and make it easier to decide whether you want to do things just as they do, or differently.

Entering metadata for individual articles

You've set the metadata for the website in the **Global Configuration** screen. This is great to help search engines to understand what your site is about. However, it's a good idea to add keywords to individual articles as well as this will help search engines analyze and rank individual pages on your site.

Time for action – add metadata information for an article

To see how it's done, let's open an existing article in the article editor and enter some metadata:

1. Navigate to **Content | Article Manager** and select any article. Click on **Edit**. In the following example, we've opened the **SRUP Welcomes New Members** article.

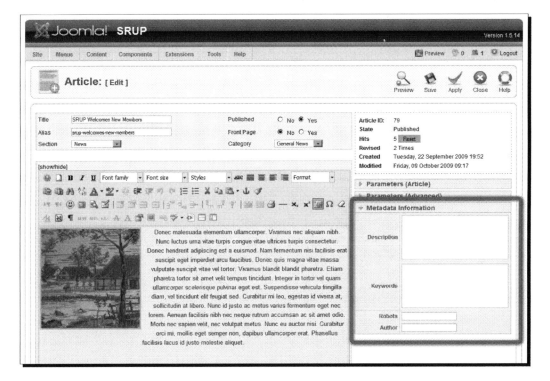

2. Below **Parameters (Article)** and **Parameters (Advanced)**, you'll find a panel called **Metadata Information**. Click on the name (**Metadata Information**) to open this panel and enter the appropriate information.

3. In the **Description** box, fill in a short one-sentence summary of the articles content. In this example, we've entered **Feel free to join SRUP, the Society for Ugly Paintings enthusiasts**.

4. In the **Keywords** box, add a few content keywords. In this example, we'll enter **SRUP Membership**, **Ugly Paintings Membership**, **Member**, and **Join SRUP**.

5. Click on **Save**. No need to **Preview**—metadata is invisible on the frontend of the site, remember?

What just happened?

You've set the metadata for the website and added some keywords for an individual article. You'll usually enter keywords and a description for each individual article as you write the article, but it's of course also possible to edit a bunch of articles afterwards. It's good to have a description for every page. Although there's some discussion whether search engines will attribute much value to keywords, they do add to the meaningful content of your web page.

 In this example, we've left the **Robots** and **Author** text boxes of the article metadata section blank. In the **Robots** box, you can enter optional instructions for robots (the programs that search engines use to crawl your site). You can tell them not to index this page or not to follow the links from this page. In the **Author** text box you can enter an article author name to be added to the page metadata. Normally, this won't be of any importance for your search engine visibility.

Have a go hero – explore the art and science of metadata

Joomla!'s metadata capabilities are fine, but if you really want full control and tweak your pages for optimal search engine visibility, there's a must-have metadata extension. It's called the Joomlatwork SEO patch for Joomla!. The patch provides you with additional fields, both in the global configuration and in the article editor, allowing you to customize the page title, the page metadata, and more. Go to www.joomlatwork.com to read more about the SEO patches capabilities and to download it.

Don't forget to choose the perfect site name

One of the first things you do when you set up a new site is entering a name for it. You'll be prompted to enter a name when installing Joomla!; after that, you can change this text in the Global Configuration screen. It's a good idea to think very carefully about the Site Name as this will appear in the browser title bar of the home page.

In the case of the example site, it's better to have some meaningful words here rather than just the mysterious abbreviation SRUP. You can change the site name as follows:

- ◆ Navigate to **Site | Global Configuration**.

- ◆ In the **Site Settings** section, enter an appropriate name in the Site Name box. In this example, we've entered **SRUP – Ugly Paintings Society**. This is descriptive and not too long; it won't take up the full browser title bar.

- ◆ Click on **Save** and click on **Preview**. The new name is displayed in the browser title bar:

> SRUP - Ugly Paintings Society - Mozilla Firefox

Coming up with a good domain name

The name of your site should of course be reflected in the domain name. Your domain name may be shorter, it may be an abbreviation, but it should be associated with the name you carry on the site itself. If you haven't already chosen a domain name, how can you come up with a domain name that's short, easy, and memorable? Unless you've got a very strong brand that visitors know and recognize, you might want to use a descriptive domain name, telling people right up front what product or service you're offering. If you're selling *bicycles* or providing *financial advice*, it's good to combine these with your business name to create a web domain name like *petersbicycles.com* or *petersfinancialadvice.com*.

To help you find a nice domain name (that isn't taken yet!), you can use many resources on the Web. On `http://justdropped.com`, you'll find expired domain names that are available again. On `http://domainsbot.com` it's easy to type several possible domain names to quickly find out if they're available. If you're really stuck, do a Web search to find a "domain name generator" helping you on your way.

Use search engine friendly URLS

Up to now, we've focused on SEO techniques you can deploy when writing content for your website. You can apply SEO techniques by presenting and formatting articles to make their contents easily findable, or by adding clear metadata to your site and its contents. Another technique that can make search engines pick up the contents of your site more easily is to make your URLs clear and readable. After all, you've probably noticed Joomla!'s default URLs contain a good deal of incomprehensible gibberish:

```
http://www.srup.net/index.php?option=com_
content&view=article&id=82:ugly-paintings-gallery&catid=39:facts&Item
id=54
```

Actually, this is not gibberish, but still human beings as well as search engines will have a hard time figuring out what all the codes, special characters, and numbers are about. That's why you'll probably want to use search engine friendly (and human friendly) URLs. This technique results in readable URLs that match the content of the page, such as the following example:

```
http://www.srup.net/ugly-paintings.html
```

Joomla! has search engine friendly URL functionality built-in, but it's turned off by default.

Time for action – enable search engine friendly URLs

Let's switch on Joomla!'s friendly URL functionality:

1. Navigate to **Site | Global Configuration**. In the **Site** tab, there's a **SEO Settings** section. Set **Search Engine Friendly URLs** to **Yes**:

2. Click on **Apply** and preview the frontend of the website. In the browser, URLs will now look something like this:

This is much better as these URLs are shorter and easier to understand. However, as you browse your site, you'll see that all URLs share the `index.php` bit. You can change this using the other SEO Settings. This requires a bit more work than just selecting **Yes**; you'll also have to rename a file on the web server. Feeling confident? Let's try it out.

If you've installed Joomla! locally you may experience some difficulties with the next step that requires renaming a file to `.htaccess` (with a leading dot). By default, Mac OS Finder and Microsoft Windows Explorer don't allow you to rename filenames starting with a dot. There are several workarounds, but it's easiest to just rename the file using your FTP program. This does allow you to use a leading dot in the names of both local files (on your computer) and remote files (on the web server).

Another point to note is that not all hosting providers allow you to use `.htaccess` files. If you're not sure whether your account supports using `.htaccess`, check with your hosting provider.

3.   Navigate to **Site | Global Configuration**. In the **Site | SEO Settings** section, make sure all three of the options are set to **Yes**:

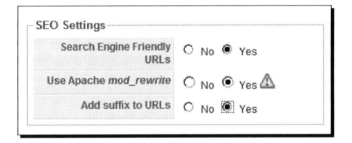

4.   The **Use Apache mod_rewrite** option may sound like technical mumbo jumbo, but it's a critical setting, allowing further customization of URLs. For this to work, you'll have to rename the `htaccess.txt` file that's installed with Joomla!. Using your FTP program, go to the root of your Joomla! site on the web server. Locate the `htaccess.txt` file:

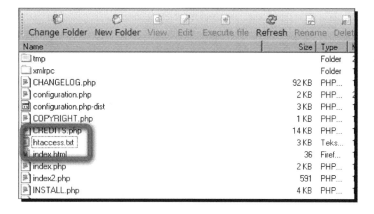

5. Rename `htaccess.txt` to `.htaccess`—yes, this file name should start with a dot and should not have a file extension (such as `.txt`)!

6. Click on **Save** and click on **Preview**. Browse your site and you should now experience the magic. Your URLs are short and descriptive, like this:

   `http://www.srup.net/ugly-paintings.html`

What just happened?

You've just fooled search engines into believing you're using good old HTML web pages. Joomla! now displays URLs that seem to point to pages, such as `http://www.srup.net/ugly-paintings.html`. Using SEF URLs will make it easier for visitors and search engines to understand the contents of the page this URL is pointing to.

As you've seen, Joomla!'s pretty URLs come in three flavors:

◆ By setting **Search Engine Friendly URLs** to **Yes**, you'll get short and readable URLs, but they do all contain the `index.php` filename.

◆ By setting **Use Apache mod_rewrite** to **Yes**, you'll tell Joomla! to make the URLs even prettier. They no longer contain `index.php`. Your hosting provider has to support this feature (called `mod_rewrite`); they should have the `mod_rewrite` module installed on the web server. This technique involves using an `.htaccess` file containing rules telling the web server how to deal with these pretty URLs.

◆ By setting **Add suffix to URLs**, the **html** suffix is added to **URLs**. This is recommended because this makes the Joomla! output look like pages in static sites. Search engines tend to prefer static pages to dynamic output, which is likely to change all the time.

What if it doesn't work?

And what if the pretty URLs function doesn't work? First check if you've renamed `htaccess.txt` properly to `.htaccess` (mind the leading dot!). If you still get error messages when checking out the frontend of the site, it's possible your web server doesn't support the advanced requirements of the second option (using `mod_rewrite`). In this case, you should try if setting *only* the **SEO Settings** option **Search Engine Friendly URLs** to **Yes** does the trick.

Have a go hero – make your URLs even prettier

Many Joomla! users are perfectly happy using the built-in SEF system. However, you'll notice that the URLs can still contain some numbers (these are Joomla!'s internal references to specific database content):

```
http://www.srup.net/ugly-paintings/39-facts/82-ugly-paintings-
gallery.html
```

If you want even prettier URLs, consider using a dedicated SEF Component for Joomla!. These usually give you more control, allowing you to modify individual URLs or shorten URLs by hiding the section or category part. There are some fine SEF components available in the Joomla! Extensions Directory; check out the details and user comments to find out which one fits your needs. All the big ones work great. It's just a question of installing the component, checking the basic settings, and enjoying the output.

Why don't you check out one of the available SEF components for your own site? Go to `www.joomace.net/free-downloads` to download the `com_acesef.zip` file. After installing, you'll find an **AceSEF** section in the **Components** menu giving access to a special Control Panel:

Enabling AceSEF is just a question of clicking the **Configuration** icon and selecting **Enable AceSEF: Yes**. After you've committed your choice (click on **Save**), you're all set. Check the frontend of your site to see the pretty URLs magic at work. Explore the various AceSEF menus and the User Manual to tweak your site links to your heart's content.

SEF comes at a cost

At the time of writing there are no free, no-strings-attached SEF components for Joomla!. Some components (such as AceSEF) are free, but they will display a link to the website of the developer on every page of your site. If you don't want this, you'll have to buy the extension—or just use the default Joomla! SEF.

Add extra links to your content

Search engines rate your site higher if it's an active part of the World Wide Web community. That means it's good to create links to other sites (outbound links) that offer relevant quality content on related subject matter.

Of course, it's great if other quality sites contain links to your site. One way to get the world to notice your site is to notify Google, Yahoo!, and others that they're welcome to come and index your content; all search engines have a service that allows you to submit your site. Another way to get others to link to your site is by submitting your site to several useful directories. Other sites or blogs might want to link to your site if you offer good and relevant content. You might also consider writing articles for related sites, providing these allow you to link back to your site. Not only will this help you build your reputation on the subject, it should also generate some valuable inbound links.

However, not only links to and from your site can influence your ranking. It's also worth adding *internal* links (that is links within your site). By adding these, you'll make it easier for both visitors and search engines to find your content. You can manually create links in your articles, but Joomla! also allows you to automatically create internal hyperlinks. It allows you to set all article titles to be hyperlinks to the main article text and it enables you to dynamically create lists of hyperlinks.

Time for action – turn article titles into hyperlinks

By default, the titles of articles displayed with intro texts (on the home page, or on overview pages) are plain text. The visitor can only go through to the full articles by clicking the accompanying **Read more...** link. From a SEO point of view, it's better to turn the article titles into hyperlinks to the full articles. Let's turn this feature on:

1. To change the title setting for all articles that you want to write from now on, navigate to **Content | Article Manager** and click on **Parameters** to open the general settings screen for articles. Set **Title Linkable:** to **Yes** as shown in the following screenshot:

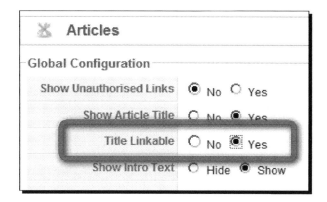

2. This setting won't change any article that has already been stored in Joomla!'s database. To change the setting for an individual (existing) article, navigate to **Content | Article Manager** and select the article you want to edit.

3. In the article editor change the **Title Linkable** setting in the **Parameters (Advanced)** to **Yes**:

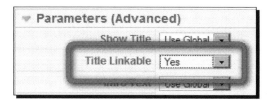

What just happened?

The site visitor now can click on the article title instead of just the **Read more...** link to go to the full article. Here's an example of this on the example website. After you've changed the **Title Linkable** setting, article headings are clickable:

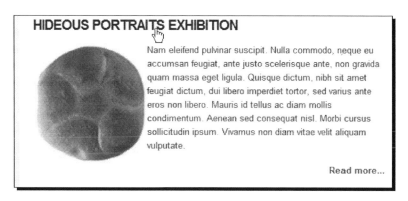

This is good from a usability point of view as visitors will expect titles to be hyperlinks, but it's also good SEO practice. Search engines understand meaningful hyperlinks better and rate these higher than generic **Read more...** links.

Creating an automatically generated list of hyperlinks

Another way to easily create internal hyperlinks in Joomla! is by adding link lists. Joomla! contains a few modules allowing you to add different hyperlink lists, for example a list of links to the most popular articles on the site or to the articles that have been added most recently.

Time for action – add a list of links to popular articles

Let's add a list of links to popular articles on the example site:

1. Navigate to **Extensions | Module Manager**. Click on **New**.

2. Select the **Most Read Content** module and click on **Next**.

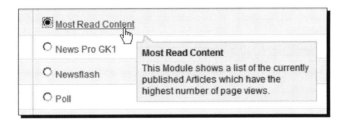

3. In the **Module: [Edit]** screen, enter the details for this module. In the **Title field** enter **Popular Articles**.

4. In the **Position** field select **right** to show this module in the right-hand side column.

5. Leave the other settings as they are. By default, the **Menu Assignment** settings will make the module display on all pages. The **Parameters** are set to show a list of 5 hyperlinks.

6. Click on **Save** and click on **Preview** to see the output on the frontend of the site:

SRUP ACTIVITIES

THIS YEARS MEETING

Meetings

Quisque dictum, nibh sit amet feugiat dictum, dui libero imperdiet tortor, sed varius ante eros non libero. Mauris id tellus ac diam mollis condimentum. Aenean sed consequat nisl. Morbi cursus sollicitudin ipsum. Vivamus non diam vitae velit aliquam vulputate. Nam eleifend pulvinar suscipit. Nulla commodo, neque eu accumsan feugiat, ante justo scelerisque ante, non gravida quam massa eget ligula.

Read more...

POPULAR ARTICLES

- Just What is Ugly Art?
- Ugly Paintings Gallery
- Bad Abstract Paintings
- This Years Meeting
- Deplorable Still Lifes

What just happened?

You've added the Most Read Content module to your site to display a list of popular articles. These are the articles that have the highest number of page views. Having lists like this on your site is again good for both your real visitors (who'll be able to find out what other visitors like to read) and for your robot visitors who appreciate regularly updated links to different articles within the site.

Have a go hero – add link lists

Have a look at the other link list modules that Joomla! contains, such as the Latest News module (displaying recently added articles, see Chapter 10) and the Related Articles module, showing a list of articles related to the current article the visitor sees. Articles are considered to be related if they share at least one keyword in the article's **Metadata Information**. If you've got lots of content on your site, it's a good idea to offer visitors several ways to find popular, related, or recently added articles.

Using a site map

A site map is a one-page overview of your site's contents containing links to all pages. Adding a site map will automatically create internal links to all pages, and both real people and search engine robots will benefit from it as it presents a clear overview of the site's contents. The site map functionality isn't part of the Joomla! core software, but there are a number of free site map extensions available for Joomla! 1.5.

:tion – adding a site map component

...Service Map, a free component and create a link to the site map from the

...your browser to `www.sefservicemap.com` and download the ZIP ...ontaining SEF Service Map 2.

2. Navigate to **Extensions**. Click on **Browse** to locate the ZIP file (in the current release this file is named `sef_servicemap_2.0.11.zip`) and click on **Upload File & Install**. You'll see a message: **"Install Component Success"**.

3. That's it; you can use SEF Service Map with the default settings now.

To get the site map to display, add a menu link from your home page to the site map:

4. Navigate to **Menus | Main Menu** and click on **New** to add a menu item.

5. In the **Select Menu Item Type** list, select **SEF Service Map**. You'll be taken to the **Menu Item: [New]** page.

6. In the **Title** field, enter a title. In this example, we've entered **Site Map**. Click on **Save** and click on **Preview**. In the frontend Main Menu, click on the **Site Map** link to see the results:

What just happened?

By adding a site map you've created an overview of links to all pages and made it easier to find content.

Have a go hero – tweak that site map

If you want to change the output of the site map, navigate to **Components | SEF Servicemap**. Here you can edit the site map structure; maybe you want to leave out some (categories of) articles. SEF Service Map offers a wide range of settings allowing you to change the appearance of the site map, display it in one or more columns, and so on.

Make it easier to discover new content: Using RSS

If you regularly add new articles to your site, you should consider using a free "subscription service" for your site visitors. People can subscribe to your site news by clicking on a special "RSS feeds" button; using special software (called RSS readers or feed readers) they can stay up to date with their favorite websites without having to actively search for new content. The feed reader usually displays only part of the news items; people will click through to your site to read on. RSS feeds are also great to help search engines to discover any new content you add very quickly.

Time for action – enable RSS feeds

Let's enable RSS feeds on the example site.

1. Navigate to **Extensions | Module Manager** and select the module named **Syndication** (the module type is **mod_syndicate**).

2. You'll be taken to the **Module: [Edit]** screen. Set **Enabled** to **Yes**.

3. In the **Position** drop-down box, select **footer**. This is the position where the hyperlink to the RSS feed will be displayed.

4. In the **Menu Assignment** section choose **Select Menu Item(s) from the List** and select just the **Home** page menu item. This way visitors can subscribe to news items that are added to the home page:

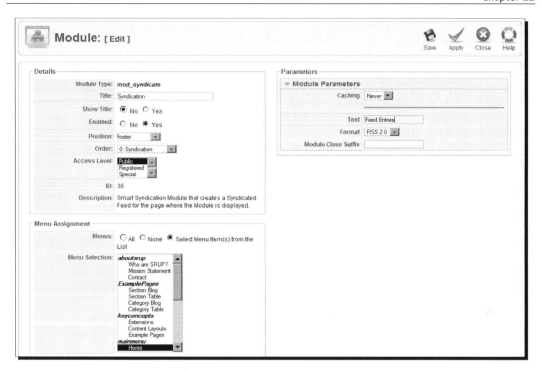

5. Click on **Save** and click on **Preview**. On the frontend of the website you'll see an RSS icon next to the text **Feed Entries**:

Clicking on this link will take the visitor to a special page in their browser. Here's an example of how Firefox will display RSS feeds:

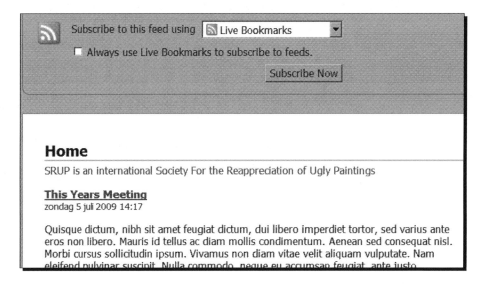

What just happened?

In Joomla!, you can add a Syndication link to any page (any menu item, really) that contains articles intros (such as the home page or category overview pages). Joomla! will create a news feed for the page on which the module is displayed. The page will contain a feed link; through this, the visitor can subscribe to this news feed to keep up to date on any changes to your home page.

Have a go hero – provide a newsletter service

Do you want to explore other ways to present new content to your site visitors? You might want to consider introducing a newsletter service. You can have visitors subscribe to the newsletter to keep up to date with anything you're publishing about on your site. It's a great way to keep visitors interested and to increase site traffic. In the Joomla! Extensions Directory, there are a great number of newsletter components.

Getting to know more about your site traffic

In this chapter, you've focused on optimizing your site to get search engines to notice its contents and to entice people to read what you have to offer and to visit your site regularly. However, the best way to improve your sites visibility is to get to know your visitors really well. Where do they come from? What search words do they use to end up on your site? What are the articles they favor, what time do they spend on your site, what are the links they follow, and where do they leave your site again? A really great (free) tool to help you discover all there is to know on your site traffic is Google Analytics.

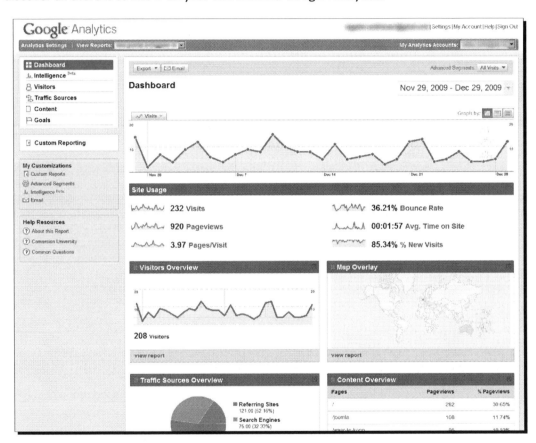

Using Google Analytics will help you understand what makes your visitors tick, and can help you to better adapt your content, the language, keywords you use, and even your choice of subjects to what your visitors care for.

It's easy to use Analytics to analyze Joomla! sites. It's free. These are the steps involved: make sure to get an account at `www.googlemail.com`, go to `www.google.com/ analytics` and sign up for this specific service. Add the domain you want to keep track of. Google will verify you're the domain owner (you'll have to upload a specific file to your site). In Joomla!, add a special code provided by Google to your template's HTML file enabling Google to start analyzing and keeping track of your site traffic.

 To get a quick overview of the possibilities of Google Analytics, visit `http://www.google.com/analytics/tour.html`. Apart from this, there are very many helpful Analytics resources and tutorials—provided both by Google and others.

More SEO resources

Using your favorite search engine to do a Web search for "Joomla! SEO" will help you on your way when you want to know more about optimization techniques. You might also want to have a look at these sites:

- A tutorial on Joomla! SEO: `www.compassdesigns.net/joomla-blog/top-10-joomla-seo-tips-for-google`.
- Joomla! SEO blogs: `http://seo4joomla.wordpress.com`, `www.alledia.com`.
- Browse the SEO and Metadata and SEF categories of the Joomla extensions directory (`http://extensions.joomla.org/extensions`) to get an idea of the many extensions available to assist you on optimizing your sites search engine visibility.

There's an exhaustive book on Joomla! 1.5 SEO by Herbert Jan van Dinther available: see `http://www.packtpub.com/joomla-1-5-search-engine-optimization-seo/book`.

Pop quiz – test your knowledge of Joomla! search engine optimization

1. What's the use of adding metadata descriptions to the articles of your website?
   a) Site visitors can quickly find out what your site is all about.
   b) Search engines can display the descriptions in their search output.
   c) They're not really useful, because search engines tend to ignore descriptions.

2. To be able to use Search Engine Friendly URLs:

   a) You have to rename Joomla! files on the web server.

   b) Check the appropriate SEO Settings in the Global Configuration (and maybe rename a file on the web server).

   c) You have to install a SEF Component.

3. What kind of links are important for SEO?

   a) Links from other sites to your site, and links from your site to other sites.

   b) Links within your site.

   c) Links to, from, and within your site.

4. The function of RSS feeds is:

   a) To increase traffic by providing your visitors with an overview of the site's contents.

   b) To increase traffic by allowing your visitors to subscribe to a newsletter.

   c) To increase traffic by allowing your visitors to subscribe to recently added articles.

5. What's the use of the Google Analytics tool?

   a) It allows you to analyze.

   b) You can't use Google Analytics with Joomla!.

   c) Using Google Analytics can increase traffic to your site through Google Web searches.

Summary

In this chapter, we've covered some common sense Search Engine Optimization techniques that will help getting your site's contents picked up by search engines.

◆ The purpose of search engines is to give quick access to the most valuable, up-to-date, and relevant web content—so making sure your site contains that good content is really the best way to optimize your site's search engine visibility.

◆ In Joomla!, you can use several techniques to increase the visibility of your site's content for search engines. You can add global metadata to the site and article metadata keywords giving search engines specific information on the contents of individual pages.

◆ By enabling Search Engine Friendly URLs in Joomla!, the browser address bar will display readable URLs that match the content of the page instead of long and hard to decipher URLs. Using SEF URLs will make it easier for visitors and search engines to understand the contents of the page.

◆ Linking is very important; it's good to link to other sites, and it's great if other sites link to *your* site. It's also essential to add relevant internal links to your site. They make it easier for both visitors and search engines to find your content.

◆ Joomla! allows you to automatically create internal hyperlinks; you can set all article titles to be hyperlinks to the main article text. You can also create lists of links to popular or recently updated articles.

◆ You can use RSS Feeds to allow visitors to subscribe to your site news; feeds are also great to help search engines to discover any new content you add very quickly.

A

Keeping the Site Secure

You've created a great site, customized its design, and added valuable content. That's an investment worth protecting. Rest assured, most Joomla! sites will run for years without any hiccups. However, it's a good idea to take some precautions to minimize the risk of your website getting broken. A few simple measures can make it a lot harder for malicious hackers to get access to your site and mess up its contents. Backing up regularly can get you out of trouble fast if you run into hardware disasters (think crashing hard drives) or software trouble (installing extensions that somehow mess up your existing site). Fortunately, these problems are rare, but it's definitely worth the little extra time investment needed to minimize risks.

How can you protect your site and how do you get your site up and running again when something has gone wrong? This appendix contains some essential tips and best practices to keep your site in perfect health (and save yourself some headaches too).

Choosing a web host that meets security requirements

In this appendix, you'll learn what you, as the site administrator, can do to keep your site safe. However, there are also some basic but critical security measures that your web hosting company should take. You'll probably have a shared hosting account, where multiple sites are hosted on one server computer, each site having access to their part of the available disk space and resources. Although this is much cheaper than hiring a dedicated server to host your site, it does involve some security risks. Good web hosting companies take precautions to minimize these risks. When selecting your web host, it's worth checking if they have a good reputation for keeping their security up to standards—it pays to be picky. The official Joomla! resources site (`http://resources.joomla.org/directory/support-services/hosting.html`) features hosting companies that fully meet the security requirements of a typical Joomla!-powered site,

Tip 1: Upgrade regularly

The Joomla! development team regularly releases updates to fix bugs and security issues. At the time of writing, the current version number is 1.5.15. This indicates it is the 15th update of the original 1.5.0 release. Try to keep up with these updates; you'll find announcements of new updates on the Joomla! site (www.joomla.org). The essential steps of upgrading are downloading the upgrade files (contained in a zip file), unzipping these, and uploading the updated files to the web server—overwriting the existing files.

Don't forget there's more to keeping your site current than just upgrading the Joomla! software itself. It's a good idea to check for updates for the extensions you use in the Joomla! Extension Database. To read more on upgrading, visit the Joomla! documentation site: http://docs.joomla.org/Upgrading_1.5_from_an_existing_1.5x_version.

Tip 2: Change the default Administrator Username

When you install Joomla!, the default username of your login account (the critical account of the almighty *Superadministrator*) is admin. By changing it to something different, you'll make it much more difficult for bad guys to gain access to the site. After all, they won't be able to guess your username anymore.

You can't change the administrator username during the Joomla! installation. After the installation is finished you can enter a different username. This is how you do it:

1. In the backend of the site, navigate to **Site | User Manager**.
2. Select the **Administrator** user record (**Username: admin**).
3. In the **User: [Edit]** screen, enter a new **Username**. Be creative!
4. Click on **Save** to apply changes.

Log out and log in to the backend with the new username.

Tip 3: Choose a strong password

Choose an administrator password that isn't easy to guess. It's best to have a password that's not too short; 8 or more characters is fine. Use a combination of uppercase letters, lowercase letters, numbers, and special characters—this should guarantee a strong p@sZw0rD.

Don't use the same username and password you use for other online accounts, and regularly change your password. You can create a new password anytime in the backend User Manager in the same way you enter or change a username (see Tip 2).

Tip 4: Protect files and directories

Obviously, you don't want everybody to be able to access the Joomla! files and folders on the web server. You can protect files and folders by setting access permissions using the CHMOD (Change Mode) command. Basically, CHMOD settings tell the web server who has access to a file or folder, who is allowed to read it, write it, or to execute a file (run it as a program).

Once your Joomla! site is set up and everything works OK, you can use CHMOD to change permissions. You don't use Joomla! to change CHMOD settings; these are set with FTP software (for more information on FTP programs, see Chapter 2 on installing Joomla!).

This is how it works:

1. In your FTP program, right-click on the name of the file or directory you want to protect.
2. In the right-click menu select **Properties**.
3. You'll be presented with a pop-up screen. Here, you can check permissions and change them by selecting the appropriate options as shown in the following screenshot:

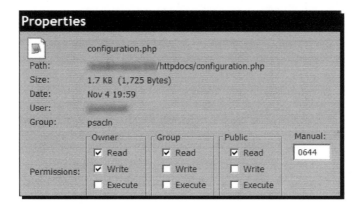

As you can see, it's possible to set permissions for the file owner (that's you), for group members (that's likely to be only you too), and for the public (everyone else). This last one is the tricky part; you should be very careful and restrict public permissions as much as possible.

When changing the permission settings, the file permissions number (the value in the **Manual:** box in the previous screenshot) will change accordingly. Every combination of settings has its particular number. In the above example, the permissions are set to 644 (the leading 0 is ignored).

4. Click on **OK** to execute the CHMOD command and set file permissions.

Choosing file permissions

What files should you protect and what CHMOD settings should you choose? Here are a few pointers:

1. By default, permissions for files are set to 644. That's a safe value:

   ❑ When your need to change the file contents, temporarily change permissions to 775:

   ❑ Once you're done, go back to 644. Configuration files (such as `configuration.php` in the Joomla! root directory) are especially vulnerable as they contain username and password details. Make sure that the CHMOD value of `configuration.php` is set to 644.

2. For *directories* a safe setting is 750 (which doesn't allow any public access):

   ❑ However, some extensions may need access to certain directories; the 750 setting might result in error messages. In this case, set permissions to 755:

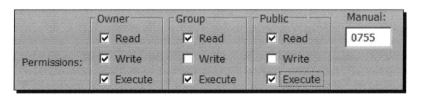

❑ Never leave permissions for a file or directory set to 777; this allows everybody to write data to it:

You can also block direct access to critical directories using a `.htaccess` file. This is a special file containing instructions for the web server—among other things, it tells the web server who's allowed access to the directory contents. You can add a `.htaccess` file to any folder on the server using specific instructions. This is another way to instruct the web server to restrict access. See the Joomla! security documentation on `www.joomla.org` for instructions.

Tip 5: Use extensions to secure your site

There are many things you yourself can do to keep your site safe, but there's also dedicated security software available for this purpose. Just like you've probably installed a firewall and antivirus software on your computer, you can install security extensions to add a layer of protection to your site and prevent intrusions and hacker attacks. Let's have a look at some free security extensions:

◆ The jSecure Authentication module keeps malicious hackers from gaining access to the backend of your site by blocking the possibility of creating accounts through the `www.yoursite.com/administrator` login page. Users can only get in using a secure key. See `www.joomlaserviceprovider.com` for details and downloads.

◆ When you enable user registration in Joomla!, anyone can register on the frontend of the site. To better control who is allowed to register, consider using the JRPassphrase module. Before they can use the site registration form, visitors must first submit a passphrase. This way, you can allow people you know (your family, your club members, and your clients) to get in while preventing access to others.

◆ To prevent spammers from using site forms (such as the contact form and the login and registration forms) consider using a Captcha extension. The Security Images component requires anyone filling out a form to type a phrase consisting of hard-to-read images before they are allowed to actually send the form data.

In the Joomla! extensions directory, browse the **Access & Security** section to see what's available and to read user reviews:
`http://extensions.joomla.org/extensions/access-a-security`.

Tip 6: Have a backup ready

Whatever precautions you take, be prepared for catastrophes. Always have a backup ready to restore your site to its most current healthy state.

There are a few great Joomla! extensions that automate the backup process. A very popular one is JoomlaPack. It will backup all necessary files (all Joomla! files and the database contents) to recover your site. JoomlaPack will allow you to restore the backup file to any location (not just to its original location).

Creating a Backup with JoomlaPack

This is how you install JoomlaPack and create a backup:

1. Go to `http://joomlapack.net` to download the JoomlaPack extension file.
2. Navigate to **Extensions | Install/Uninstall** to install the extension.
3. Navigate to **Components | Joomlapack** and click on **Backup Now** to make a backup using the default settings. The backup should start immediately:

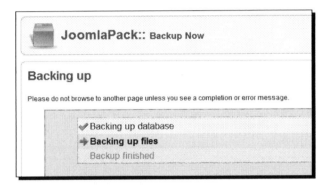

4. When the backup is complete, you'll see the following message:

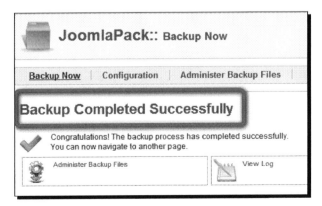

5. To save the backup file on your computer, click on **Administer Backup Files**. Select the backup file and click on the **Download** button.

Restoring a backup

This is how you restore a backup file:

1. Unzip the JoomlaPack backup file that you downloaded to your computer earlier.

2. Using an FTP program, upload all of the files from the backup ZIP file to the original location: the web server directory where you installed Joomla!.

3. When all files have finished uploading, point your browser to the URL of your site adding `/installation/index.php`. For example: `www.yoursite.com/installation/index.php`.

4. The JoomlaPack installer screen will appear. Follow the instructions of the installer.

There's a step-by-step tutorial on using JoomlaPack for backing up and restoring Joomla! sites at `http://joomlapack.net/help-and-support/documentation/joomlapack-user-guide.html`.

Before you upgrade Joomla! to an updated version, it's a good idea to create a backup of your current site. If anything goes wrong, you can quickly have it up and running again.

Tip 7: Stay informed!

Obviously, there's much more to learn about keeping your site secure. For more tips, have a look at:

◆ Joomla! Administrators Security Checklist: `http://docs.joomla.org/Joomla_Administrators_Security_Checklist`

◆ The official Joomla! security forum at: `http://forum.joomla.org/viewforum.php?f=432`

To keep up to date with the latest news on Joomla! security issues, visit:

`http://developer.joomla.org/security/news.html`.

If you use news reader software, you can subscribe to Joomla! Security Announcements there.

B
Pop Quiz Answers

Chapter 2

Installation: Getting Joomla! Up and Running

1	2	3
b	b	c

Chapter 3

First Steps: Getting to Know Joomla!

1	2	3
c	b	b

Chapter 4

Web Building Basics: Creating a Site in an Hour

1	2	3
b	b	a

Chapter 5

Small Sites, Big Sites: Organizing your Content Effectively

1	2	3
c	b	b

Chapter 6

Creating Killer Content: Adding and Editing Articles

1	2	3	4	5
all three are correct	b	c	b	c

Chapter 7

Welcoming Your Visitors: Creating Attractive Home Pages and Overview Pages

1	2	3
b	c	c

Chapter 8

Helping Your Visitors Find What They Want: Managing Menus

1	2	3
b	b	c

Chapter 9

Opening Up the Site: Enabling Users to Contribute and Interact

1	2	3
b	a	b

Chapter 10

Getting the Most out of Your Site: Extending Joomla!

1	2	3
a	c	b

Chapter 11

Creating an Attractive Design: Working with Templates

1	2	3
b	b	c

Chapter 12

Attracting Search Engine Traffic: Tips and Techniques

1	2	3	4	5
b	b	c	c	a

Index

K

Kunena 275

L

latest news module 258
layout, Joomla! site
  Cascading Style Sheets (CSS) 83, 84
  color scheme, customizing 77
  color variation, selecting 77, 78
  customizing 77
  layout settings, exploring 85
  new header file, creating 79-81
  new header image file, displaying 82, 83
links
  adding 119
List Layout
  about 183
  Blog Layout, changing to List Layout 184, 185
  Category List Layout 189
  Category List Layout, parameters 189
  Section List Layout, parameters 186
  Section Lists, creating 184
login module 258

M

mainbody 43
main menu
  about 195
  hyperlinks, adding to new menu 198, 199
  menu, displaying 200-202
  menu items order, changing 195-197
  menu position, tweaking 204
  menus, arranging 210
  menu styling, tweaking 203
  new empty menu, creating 197, 198
  new menu, adding 197
  orientation, tweaking 204
  secondary menu item, creating 207, 208
  split submenus, creating 208, 209
  submenu items, creating 206
main menu module 258
managers 225
menu items
  order, changing 195, 196
menu links

alias-links 216
creating 215, 216
external link 216
internal link 216
menu item types 217
separator 216
types 216
menu manager 194
menu module
  details section 211, 212
  module parameters 213
  other parameters 214
  settings 210
menus
  deleting 76
metadata
  about 318
  finding, to fit site 321
  information, adding for articles 322, 323
  site metadata, personalizing 318-320
  site name, selecting 323, 324
mod_archive module 258
mod_breadcrumbs module 258
mod_custom module 258
mod_feed module 258
mod_latestnews module 258
mod_login module 258
mod_mainmenu module 258
mod_mostread module 258
mod_newsflash module 258
mod_random_image module 258
mod_related_items module 259
mod_search module 259
mod_sections module 259
mod_stats module 259
mod_syndicate module 259
modules
  about 248
  hiding 72, 73
mod_whosonline module 259
mod_wrapper module 259
multi-page articles
  alternative page display, techniques 152
  article splitting, page breaks used 149
  creating 149

Packt Open Source Project Royalties

When we sell a book written on an Open Source project, we pay a royalty directly to that project. Therefore by purchasing Joomla! 1.5: Beginner's Guide, Packt will have given some of the money received to the Joomla! project.

In the long term, we see ourselves and you—customers and readers of our books—as part of the Open Source ecosystem, providing sustainable revenue for the projects we publish on. Our aim at Packt is to establish publishing royalties as an essential part of the service and support a business model that sustains Open Source.

If you're working with an Open Source project that you would like us to publish on, and subsequently pay royalties to, please get in touch with us.

Writing for Packt

We welcome all inquiries from people who are interested in authoring. Book proposals should be sent to author@packtpub.com. If your book idea is still at an early stage and you would like to discuss it first before writing a formal book proposal, contact us; one of our commissioning editors will get in touch with you.

We're not just looking for published authors; if you have strong technical skills but no writing experience, our experienced editors can help you develop a writing career, or simply get some additional reward for your expertise.

About Packt Publishing

Packt, pronounced 'packed', published its first book "Mastering phpMyAdmin for Effective MySQL Management" in April 2004 and subsequently continued to specialize in publishing highly focused books on specific technologies and solutions.

Our books and publications share the experiences of your fellow IT professionals in adapting and customizing today's systems, applications, and frameworks. Our solution-based books give you the knowledge and power to customize the software and technologies you're using to get the job done. Packt books are more specific and less general than the IT books you have seen in the past. Our unique business model allows us to bring you more focused information, giving you more of what you need to know, and less of what you don't.

Packt is a modern, yet unique publishing company, which focuses on producing quality, cutting-edge books for communities of developers, administrators, and newbies alike. For more information, please visit our website: www.PacktPub.com.

PUBLISHING

Learning Joomla! 1.5
Extension Development

Creating Modules, Components, and Plug-Ins with PHP

A practical tutorial for creating your first Joomla! 1.5 extensions
with PHP

Joseph LeBlanc

PACKT

Learning Joomla! 1.5 Extension Development

ISBN: 978-1-847191-30-4   Paperback: 176 pages

A practical tutorial for creating your first Joomla! 1.5
extensions with PHP

1. Program your own extensions to Joomla!

2. Create new, self-contained components with
   both back-end and front-end functionality

3. Create configurable site modules to show
   information on every page

4. Distribute your extensions to other
   Joomla! users

Joomla! E-Commerce
with VirtueMart

Build feature-rich online stores with Joomla! 1.0/1.5 and
VirtueMart 1.1.x

Suhreed Sarkar

PACKT

Joomla! E-Commerce with VirtueMart

ISBN: 978-1-847196-74-3   Paperback: 476 pages

Build feature-rich online stores with Joomla! 1.0/1.5
and VirtueMart 1.1.x

1. Build your own e-commerce web site from
   scratch by adding features step-by-step to an
   example e-commerce web site

2. Configure the shop, build product catalogues,
   configure user registration settings for
   VirtueMart to take orders from around
   the world

3. Manage customers, orders, and a variety of
   currencies to provide the best customer service

4. Handle shipping in all situations and deal with
   sales tax rules

Please check **www.PacktPub.com** for information on our titles